To Tiffany
with love

[signature]

Teen Voices

Also by Maurizio Andolfi

Family Therapy:
An Interactional Approach
1979: Plenum Press, New York

Dimensions of Family Therapy
(co-edited, with Israel Zwerling)
1980: Guilford Press, New York

Behind the Family Mask:
Therapeutic Change in Rigid Family Systems
1983: Brunner/Mazel, New York

The Myth of Atlas:
Families & the Psychotherapeutic Story
(with Claudio Angelo and Marcella de Nichilo)
1989: Brunner/Mazel, New York

Please Help Me with This Family:
Using Consultants as Resources in Family Therapy
(with Russell Haber)
1994: Brunner/Mazel, New York

Teen Voices

Tales from Family Therapy

Maurizio Andolfi & Anna Mascellani

Wisdom Moon Publishing
2013

TEEN VOICES

TALES FROM FAMILY THERAPY

Published by Wisdom Moon Publishing LLC
San Diego, CA, USA

Wisdom Moon™, the Wisdom Moon logo™, *Wisdom Moon Publishing*™, and *WMP*™
are trademarks of Wisdom Moon Publishing LLC.

www.WisdomMoonPublishing.com

ISBN 978-1-938459-27-6 (hardcover, alk. paper)
ISBN 978-1-938459-30-6 (softcover, alk. paper)
ISBN 978-1-938459-34-4 (eBook)

LCCN 2013955404

Table of Contents

PRACTICE ILLUSTRATIONS

To Lorena, Jonathan,
Carlo, and Giulia

Introduction

What does it mean to raise adolescents in an age when family fragmentation, single-parenthood, and absent fathers are becoming predominant?

How can adolescents develop a sense of belonging and trust when parents fight all the time or continue their hostility long after they have divorced? How do adolescents learn to feel safe in new step-families?

How can parents learn to deal with adolescents' ambivalence and anger? How can they recruit the support of families and friends when they are worried or confused about their teenagers? When does adolescence begin and when does it finish? Is adolescence a "disease" or is it rather the most-misunderstood phase of the family's life cycle?

What is behind the adolescents' violent and aggressive behavior? Why do they act out when they feel alone, left out, triangulated, or when nobody in the family pays attention to their real needs? What are they communicating with their angry voices and their body language?

Why are many adolescents unable to develop healthy dependencies inside their families and substitute them with alcohol, drugs, food, or technological addictions?

How do we deal with their sadness after sudden losses or dramatic family separations without labeling the behavior as pathological depression? Why do we put more trust on medication than on family resources? How do we listen to the adolescents' voice, especially when it speaks of despair and isolation? How can we contain their pain and confusion and look at suicide attempts in adolescence as an eloquent developmental crisis? What do their extreme actions signal, and to whom?

These are some of the fundamental questions about adolescence addressed in this book, in our attempts at finding answers through psychological understanding and clinical experience.

We will not be looking at adolescent issues as individual traits and therefore we won't focus on individual diagnoses as in a medical model; we won't do "one-on-one" therapy; on the contrary, we believe in enlarging the system and considering the family as our "client" as well as our main resource to resolve their children's problems. We adhere to the philosophy of traditional family therapy, which in fifty years brought revolutionary results in Mental Health and in the healing professions. Our approach is inter-generational and aims to integrate systemic and developmental theories; therefore, the family's developmental history and life cycle are the framework we use to understand and assess adolescent misbehavior and symptoms. Consequently we are interested in linking the teenager's presenting problem to relevant family events by observing the connection between past traumas, family disconnections, marital crises, sudden losses, and the adolescents' present actions. In so doing, we have been greatly inspired by the pioneer work of Murray Bowen, James Framo, Donald Williamson, Carl Whitaker, Salvador Minuchin, just to mention a few of the most outstanding inter-generational writers and clinicians who influenced the family therapy movement for decades.

The three-tier inter-generational family system is the core of our observation and intervention; we look at relational patterns and inter-generational blockages within the family to deal with the adolescent's problems: instead of looking at dyads, as happens in individual therapy, we have applied the triad as the unit of observation of evolving family relationships.

The primary triad (Mother-Father-Child) and its distortions have been described first by Minuchin as "rigid triads" and by Haley as "perverted triads." The role-reversing triads and the consequent parental-child function, especially, have been illustrated by a number of outstanding authors (Bowen, Whitaker, Selvini Palazzoli, Andolfi, etc.).

If Attachment Theories have been fundamental in describing the child's primary needs in developmental terms, Systemic-Relational Theories have added a triadic dimension in the early observation of children. A developmental-systemic view of Mother-Father-Infant was introduced by Fivaz-Depeursinge's seminal research work, known as The Lausanne Trialogue Play.

The model of therapy described in this book is experiential, that is to say, a special personal/professional encounter shared by therapist and family in a safe and active context: we have been greatly influenced by Satir and Whitaker who long ago described a model of intervention called "symbolic-experiential"; and more recently by Daniel Stern, a very inspired psychoanalyst who made a great contribution to the field with the concept of inter-subjective experience and implicit knowledge, embracing and enriching many systemic principles.

The goal of therapy is not only the remission of symptoms, but rather the change of inter-generational distortions that produce those symptoms. The therapist plays an active role: he is direct, authentic, empathic, and able to remain close to the clients' pain and despair, as well as to respond positively to their hope and desire for change. He explores first the adolescent's development within the family and social context and very quickly establishes a therapeutic alliance with the teenager through the description and reframing of his/her symptomatic/pathological manifestations. Therefore he re-directs negative, destructive actions into positive connections with family members.

Often, adolescents who present psycho-relational symptoms or psychiatric disorders grow up in family contexts where inter-generational dysfunctions and traumas have never been resolved, and are often buried or not spoken about for years.

By circumventing blame and anger in the session, the therapist engages the family in a constructive process that allows the adolescents to change and grow in healthier ways and the parents to share the pain and sorrow of their own issues and responsibilities for their children. This re-establishes more functional generational boundaries, produces a clearer and productive co-parenting alliance, and creates sibling support.

Several Practice Illustrations are included in each chapter in order to assist the reader in understanding and following the main therapeutic interventions: in particular, the dialogues included demonstrate how to build trust and safety in session, and how to create an alliance with the family to produce important and steady changes.

The segments of therapy/consultation are taken from Andolfi's 40 years of experience working with problematic adolescents and families, coming from diverse socio-cultural backgrounds and conducted in many different parts of the world.

Violent behavior, bullying, drug-alcohol addictions, eating disorders, reactive depression, and suicidal attempts are addressed with the same openness and compassion in order to "reach and touch" the adolescents in their core-Self behind their façade. Symptoms are useful guidelines that help us to enter into family dilemmas and conflict, and to overcome negative or painful events, finding new alternatives for personal and family growth.

Provocation, support, metaphors, curiosity, humor, playfulness, free asso-ciations, self-disclosure, and sculpting are the main therapeutic tools used to explore the family life cycle and to look for resources and new openings.

Family of origin, siblings, friends, pets as well as community members and hospital workers can be recruited and included as consultants in the therapeutic process to enlarge the social resources of the family and find emotional support and solidarity.

We have collected and included in this volume several long-term family-therapy follow-ups which have been very informative; in particular, we have learnt that even severe disturbances and illnesses like anorexia, depression, suicidal attempts, and so on, can be treated successfully in adolescents without, or with very limited use of medication and hospital admission; we have also learnt that we can work with symptoms indirectly, without focusing on symptomatic manifestations and labeling them, and that by caring for adolescents and listening to their voice, we were able to elicit unexpected resources and relational skills. But even more importantly, we understood that families become "the best Medicine" when they are encouraged to move from a passive, helpless position to an active role, functioning as a team of experts in a safe therapeutic context. Mutual love and care will always have a powerful healing effect and the adolescent's misbehavior and symptoms will soon disappear.

We recommend this book, first of all, to adolescents and families in general, with or without specific presenting problems: they can discover something of themselves in these pages, and through the therapeutic vignettes they can identify obstacles and impasses, as well as hope and care for personal and relational well-being. Secondly, of course, this is a book for the "experts" who work in the field of what we term the healing professions: psychiatrists, psychologists, psychotherapists, counselors, social workers, nurses, and other caring professionals can enjoy this provocative book and find very useful tools to add to their professional toolbox. But even more importantly, they can get a different, creative, and human way of looking at a family's difficulties, strengths, and resilience, if they find the courage to move out of rigid diagnostic and therapeutic ways of labeling adolescent acting-out. Love and care are not only family guidelines for a good life, they are also a very basic requirement for good and enriching professional work.

Maurizio Andolfi & Anna Mascellani

Acknowledgments

Many thanks to Cecilia Tinto for the translation of this book from the Italian language and even more to Chiara Hunter, who has been editing and adapting the text for the English reader and language with a great competence and dedication. We want to express a very sincere thanks to Francesca Ferraguzzi who has been editing several case illustrations and to Laura Bruno for assisting the authors in the transforming and enriching the English Edition of this volume. Thanks to Glenn Larner, Editor of the *Australian and New Zealand Journal of Family Therapy*, for some suggestions and positive criticism. Very many thanks to Mitchell Ginsberg for accepting our book in his editorial House with great enthusiasm during a period in which Family Therapy books seem to appeal much less to the general public and to the most-known Publishing houses in the field, very afraid to take risks because of the increasing conformism in the Scientific Community and medicalization of human sadness and other human adverse conditions.

The most important acknowledgment goes to the many families and adolescents who are present and alive in this book: we learnt from their stories about their pain and suffering as well as about their strengths and resilience and through that we shaped this book; in the English Edition we were also able to add more recent cases and follow-ups.

Chapter 1
Adolescence: a critical phase
in the family's life cycle

DEVELOPMENT AND DICHOTOMIES WITHIN THE SYSTEMIC
MODEL: THE TWO SIDES OF FAMILY THERAPY

The sharing of a theoretical frame of reference within systemic-relational psychology during the last fifty years has not been sufficient to delineate a common conceptual and operational model. A fundamental difference concerns the value given to the individual and to historical and subjective aspects, including those regarding the therapist, in the conceptualization of the family system and of the therapeutic model.

The development of family therapists' clinical practice has, over time, outlined substantial differences in intervention methodology which, in the initial phase, were situated in the East and West Coast of the United States, and later reflected further dichotomies in Europe and above all in Italy, where different operating modalities can be found between Rome and Milan.

During the sixties, two sides started to appear within the nascent family therapy movement: *conductors*, those therapists who used their own personality, including intuition and creativity, as evaluation and intervention tools (see Ackerman (1958), Satir (1964), Whitaker (1989), Minuchin (1974)), and *system purists*, those who studied the family as a relational system, and put themselves in a relatively removed position from any kind of personal involvement and emotional resonance. See the Palo Alto Group (Watzlawick, Beavin Bavelas, Jackson, 1967), Haley (1973), Sluzki (Sluzki, Ransom, 1974), Hoffman (Haley, Hoffmann, 1967), and the Milan School (Selvini Palazzoli, Boscolo, Cecchin, Prata, 1975) during its initial research phase.

At the beginning of the eighties this debate became even more heated after a series of articles appeared in *Family Process*, where the main question was whether the therapist should practice therapy from a pragmatic or an aesthetic position: the first assumed that therapy should resolve the symptoms as they are presented initially, clearly defining the goals; while the second orientation considered therapy as a creative and growing process, aimed at promoting the development of the family and its ecosystem.

Over the years this debate has encouraged many family clinicians to take the side of one approach or the other, without managing to integrate harmonically the *role* with the *person* of therapist, and taking responsibility for addressing symptoms while, at the same time, facilitating the development of the family and its relational world.

In more recent times the dichotomy seems even greater. Let us consider the strong development of the so-called narrative family therapies and the trouble many scholars and family therapists have in accepting the point of view of postmodern theories, in particular that of social constructivism, to understand the family.

A critique on this way of viewing reality came from Salvador Minuchin, who titled a work he published in the *Journal of Marital and Family Therapy* in 1999, "Where's the family in narrative family therapy?" He debated the basic and mainly political assumptions of social constructivism and its therapeutic usefulness and maintained that the individual and the social environment are the main interlocutors, while the family, as mediator between the two, disappeared. Moreover, Minuchin criticized the newly neutral position of a narrative therapist who mustn't have any kind of influence or personal involvement within the therapeutic situation.

In the vibrant answer by Carlos Sluzki to Minuchin's provocative article, Sluzki insisted that the family is no longer the only focus of attention of systemic therapists and that the individual has acquired a more relevant position within the therapeutic process.

From then on, so-called *individual systemic therapies* and family therapy carried out in the presence of a single subject—who carries inside himself the representation of the family—began to thrive!

Vincenzo Di Nicola (1990), examining the differences between the Milanese models, one by Selvini Palazzoli and collaborators, on the one side, and that of Boscolo and Cecchin, on the other, described two kinds of therapeutic models confronting one another within the main schools of family therapy: the *technocratic* model and the *phenomenological* one.

The first kind (of which Haley and Strategic Therapy are good examples) focuses on therapy, favors technique, and bases intervention on the principles and precise rules according to which the family system organizes its behavior. The therapist's affective resonance and counter transference are kept absolutely outside of the therapeutic scenario.

On the other hand, the phenomenological therapist is constantly mindful of the pain endured by the family and the ways in which the the family deals with it. His interest is focused on understanding the essence of the family, not only its functioning and malfunctioning. His research isn't so much guided by the head, but originates from the experience generated by the therapeutic encounter.

These two models do not have much in common. It's basically about choosing whether to intervene in a focused way to modify behaviors or to use the behaviors actively to understand the emotional world of the family and to improve its expression.

SYMBOLIC-EXPERIENTIAL THERAPY: WHITAKER'S MODEL

In the beginning of the forties, Carl Whitaker (Whitaker, Keith, 1981) started to practice and teach a model of family therapy called symbolic-experiential therapy. This model was born mainly to treat psychotic patients and their families; it was later used in the treatment of families that had been deeply stressed by strongly destabilizing environmental events, such as wars.

This new therapeutic procedure required the development of methods for dealing with intense transference reactions and strongly regressive behavior; this type of symptom requires the capacity to resonate with the patients' emotions from a therapeutic position that is more proximal that distal, to be able to contain emotionally and reassure.

This aspect of the historical development of symbolic-experiential therapy had a considerable influence on the role taken by the therapist and separates this model from models that postulate a greater distance and neutrality in the therapist, especially the systemic and the strategic ones.

The first applications of this model with anxious people who had lived through traumatic war situations influenced the former authors, inducing them to ponder the fact that in life events, the "primary emotional symbolic experiences derive from the awareness of the uniqueness of the perceptions, of the vulnerabilities, and of the limitations of each individual" (Whitaker, Keith, 1981) within different social and cultural contexts and specific times.

The central role of emotional experience in therapy requires the therapist to be willing to include himself and to participate emotionally with the family, which is considered a vital organism, rich in resources. The therapist bears in mind that there is a longitudinal family, articulated into subsystems, that rewrites its developmental history during therapy. The tri-generational genogram guides the sessions as a reference grid, no matter who participates in any particular, single session. The goal of symbolic-experiential interventions isn't just the remission of symptoms, but rather the change of inter-generational models that produce the symptoms (Whitaker, Keith, 1981).

In symbolic-experiential therapy, "while facing real difficulties during the session, relational impasses, individual pathologies, mental illness, everybody, including the therapist, can get in touch with parts of the self, often disguised or compressed into repetitive and unfruitful relational schemes, where there's no room for creativity and growth. Being able to allow oneself to remain present in a vital way produces an expansion of the spirit, which then creates a new kind of harmony between oneself and others" (Andolfi, 2002, pp. 68-69).

To do so, Whitaker reached for his own cognitive, emotional, and affective resources, widely using his own Self. Even though he never used the term *self-disclosure*, he doubtlessly often used fragments of the therapeutic experience, personal thoughts, examples of episodes or "crazy ideas" to highlight family distortions and create moments of deep connection with the family's pain and difficulties. Helm Stierlin defined this behavior *cure through encounter*, a process in which the therapist induces change not through the reorganization of family bonds, but through some kind of participating observation (Stierlin, 1981).

THE EXPERIENCE SHARED WITH THE FAMILY IN THERAPY

When Jim Framo[1] returned to Italy—his homeland—in 1971 to present his clinical work in Rome, what surprised his audience was the deep humanity and warmth he showed while interviewing a couple of family therapists in front of everyone; above all, what was particularly surprising was his emotional participation in the couple's suffering: they had gone through the pain of several abortions, without managing to have children. It seemed as if he could enter into the depth of their loss in a direct and authentic way, without using any particular technique.

---

1 James L. Framo was the first pioneer of the family therapy who came to Italy to talk about his work. He was of Italian descent and worked in Philadelphia until the Eighties with Ivan Boszormenyi-Nagy and later in San Diego, California.

His statement *"Therapy is an experience!"* also made a deep impression; it also created some doubts for his simplicity.

It was unusual for such painful and personal couple difficulties to be exposed in front of an audience of professionals, without any protection for their privacy. It was only some decades later that we rediscovered the value of *shared experiences with the family during the session* as a fundamental premise in the whole therapeutic framework.

Fifteen years spent in close contact with Whitaker and his clinical work, from 1977 to 2002, have helped us to incorporate many of his ideas on the therapeutic relationship, such as the usefulness of widening the family system to look for resources in the developmental history of the family, the normalization of the patient's symptoms, and the value of *being* and not *acting* the therapist. It's nevertheless very difficult to describe the essence of what it means to be a therapist without trivializing its most profound meaning or, worse, turning everything into a religious dogma, running a different risk: that of losing the sense of this work, which remains that of a caring profession. Kitty La Perriere wrote, as far back as 1999, in the volume *La crisi della coppia*: "Family therapists have too often been seduced by the need to change people, dysfunctional relationships, and behaviors, thus losing the spiritual value of staying with the pain, the suffering and impotence."

Perhaps it is this search for the highest aspects of the individual and the ability to stay in touch with this person's deepest emotions that allows this process of normalization, where the boundaries of the subject's psychopathology are lost, in the search for the understanding of each person's inner world, within the longitudinal history of the family.

In his last work, *The Consultant's Inner Life,* Whitaker declared that he was searching for those fragments of the client's past experience which hadn't yet been revealed or assimilated; as these experiences are brought to the light of our consciousness they cast shadows on what has been said or seen before in therapy. "And naturally," says Whitaker, "I also bring to the therapy my own *context shadows* from past therapies, so that this new experience becomes for me an opportunity to discover new parts of myself" (Whitaker, Simons, 1994).

The idea that the therapeutic space can be the place to experience together something both deeply human and creative has informed our clinical work for many years. The expectations with which the family seeks help, together with the feeling of impotence or failure experienced by the family as a group before entering therapy, are the first vital elements on which to build the therapeutic encounter. That is why we need to ask ourselves: "What does the therapist need to bring, of his own, to create this shared experience?" It is too easy and risky to answer "his professional competence," since this would weigh the balance of the relationship in favor of the therapeutic role and would deprive it of its most authentic and human side, which cannot fully express itself within a role.

The dilemma between role and person has always been present in the so-called helping professions, including psychotherapy. Doubtlessly, therapies based on elements of strong dependency, such as individual therapies, will tend to organize the session on bases that are more hierarchical and asymmetrical, where the therapist might feel compelled to play a parental role strongly elicited by a clearly defined setting. In group therapy, and especially family therapy, the concept of dependence is absolutely out of place; a family can decide to stop coming to sessions after a few encounters and, actually, anytime they wish, just as a member of the group can slam a door and leave during a session, if he feels like it; moreover, a patient chooses to go to individual therapy, while a family never does, as the choice and the agreement of the group are subject to considerable compromises and to a constant dialectic. The first goal of a family therapist is to create a joint motivation to build a therapeutic system. This isn't easy, since often parents, a couple, or a troubled adolescent come into therapy without sharing the same sense of the problem or the possible search for solutions. We have explained in many previous works how to motivate various family members and will describe this issue further in the following chapters of this book (Andolfi et al., 2007; Falcucci et al., 2006).

Here we are interested in exploring what happens in the mind and in the guts of a therapist who welcomes a family. In the space of a few moments an encounter takes place between two family worlds, that of the family, present in the session with all its difficulties, and that of the therapist's "inner family": the therapist might receive countless stimuli from his clients which can reactivate, in the present moment, images, expressions, gestures, words, questions, jokes, feelings, or physical reactions that have to do with his own family world or previous therapeutic experiences. Not to mention life events brought into therapy by the family, such as losses, separations, births, illnesses which can overlap similar events the therapist has gone through during his own existence.

Some authors, such as Mony Elkaim (1990), have spoken about *therapeutic resonance* or *emotional reactions*; Whitaker spoke about *context shadows* which are born from previous experiences, in family or in therapy, to describe the same thing, that is: the very special nature of the experience that the family and the therapist will share.

Since the time of the so-called *joining* with the family, described so well by Minuchin in his classic work (Minuchin, 1974; Minuchin, Rosman, Baker, 1978), it has seemed inadequate to consider it as a kind of social pleasantry or some sort of reassuring start, aimed at diminishing the family's anxiety. The observation of the family from the beginning, the ways in which each member takes a seat and interacts with the others, can help the therapist to imagine the way it functions and, most of all, to sense the areas of difficulty, often hidden behind the *family mask* and, in any case, underlying the patient's symptoms; all this can encourage the therapist to assert or investigate issues not apparently visible or appraisable, in an attempt to reach the solid core of their disquiet. In this search for the markers of the pain in the family, it's useful to let oneself be guided by a family member, usually the identified patient. It is often a child or an adolescent with whom it's possible to create a very strong bond from the beginning, always based on the observation of what is unspoken or implicit and with the conviction that the whole family's feelings and emotions revolve around his problem.

It is therefore possible, on the one hand, to build a strong therapeutic alliance with the identified patient, anchoring aspects of the entire family's emotional world to him, and, on the other, to begin an inner dialogue with ourselves, aimed at making sense of the emotional reactions that inevitably accompany our search within the family. This dialogue helps us to select, almost unconsciously, fragments and images of our own family experiences or of previous therapies and to associate only to those feelings that seem more appropriate to the actual situation, presenting them to the family implicitly through a question, a metaphor, or gentle humor. Only occasionally, to make a connection to the family's experience, we might explicitly talk about previous experiences we had in our own family or in previous therapy sessions. Thus begins the construction of a puzzle where everyone, including the therapist, contributes parts of the self to finally create the therapeutic system. This could be the beginning of the construction of the inter-subjective conscience that has been described by Stern (2004).

Perhaps it is the persistence in time of these internalized fragments of the therapist's experience that enables families to recall very clearly the touching moments in therapy, made up of images, metaphorical objects or long unanswered questions, years after therapy has ended. The same happens to the therapist, who will also remember, years later, the significant moments of each therapy; it is probably this emotional baggage of intimate experiences, lived with the families, that favors his own personal growth and gives meaning to his professional role. Moreover, the moral strength acquired by going through human suffering gives the therapist that serenity, so eloquently described by Roustang (2004), that allows him to contact the depth of other people's pain, without carrying it.

Obviously in situations where one deals with the pain and sense of impotence felt by so many families when they try to solve their conflicts and relational problems, we must be very careful not to super-impose the therapist's own unresolved or unsettled emotional problems onto those brought into therapy by the family. What's more, the thera-pist might not be aware of his own *counter-transference*, thus risking the totally unconscious projection of parts of his Self into the therapy. This is the reason why co-therapy and group work has always been recommended in family therapy, in order always to have a cross-refer-ence and a critical eye which is not self-referential.

It is then possible, through time and experience, to build what we refer to as an *internal supervisor*, a part of ourselves which observes the other on a *meta level*, while interacting with this or that family member.

In the world of systemic theories, it isn't easy to deepen these aspects we regard as fundamental to becoming therapists, perhaps because said theories still show traces of a strong technicality and a certain difficulty in observing the family from a developmental point of view, and to give full value to the *rewriting of the story in therapy*. The work of Daniel Stern is interesting for our personal and professional growth and is, above all, fundamental in the scientific community. He can enlighten us with his research and help us to define better the essence of therapy, even though he was not a family therapist.

DANIEL STERN'S IMPLICIT KNOWLEDGE AND INTER-SUBJECTIVE CONSCIENCE

Daniel Stern devoted himself, particularly in later years, to the study of the value of *implicit knowledge*. In his book *The Present Moment* he emphasizes the transient events which constitute our world of experience, mainly interested in "especially those fleeting moments, shared by two people, which generate consciousness, as they represent fundamental experiences of change in psychotherapy and provide a reference point in the plot of our most intimate everyday relationships" (Stern, 2004, p. xi). The basic assumption to which Stern refers is that change is founded upon real-life experience and that much of what is experienced in the present moment forms part of the implicit knowledge.

He went so far as to state that "the present and the conscious are the centers of gravity, rather than the past and the unconscious."

"The field of implicit relational knowledge is non-verbal, non-symbolic, unspoken and unconscious. It consists of movements, affective patterns, expectations and even cognitive schemes. Most of what we know about our relationship with others, including transference, forms part of this implicit relational knowledge" (Stern, 2004, p. 200).

The phenomenon of implicit knowledge is of vital importance in psychotherapy. Eighty percent of what happens during the session takes place on the level of phenomenological consciousness, which is informed by experiences we're aware of only in the moment they take place, after which they disappear and do not become part of memory. But when two individuals co-create a shared inter-subjective experience in the present moment, the phenomenological consciousness of one overlaps that of the other, generating a synchronicity between what one of them shows of himself and what the other gathers.

"This experience is lived by both, in the sense that each one intuitively participates in the experience of the other. Both grasp the inter-subjective sharing of their reciprocal experience without necessarily putting it into words and this becomes part of the implicit knowledge in their relationship. This creates a new inter-subjective field between participants, which modifies their relationship and induces them to undertake new itineraries together. The moment generates a particular form of consciousness, the inter-subjective consciousness, and this is coded into memory and, most notably, rewrites the past. Transformation in psychotherapy, or in any other relationship, takes place thanks to these sudden and unpredictable changes in the way we are with others" (Stern, 2004, p. 19).

Reading these thoughts by Daniel Stern, it seems appropriate that we should borrow his words to describe the essence of forty years of clinical work with families. While the concept of implicit knowledge is a legacy of systemic-relational therapies based on experience, the concept of inter-subjective consciousness and the rewriting of the past in the present, as formulated by Stern, is extraordinary.

We have always intuitively stated that, in family therapy, it is *the story* that heals. It now seems that Stern allows us to go beyond intuition and opens an extraordinary field of study and research, greatly widening the parameters of the systemic-relational model.

A very efficient way to understand the unsaid on an experiential level through action is *family sculpture*, introduced by Virginia Satir (1964).

The sculpture consists of one or more family members building a visual and spatial representation of family relationships during the session; the "family drama"—with all gradations of emotional expressions—comes to life through the arrangement of bodies in space, poses and facial expressions, the play between proximity and distance, and the direction of gazes. Through the sculpture of family relationships, it is possible to bypass language and overcome the restrictions of rational logic, allowing for deeper exploration, more intense and more unconscious emotions, and the widening of the interpretation of reality.

TRI-GENERATIONAL THEORY OF ADOLESCENCE

Following Murray Bowen's (1979) and James Framo's (1992) pioneering studies, the systemic-relational approach has given profound importance to the *process of differentiation of the Self from the family of origin*. In other words: within the dynamic equilibrium between affiliation and separation every person, in the course of their life, should be able to individuate from their family and overcome dependency needs.

The tri-generational model, as proposed by several pioneers of family therapy—among whom Whitaker (1989), Bowen (1979), Framo (1992), Williamson (1981), and later elaborated by Andolfi in several scientific publications (Andolfi, 2000a, 2003; Andolfi, Angelo, D'Atena, 2001; Andolfi et al., 2007)—requires the observation of family relations over time. It is a model that considers both the structural dimension (Minuchin, 1974) and the historical and developmental dimension with which the therapist interacts. This happens not only for the problem-adolescent's personal history, but also for that of his parents, their relationship and their respective families of origin, along paths of enquiry which aim to connect—on a vertical axis—as many planes as the generations examined (Andolfi, Angelo, D'Atena, 2001).

Within the field of systemic theory many authors have proposed the triangle as the unit of measurement of evolving family relationships: Bowen (1978), Framo (1992), Whitaker (1989), Walsh (1982), Haley (1980), Hoffman (1981), Minuchin (1974), Scabini (1985), Andolfi (1987), to name only the most relevant, while in the field of research it's important to mention the most recent studies by Elizabeth Fivaz on the *primary triangle* (Fivaz-Depeursinge, Corboz-Warnery, 1999). Once the triad is adopted as the unit of study of human relations, of functional patterns within the family and, most of all, of the emergence of psychopathology in a family member, the observations about what is real will deeply differ from those made using the dyad as a lens. Obviously, the modalities of clinical intervention and research will also be influenced by these different assumptions: suffice to think, for example, about the theory of attachment, which is based on the observation of the mother-child dyad.

Relational triangles are thus understood as the elementary structure of all relations, including those in which, apparently, only two people are involved. Even in this case we find that, for each of these subjects, there exists a figure of reference who acts as a third person in the relationship, though belonging to a different space and time or, more frequently, to a different generational level.

As described in many books (Andolfi, Angelo, de Nichilo, 1987; Andolfi, 2003; Falcucci et al., 2006), we define "tri-generational" those relational triangles in which those who are involved are placed on three different generational levels, e.g., grandfather, father, (grand)son. By a tri-generational family we mean an enlarged family map arranged along a vertical plane, intersected by at least three horizontal planes. Those who belong to the same generational level are placed on the same plane; therefore, going top-down, we will find the generation of the grandparents, their children, and grandchildren respectively, linked in various ways by relational triangles, identified spatially by family coordinates indicating the people involved and the level they belong to.

We stated several times that the construction of an observational diagram makes the understanding of the individual and of his developmental processes easier. This diagram should enable us to view a person's present behavior as a relational metaphor, that is, as an indirect signal of past needs and emotional involvements which find concrete expression within present relationships (Andolfi, Angelo, de Nichilo, 1987). Thus, verbal or analogic information on how a relationship between a father and adolescent son is expressed today (we will now refer to these levels as second and third generation) contains an implicit and complementary aspect, which also informs us about how a parent perceives his past relationship with his own father today, thus moving the emotional content of the information to the upper level, between the first and the second generation.

The complexity increases if all this is then connected to the abstract and idealized images of "being the father and being the son" which everyone adopts more or less strongly from their own cultural and family context, and which, at times, assume the value of real behavioral codes.

In this web of personal and cultural values and meanings, it can be of a great usefulness to study family myths and their evolution in the "becoming" of relationships. The myth becomes a scheme through which reality is interpreted and in which real and fantasy elements coexist, inherited in part from the family of origin and partly constructed by the current family (*ibidem*). Specific events of family or individual life, especially during critical phases (births, deaths, weddings, marital separations, chronic disease, economic crises, accidents etc.) can arouse strong emotional reactions and huge family tensions, causing each family member to assume a different role and function according to his or her position in that specific *mythical constellation*.

The myth can be constructed and developed over the course of at least three generations, becoming a matrix of knowledge, representing union and cohesion to those who believe in its truth. However, in other situations, the weight of family myths can lie heavily on the younger generations and render a healthy and autonomous developmental process difficult. In adolescence this can lead to reactive depression, as in Ciro's case.

Practice illustration: Ciro and the choice of names

Ciro, a fifteen-year-old boy, was brought to therapy because of depression. During the interview with the family we discover that he was born two years after the loss of the firstborn, an eight-year-old boy who drowned in a lake not far from their home. Ciro's task since his birth has been to fill a tragic family void: the loss of this drowned child. Moreover, the name chosen for him at birth complicates his growth even further. Ciro was, in fact, the name of the grandfather on his father's side, an outstanding man who was the mayor of the town that the family originates from. The firstborn grandson has received this name in memory of the heroic grandfather. Now the name has been passed on for the third time and with it come the expectations this family attaches to it: we can easily imagine how difficult it must have been for Ciro III to grow up healthy, while bearing on his shoulders the weight of heroic figures and tragic losses! It would be possible to write a treatise on the choice of names in families, and discover a great deal about family myths and their inter-generational transmission.

The tri-generational point of view of relationships doubtlessly allows us to grasp differences and similarities, creating connections between the relationships' various historical dimensions. Just as there is a history of the relationships, built over time between those who belong to the same generational level, which influences the choices of each individual, concurrently there is also a history of relationships between individuals who belong to different levels but exert a reciprocal influence on one another. One of the most common mistakes is to consider only the horizontal plane of relationships: for instance, it is possible to keep believing that repeated emotional failures are caused by a series of unfortunate events in the couple relationship, without realizing how greatly such relationship is vertically burdened by the conflict with parents or with other significant members of the family of origin.

Things get even more complicated when we enter the world of adolescence without a multigenerational point of view. If adolescence represents the first important phase in which the dynamic relation between belonging and separation from one's family roots seems to tend towards the second option, it's also true that the adolescent, in an often contradictory and provocative way, is looking for containment and belonging: as if to test his parents' capacity to resist being excessively manipulated by his requests for absolute freedom and autonomy (Andolfi, 2000b). For example, the clash between son and father — when the former provokes the latter — is necessary for the growth of the adolescent, who appreciates his father when he doesn't back out of the test and succeeds in holding his need to break away.

We can safely affirm that many prejudices need to be disproved, as they are not sufficiently challenged, generally speaking, in individual therapy, such as the cliché that adolescents are focused only on themselves and on their often material needs, and have no interest in their parents or family (Andolfi, Angelo, D'Atena, 2001). On the contrary, in therapy we observed that teenagers do everything they can to help their parents face their marital problems, to defend the weakest, acting at times as mediators, at times as barriers in situations of great hostility and violence between their parents. And it is they, with the therapist's help, who assist their parents to get in touch with their own adolescence and remember their own developmental processes, including the relational difficulties with their own families of origin. This journey backwards through memory enables them to return to today's problems with a kinder and more realistic vision of current difficulties and, most importantly, to support an emotional alliance between parents and children.

Finally, we believe that the tri-generational model is a fundamental lens for exploring the developmental processes and the life cycle of the family and looking for those problematic issues which, once identified, allow the therapist, and above all the family, to use the resources and the skills of each individual. In this way, the illness and psychological or relational disorder of the adolescent, as well as the consequent suffering, become not only a cause of uneasiness in the whole family, but also *links of knowledge* and vital opportunities to recover the sense of Us and rediscover the value of solidarity and reciprocal support.

ADOLESCENCE AS A TIME OF INSECURITY AND FEAR

Yet another author who dedicated himself to the study of adolescence is Vittorino Andreoli. He comes closer to a developmental idea of psychopathology and considers adolescence as a time of metamorphosis: it's acute, sudden, and combines somatic changes with emotional personality changes (Andreoli, 2006). Adolescence therefore represents a complete turn-around of all points of reference. Somatic metamorphosis implies a hormonal change, and therefore a body transformation: teenagers don't like themselves, and thus apply various solutions to camouflage their unwanted body through makeup, piercings, and tattoos. The metamorphosis of personality has to do with Ego transformation and inter-generational relationships: this means parents are perceived differently. In the final analysis, social metamorphosis puts adolescents in closer connection with their peer group than with their family world. The relationship with the school changes, as do meeting places: coffee shops, hangouts, squares. Finally, the relationship with adults also changes. These fundamental changes lead the adolescent into the depths of an identity crisis, in which previously known and stable landmarks lose their value and their functions.

According to Andreoli this identity crisis ensures that adolescence can be defined as a time of insecurity and fear. The latter produces typical defense mechanisms: escape or violence. Escape can manifest as an actual escape from home or as a more or less severe psychological escape: depression as an escape from oneself, isolation at school as an escape from others, one's own room as a shelter, attempted suicide as an escape from the world. On the other hand, violence can be enacted against others, through destructive actions against the family or society (bullying), or against oneself through drugs, alcohol, eating disorders and self-harm.

Andreoli's ideas are very stimulating for a family therapist. Above all, the concept of "transformation of family relationships" leads us to think about how parents must feel when their child undergoes such a radical change. It is a dramatic experience. Much of the work should actually be aimed at parents, who need to learn to tolerate anxiety, fear, insecurity, and, most of all, feelings of inadequacy in relation to a child "who is no longer the same"! Indeed, parents view this period as a price to pay, a "test" by their child, who is torn between staying in and staying out of the family.

Insecurity and fear during adolescence constitute neither a disease nor a psychopathology, as they are fundamental ingredients for growth. Those who have never experienced them were never adolescents, as they skipped this developmental phase. These individuals stand a good chance of living their adolescence later on, in adulthood, when they will take much greater risks.

THE ADOLESCENT SELF SYSTEM

The individual's psychodynamic changes during adolescence doubtlessly have a specific value: the developmental process follows a winding road, with straight tracts, bends, accelerations and slow-downs. The *Internal* and *External Self* pursue harmony along the same axis. If psychoanalysis, with the exception of a few examples mentioned above, wrongly underestimates the individual's relational world in this phase of development, many systemic clinicians and theoreticians who deal with adolescents seem to underestimate the importance of the intra-psychic and endogenous principles, and examine reality only through the relational lens. Adolescence is predetermined by nature, not by family or couple dynamics.

Paradoxically, the characteristics of adolescence place it in the grey area that separates psychoanalysis from systemic theories: psychoanalysts are oriented towards the intra-psychic world, while systemic theoreticians are oriented towards relationships.

Luigi Baldascini is a systemic author who has attempted to integrate the intra-psychic with the relational dimensions of adolescence. In his book *Vita da adolescenti* (1993) he constantly strives to unite the particular with the universal, to trace the connections between the worlds within which adolescents live in search of their own identity. "Adolescent psychopathology" — he affirms — "is often located within families, sometimes in schools, very often within the adolescent himself but, upon closer examination, it always includes all these systems. It is therefore reasonable to look for a theoretical model which accounts for this complexity" (*ibidem*).

The Self System, according to Baldascini, is the only organizer that connects all intra-psychic systems to one another and these to the interpersonal. It is a kind of of dynamic receptacle of everything that happens as a result of what the author defines as the *inter-systemic articulation*.

The intra-psychic subsystems include: the *cognitive system*, that is, the thought function; the *emotional system*: feelings, spiritual drive, blushing, smooth muscle contraction; the *autonomic nervous system*: mainly the instinctive and motor functions, the drive to action, aggression, the sexual drive.

The interpersonal subsystems include: the *family system*, with its bonds, its flexibility, and its relational imprint; the *peer system*, where it's possible to experiment with action, emotional well-being ("we are good together"), and cognitive co-validation ("we all think alike"); the *adult relational system*, that is to say, the drive toward constructive competition, the care of others, the assumption of responsibility and possible evolution of the adolescent's ambivalence.

The inter-systemic articulation, according to this theory, allows for two possibilities, on a continuum which goes from normality to pathology: one is *inter-systemic mobility*, understood as a synchronic articulation of the different affiliation systems. This mobility allows the adolescent to utilize—with the aim of harmonic development—the resources which originate within his various reference systems, according to their functional characteristics. The other possibility is *inter-systemic immobility*, which leads to several forms of psychopathology.

KEY POINTS IN UNDERSTANDING ADOLESCENCE

Adolescence is not a disease

For many parents the perception of adolescence—when their child hasn't yet entered it—is more akin to the fear of a disease than to the pleasure of entering a new phase of growth. "What will happen when he becomes a teenager?" is a question they often ask themselves when the child is still small. The concern for the future, in these cases, takes precedence over current events and there's a tendency to interpret what happens to the child as an indicator of what will happen in later years. Although this attitude can't be considered adequate, we have to admit that adolescence expresses itself through the exaggeration of everything and, as such, can be feared like a bomb ready to explode.

The peer group—so fundamental in the adolescent's growth—is often perceived by the parents with apprehension and is generally regarded as a risk of falling in with a bad crowd. In short, the prejudice grows at the same rate as the fear of losing one's child and, consequently, increases the control over the adolescent's behavior and friendships. Mass media makes matters worse by constantly describing an appalling reality of adolescence: bullying, chemical highs, addiction to drugs and alcohol, Saturday night deaths.

The adolescent is not an overgrown child

The evolutionary processes of an individual do not correspond to an overlapping of phases, rather, each should be considered as an individual process, taking place through several phases of discontinuity. If the child isn't a miniature adult, it is equally true that an adolescent isn't an over grown child. Often, when a family with a problematic adolescent comes to therapy, the family members consider the teenager as a child who doesn't want or doesn't know how to grow up. But this isn't so. Even the child is a subject with competence (Andolfi et al., 2007), although his language is more simple and straightforward, while the competence of the adolescent is completely different from that of the child and is strongly based upon ambivalence. Parents and therapists should be able to appreciate this duality and observe the various phases between one stage and the other, as problems can arise precisely during these critical moments. It's important to remember, however, that a regressive fluctuation during the adolescent's period of transformation is totally physiological and predictable, and should be understood as a going backwards to take a run-up before the leap forward.

Adolescence is not the age of individuation: the adolescent's need for separation is as strong as his need to belong

Jay Haley in *Leaving Home: The Therapy of Disturbed Young People* (1980) speaks about adolescence as the phase of individuation. He talks about this within the context of the U.S., where eighteen-years-olds leave their homes to go to college. In our country (Italy), very few young people leave the family to study elsewhere and, even so, the separation from the family to go and study elsewhere can't be considered a downright individuation, as the economic dependency from the family still persists, often accompanied by an emotional one. At most, the physical separation from parents can be considered as an autonomy exercise as far as the management of everyday life is concerned, starting from the organization and administration of the house.

Military service, which hasn't been compulsory for the past few years in Italy, despite its negative characteristics had some merit: young people had to abandon their security to enter a different world from their own, in which they were forced to coexist with people coming from different places and cultures, even though they were all Italians.

In the most primitive cultures there are often important propitiatory rites corresponding to rites of passage in the life of individuals, especially during male adolescence, whilst in our culture there is no longer a rite which focuses on the transition between childhood and adolescence and, later, on the passage to adulthood. At one time, marriage was the rite of passage, because people married young; today, adolescence is so long that marriage cannot constitute a rite of passage before the age of thirty. In northern Europe young people actually move out at eighteen or twenty. This is unthinkable in our context. Ours can be considered as a social problem: there are no rites to celebrate the exit from the family and the latter tends to keep its children longer due to its caring, controlling, and enmeshing characteristics. Just on the other side of the border, in France, for example, the models of growth are totally different, while in Italy changes are never rapid, due also to the precarious economic situation affecting young people today.

Bowen and Williamson, like Haley, lived in the United States. In contrast, they both maintained that individuation occurs between the ages of thirty-five and forty-five, and not at eighteen. This is the time when individuation is complete and what Williamson (1981) describes as *inter-generational intimidation* loses its strength. It's important to take into account that the physical separation from the family of origin strongly differs from the development of an individual into adulthood: the latter requires a much longer timescale. In therapy, we often find individuals who, at this age and later, have not individuated at all. Let's consider how many adults are still subject, in a humiliating and alarming way, to their families' affective and emotional rules, or how many adult men, after marital separation, go back to their mother.

In reality, individuation should actually be characterized according to Baldascini's (1993) inter-systemic theory and be a detachment on various levels: the affective, the emotional, and the economic.

How often do we see, in therapy, siblings who are distant from each other because they have somehow been trapped in their own family dependencies, and have ended up manipulating them! Being children is about a vertical inter-generational relationship (how our parents programmed us), while being siblings is about another kind of relationship, set on an horizontal plane, which becomes a true achievement if we manage to discover a generational alliance and free ourselves from parental mandates and pressures.

Another important concept to bear in mind concerns the authorization to move out of home: it is not the parents who should give it to their children, it is the children who must take responsibility for doing so. The attainment of personal autonomy is defined as "achievement" (Williamson, 1981) because it is a demanding task, especially when parents would like to keep their child longer. Autonomy is a part of the differentiation of the Self from the family of origin (Bowen, 1978) and of an integrated personality that is aware of how to place itself in the world.

A good therapist is able to understand that whenever a teenager shouts his independence, assumes a contemptuous attitude towards the family and its rules, affirming that what is outside is better, he's actually stating the opposite: his fear of growing up is so great that his greatest need is to feel he has to repair his affiliations.

From the point of view of symptomatology we should ask ourselves whether the pathological dependencies often shown by young people are not desperate attempts at substituting a *healthy dependency* which is now missing. How many parents, how many fathers, are substituted by a bottle of wine, a needle or a video-game? In therapy it's easy to see that as soon as a sense of family is restored, alcohol and drugs can quickly be downsized. During several follow-ups, after the conclusion of therapy, we asked adolescents: "What is it that allowed you to change?" they answered: "It's simple, it was my parents' love!"

It's important to ponder on this kind of observation because, while the concept of separation and autonomy is more visible and more socially obvious, the concept of affiliation, which is also fundamental, is more hidden and implicit and, as such, more difficult to understand for families, educators, and therapists.

The family history is engraved inside the adolescent

Parents often think that a child lives his life independently from what has happened and is happening in his family. There are many events that children are not aware of concerning their parents and their family, especially those which happened before they were born. The situation in reality is not like this and adolescents are always very curious about family events pre-dating their birth, even though they might appear totally indifferent.

Teenagers are actually self-educated experts of their families, they "studied" their parents all their lives, observing their relationship, their emotional states which, as we know (Andolfi, 2003), are the result of the encounter between two family histories. To clarify: what the adolescent knows about the past and, therefore, about the present of his own family isn't so much a body of facts or events as it is a *relational product* created in his family by the meanings given to such events. In this sense, we can state that the child is the depository of the family history.

During therapy we should listen to the adolescent as someone who is competent regarding his family's world.

Therapists are rarely interested in listening to the adolescent as a family expert, because they are too busy curing his illnesses and controlling his aggressive or deviant behavior. How do we then give back the voice to adolescents who are brought into therapy to resolve their problems? Is psychopathology our framework of knowledge, or are developmental processes the framework we need to interpret psychopathology? This is a very important therapeutic question. The majority of professionals are unconsciously more interested in understanding the manifestations of a psychosomatic, emotional, or behavioral disorder and in treating them, possibly in a few sessions, rather than in looking for the relational competence of the adolescent. Therefore individual cognitive-behavioral interventions or brief focal therapies which tend to make the symptoms disappear are very common: the focus, in these cases, is on modifying a dysfunction rather than on searching for the familial and relational components of a phenomenon.

The adolescent is the strong-arm of family conflicts

The violence expressed by the adolescent is frequently connected to the covert and, above all, unexpressed violence in the parental couple. It is not unusual to see families who come to therapy because they're very concerned about their aggressive child and to realize that we're in the presence of a conflict which concerns the parental couple, who completely denies it. In these cases we speak of *disguised couple therapy* (Andolfi, Angelo, D'Atena, 2001): these are situations in which a child, through some issue of his own, brings his parents to therapy to allow them to face their own couple issues.

In families it's difficult to realize that the conflict is often on a parental level and that the adolescent's disorder is the smoking gun, the evidence of what happens in the older generation; it is a war to which the adolescent also belongs, but in a reflected way, as the product of the whole. There are many therapists who, much like the police, intervene directly with the violent person: it is easy to assume that, as he is the strong-arm, he's also the most dangerous!

The adolescent's verbal signals are contradictory

When the adolescent speaks it is more important to listen to what lies hidden behind what he is saying, rather than to the simple verbal content. As already mentioned, we should never forget that ambivalence is the most typical characteristic of adolescence and its most common form of communication. The adolescent needs ambivalence to be able to practice being constantly on one side or the other of the *belonging/individuation* axis, in his search for the correct balance. Let's not forget that regulation of distances, acceptance of the Self and coherence are ever his objectives from the moment he begins to develop his identity. We should always bear in mind this concept when we speak with adolescents, so as not to lose awareness that what the adolescent says is only what he's able to say, in line with the role he's playing in his family. To understand the real situation, it might be more useful for a therapist to listen to what the young person does not say; for example, if an adolescent speaks about strong self-confidence, the first thing we should think about is where he is hiding the exact opposite, his lack of confidence. If an adolescent yells *no* to an affective request from family members, we should also ask ourselves which part of *yes* he might be looking for.

The non-verbal signals of the adolescent are complex and contradictory

Consistent with what we stated above, non-verbal signals can also be strongly ambivalent: the need for a relationship, for intimacy, is easily disguised by oppositional behavior that conveys defiance and distance. The language of the adolescent's body often underlines those provocative attitudes connected to what he would like to be, rather than relational modalities and postures that might uncover his real needs for affection and intimacy. The adolescent, in his exaggerated push towards independence, is often driven to deny his own needs, because he sees them as vulnerable parts which get in his way. This does not mean that we therapists should also deny these parts in an attempt to help him; on the contrary, it's our duty to listen to them, welcome them, and render them more explicit and visible within the family. During this process, it's very useful to be able to play on both extremes of ambivalence at the same time, in order not to miss the possibility of an encounter with the adolescent.

For the adolescent the peer group is a lab of fundamental knowledge and experience

Often parents don't realize that the fear they feel when facing children who have changed would diminish if they would only allow them to listen to loud music, have friends over, and basically invite adolescence into the home. They would allow themselves to understand a reality they have often imagined as threatening, because never encountered directly, and thus acquire more adequate skills to face this period of great family instability. This does not mean that parents need to be their children's friends, a quite confusing and useless role; it rather means they should enter (as observers) into that part of the adolescent which is unknown because only enacted in the outside world. In adolescence, it is fundamental to associate with peers, because this constitutes the other polarity of reality, as necessary for development as the family.

Following the original experiences of Russell Haber, well described in *Please Help Me With This Family* (Andolfi, Haber, 1994), for several years we have included special sessions with friends in all family therapy where adolescent difficulties are an issue. These encounters with peer groups are an important resource and allow us to observe other dimensions of the teenager, which are difficult to contact during family sessions. We will describe this in subsequent chapters.

"Gang Culture" in our society is directly connected to the father's absence

It is a common belief that male violence manifesting within gangs is directly proportional to the absence of the father in the modern family and in society. Violence comes from fear and insecurity. The father, especially for male children, is an important source of reassurance and his absence increases insecurity and fear, which transmute into violence. Our society, so very keen to detect the problems of adolescents, does not seem as interested in the problem created by the absence of the father, a sure and incontrovertible fact. Society does not identify a father's absence as problematic; it simply accepts it passively as fact of life.

If we were to return to fathers their function as competent parents, we would find that things could change a great deal, especially in the upbringing of male children, who are otherwise only influenced by the maternal side. The nature of a mother-male child relationship is, in biological terms, fusing and passionate. If this relationship does not change in due time, in childhood, and, most importantly, in adolescence, there will be notable risks for the child. In this sense, the father has a protective function towards the child, as he disengages the mother-child relationship.

Avoiding a pathological stigmatization of the adolescent's behavior: pathology must be diagnosed and classified according to developmental criteria

If we were able to get rid of the Cinderella syndrome which still affects the world of psychology, we would realize how useless it is to refer exclusively to a medical-psychiatric model for understanding and helping families with difficult adolescents. Obviously diagnosis is very important in our work, but this doesn't mean the static, classificatory diagnosis of DSM V, but rather a structural and developmental one. Structural diagnosis will inform us about the extent of the problem in the present moment within the family context and will be based upon the concept of clear or permeable generational boundaries and conflict deviation (Minuchin, 1974); while a developmental diagnosis will allow us to assess the current psychopathology of the adolescent within the developmental cycle of the family and of life events (Scabini, 1985).

This way of proceeding and gathering knowledge (diagnosis) has a relational value, which carries deep meanings. If these meanings are understood, they will provide all the necessary resources to overcome the *impasse* created by a psychological problem. We should therefore focus our attention on the whole person, especially when the subject is still developing and everything is very plastic and strongly transformative. A phobic, drug-addicted, suicidal teenager isn't wholly described by these adjectives rather, he is a person who is growing up and presenting a specific problem within many potential resources.

BUILDING A THERAPEUTIC ALLIANCE WITH THE FAMILY THROUGH THE ADOLESCENT

The therapeutic alliance is the necessary and main ingredient of every clinical intervention. If a therapeutic alliance is not established, therapy does not happen; it is necessary to build a relationship founded upon trust, which is then consolidated through the experience of therapy itself. Since we're talking about a group, the bonding process will necessarily be multiple. We've shown in many works (Andolfi, Angelo, de Nichilo, 1987; Andolfi, 2003; Andolfi et al., 2007) our way of building therapeutic complicity with the problem child or teenager for whom therapy was requested. Unlike individual therapy, where the alliance is clearly formed by the dyad patient-therapist, things get a little more complicated in group situations.

So, how do we build a therapeutic alliance with the entire family? The starting point is always represented by the person for whom the intervention is requested, in this case, the teenager. We have always argued that the direct intervention the therapist makes with a single patient has a great relational importance and relevance for all family members. The entrance to the affective world of the family is therefore made through the adolescent.

Using a triadic model to understand human relationships

The use of a triadic model is fundamental to understanding that the therapist does not bond with the adolescent within a dual dimension: on the contrary, the alliance is built as the entire family gets involved through the relationship with the adolescent.

Many relational triangles are formed during our growth and accompany us throughout our lives, starting with the primary triangle formed when we are born. In *The Myth of Atlas* (Andolfi, Angelo, de Nichilo, 1987), we describe clearly the inter-generational networks that accompany our development: it is precisely the possibility of reactivating or modifying relational schemes in therapy that allows for change.

Directness as an antidote to protectiveness

Protection is essential in the care of minors; protectiveness is, on the other hand, a relational scheme of hiding, a kind of defense to avoid facing conflicts and problems in affective relationships. Being direct is very different from being directive, which implies a certain authoritarianism and imposition. Rather, it implies the ability to be authentic and to go to the heart of the matter, without beating about the bush. It's a relational scheme whose aim is to relate to everyone with true curiosity and openness, by being open about our own opinions and intuitions, by getting in touch with our patients' conflicts and suffering without hesitation or prejudice.

Being direct does not imply that the therapist should be the protagonist in session; on the contrary, he represents a safe guide who allows each family member to experiment interacting with others in a different and more authentic way. Perhaps, in so doing, we may lose something of the circular causality that systemic therapists are so fond of, but surely this attitude is created within the relationship and represents a personal reply to affective requests originating from the therapeutic experience. In this sense, being direct really represents an antidote to protectiveness, which is understood as self-censorship in expressing thoughts and feelings for fear of threatening the other and putting the relationship in jeopardy. Protectiveness, especially between parents and adolescent children, can be very harmful as it can collude with substitute caregiving: in so doing the main actors (the parents) deprive themselves of the chance of playing an active role and experiencing real intimacy with their children. In this sense the therapist's directness becomes a *modeling* during the session, a kind of educational model for the parents.

Empathy and support of the adolescent as a person

Empathy and emotional support of the adolescent constitute the foundations upon which all therapeutic interventions need to be based in order to be accepted by the client. The more these factors are present in the relationship with the adolescent, the better will the therapist be able to use his instruments.

Empathy is not just a kind and accepting modality used to create a relationship with others, it is more importantly a creative way of interacting moment by moment, by listening, observing, asking questions, never taking anything for granted. It's about paying attention to the adolescent's words, gestures, and silences, and giving him feedback on what we've understood of him. It is the ability to identify oneself with someone so closely as to grasp his thoughts, his innermost states of mind, and his emotions, without feeling overwhelmed.

Valuing the adolescent's relational skills: the adolescent as a co-therapist

We already described in detail the importance of identifying and using the relational skills every adolescent carries within his family to enter into the history of the family. We have always considered children and teenagers as valid co-therapists and, for this reason, we ask them to move throughout the session, often placing them close to us and encouraging a physical connection which strengthens the message of collaboration such as: "You really can help me!" Asking them to move also helps us to check their willingness and freedom of action within the therapeutic space, informing us directly about the level of rigidity of family relationships.

A further benefit will be gained when the therapist recognizes and supports these skills from the beginning of the first session: he will then be able to build the therapeutic alliance more easily through direct contact with the teenager, in a totally unexpected way to him and his family, who are often too focused on the problem which brought them to therapy.

The idea of involving the symptomatic adolescent, viewing him as a connection to reach existential and developmental dilemmas in the family, goes back over twenty-five years, when we first thought about considering children and adolescents as *points of entry* to the family system (Andolfi, Angelo, 1985). The idea of seeing young people as actual co-therapists, thus giving full value to their relational skills within the family, was coined only a decade later (Andolfi, Haber, 1994).

Amplification of the problem/pathology presented by the adolescent and its redefinition in an inter-generational perspective

You might think that enlarging a problem, an embarrassing issue, a violent or irrational behavior during a session, could be perceived as a lack of respect or even as a risky operation. In reality the amplification of the symptom represents its staging, and while it is magnified we can find the most adequate ways of reducing the meaning connected to the problem, which until then was, so to speak, "life-sized." By widening the perspective, it's possible to appreciate all of its facets, to directly or indirectly redefine the problem, and to view its seriousness with a sense of proportion.

Our therapeutic experience itself shows that, once the problem is magnified and its connections with other realities of the family are seen, we are able to understand its inter-generational and historic dimensions. Of course, what we just stated implies a provocative intervention procedure (Selvini Palazzoli et al., 1975; Andolfi et al., 1983; Andolfi, Angelo, de Nichilo, 1987), but this approach, together with strong support for the adolescent's integrity, allows the opening of the therapeutic scenario to new forms of relationship and reciprocal assumption of responsibility.

Valuing the adolescent's ambivalence through play and humor

Play and humor, as we already saw when discussing couple dynamics and, most of all, childhood problems (Andolfi et al., 2007; Fal-

cucci et al., 2006), are two ingredients without which therapy cannot proceed too far: we become bored, and are unable to build a creative context
which allows physical as well as mental and emotional movement.

Ambivalence is a fundamental existential reality which is present
in all stages of growth and has nothing to do with hypocrisy or deceitful-
ness: it is an often confusing and uncertain way of dealing with choices
in life and in most significant relationships, both within the family and
the social context, which changes along with circumstances.

As adolescence is an evolutionary phase marked by strong transformations, ambivalence is consequently accentuated during this time of
life; therefore, the therapist should learn to play with the adolescent's
ambivalence and respect both its polarities.

Building metaphors and *as if* language

The metaphor is a figure of speech that consists in transferring to
an object the proper meaning of another object, using an analogy. One of
the main characteristics of metaphors is that of creating an image for
emotions, behavior, and types of relationships that a person has within a
system. Metaphors are built together, during a session, to express images
or family roles that are deeply rooted in the family. These symbols often
contain feelings that were hidden and allow difficult to express relational
aspects and contents to emerge.

The metaphor does not belong to the one who introduces it, be it
a family member or the therapist, rather it belongs to the entire group
that participates in the *metaphor-building process* (Whitaker, 1989). The
therapist introduces an image generated from what he has understood
about the family, and he needs to verify the impact of such an image on
the family.

Adolescence is, surely, the developmental phase in which analo-
gies are used more than direct language; therefore, it is very easy to use
the metaphor as a mean of communication with teenagers, as is the *as if
language* (Andolfi, 2003), which enables us to circumvent the verbal defenses of the adolescent.

Intuition, joining and imagination during the session

Intuition is unconscious, instinctive, and hard to intellectualize,
because as soon as one tries to rationalize intuition, it ceases to be such.
It's very difficult to teach how to use intuition, at least in a direct form,
because it is part of the creativity we're born with. Nevertheless, intui-

tion helps us to connect deeply with others and is, therefore, fundamental to therapy.

Joining has to do with knowing how to persuade others to our
reasoning and is, like intuition, a vital factor in affective relationships
and in building significant therapeutic connections. It's a two-way path:
not only is it necessary to know how to enter the world of the other, we
must ensure that the other can enter ours, to allow an exchange of creativity to begin.

Imagination is just as fundamental, but is often limited as a
result of rigidity in facing life's problems. There's no doubt that the more
severe the problem brought by a family to therapy—perhaps caused by
an adolescent child—the less you can use imagination, because the negative reality of the present absorbs everyone's energies. The reactivation
of the capacity to imagine is an amazing medicine in therapy, and it is
facilitated by the use of the *as if language* (Andolfi, 2003).

Lynn Hoffman (1981), in referring to deep connections with
families, stated that Whitaker was able to pass from the unthinkable to
the unimaginable. It is as if there were different levels: what is known,
what can be known and, on a deeper level, the unimaginable. Being able
to join with members of a family, to allow the unimaginable to emerge
from within them, is a great resource. An even deeper level of knowledge is reached when you are able to speak about what cannot yet be
imagined.

Chapter 2
Violent adolescents and family crisis

ACTION AND KNOWLEDGE

Is action determined by thoughts, or are thoughts caused by action? This is often a controversial question for researchers in childhood development and family relationships. Daniel Stern (2004), in his outstanding book, *The Present Moment in Psychotherapy and Everyday Life*, describes action as a main road to knowledge. While Stern is criticized by psychoanalysts for giving primary value to action rather than thought, the recent paradigm shift in the cognitive sciences suggests the mind is not separate from the body. Rather, thought is born and thrives on bodily sensations as well as on movement and action (Clark, Fairburn, 1997; Damasio, 1999; Varela, Thomson, Rosch, 1991). As Stern (2004) added: "in therapy, the inter-subjective encounter in the present moment takes place between two incorporated minds that interact physically and mentally" (p. 146). The innovation in his approach is that the present moment is pivotal to the therapeutic enquiry. What's more, by recognizing *implicit knowledge*, a change takes place in the way in which the relationship between action and language is considered. The balance shifts towards the *nonverbal* level of communication and, in so doing, it becomes possible to recover knowledge and therapeutic experience developed by systemic and gestalt-oriented approaches.

The value of action has been clearly outlined by a well known criminologist, Gaetano De Leo (1989) who defined it as forming and creating identity in its social, communicative and relational dimensions. Action is a communicative construct within a systemic perspective. It is a communicative "language" and "discourse" linked to the relationship between the individual and the Self, his family, his other relational systems, and the complex system of the observer.

BOWLBY AND FAMILY VIOLENCE

In the article "Violence in the family," John Bowlby (1984) stepped beyond the boundaries of his own area of expertise to offer rather suggestive interpretations for a series of common behaviors within the family. He came very close to a family therapy approach by considering behavioral systems, observing relationships and interactions, although mainly on a dyadic level and referring to "family attitudes." Bowlby saw family violence as a distorted and exaggerated version of potentially functional behavior: attachment behavior on the one hand and care-giving on the other. He turned around the more obvious explanations for violent behavior, such as the fight for power, the expression of aggressive instincts, the reaction to frustration etc., by connecting violence to significant bonds and observations on attachment needs, separation and mourning.

Violence is therefore an answer — distorted because of its intensity, but natural from a qualitative point of view — to the behavior of the person implicated in the relationship, whenever this is perceived as threatening to the relationship itself and the need for dependency by the person who reacts violently. It's an attempt to preserve the bond or recapture the qualities that have been compromised by a certain kind of behavior. Bowlby gave the example of mothers who harshly reprimand or hit their children when the youngsters' careless actions put their lives in danger, thus threatening the emotional connection.

Taking Bowlby's perspective, anger and violence can be provoked when family bonds involving long-term relationships charged with strong emotions, such as those involving a partner, parents, and children are threatened. What this suggests is that underlying adolescent violence may be a feeling of loss, whether real or imagined, and that the violent action is only the tip of the iceberg.

REACTIVE VIOLENCE IN ADOLESCENTS

Violent behavior in adolescence can be present in severe psychiatric disorders, such as psychosis, alcoholism, bipolar disorder, substance abuse, and addiction or sociopathy. We cannot use the same parameters for violence associated with psychosis as for an adolescent who reacts to repeated conflict and hostility between parents. Such *reactive violence* in the adolescent's familial and social context is the focus of this chapter.

From a developmental perspective, Andreoli (2006) describes adolescence as a stage of insecurity and fear connected to an identity crisis caused by the destabilization of landmarks, through the growth process, which were previously functional for the individual, when he or she was still a child. One of the most common defense mechanisms in the face of fear is attack. This can be directed towards others, through destructive acts in the family, or outside (at school, in the street, in a pub), often developing into bullying. In other cases, violent acts may be directed towards themselves, through self-harming, the use of drugs, alcohol, or refusal of food leading to severe eating disorders.

A violent action isn't limited to acting-out: it expresses and conveys other interpersonal meanings on an implicit level. In this sense it can be viewed as a provocation—often difficult to interpret, sometimes desperate and dramatic—which the adolescent uses to communicate to the world his primary needs for care and appreciation. The violent male adolescent can become the "strong-arm" of the family when facing severe marital hostilities or inter-generational distortions; in other cases, the behavior is a desperate cry for acknowledgment by parents. His bullying or deviant behavior can also convey an identity void or a lack of family and social support. The male adolescent's identity is, in effect, built within the family and the social contexts he belongs to, and takes different forms and expressions, which can vary according to role, gender, and generational distortions present in the family.

ADOLESCENT VIOLENCE AND INTER-GENERATIONAL DISTORTIONS

The author has previously described various aspects of family functioning and inter-generational networks within which persons develop (Andolfi et al., 1987; Andolfi, 2003; Andolfi at al., 2007). In this chapter the triangular dimension of intra-familial relationships will be outlined through clinical examples. The triad is indeed a fundamental and well-structured unit of measurement to observe the development of a child or an adolescent, surely more complete than the dyad, which inevitably leaves out the third element—in effect excluding the father or other parent as a significant co-presence in the process of care-giving and upbringing of children. Such exclusion not only concerns the other parent's protective and attachment functions towards the children, but also disregards the quality of the marital dimension and its influence (positive or negative) on the parent-child relationship. At the same time, if we add another generation, we can observe how the dynamic of actual couple relationships, is strongly correlated to the quality of the bonds each partner has with his own family of origin and his process of differ-entiation, so well described by Bowen (1978), Framo (1992), and others.

These complex three-generational dynamics provide a means of both examining and treating the violent behavior of an adolescent in a family. Family dysfunctions are generally connected to confusion in generational boundaries and sub-systems that one belongs to: children, parents, or grandparents, and the violent behavior expressed by the ado-lescent can represent the "strong-arm" of unresolved or negated genera-tional conflicts.

In every rigid and severely dysfunctional family situation, when an appearance of normality must be preserved at all costs, arrogant and denigrating actions from an adolescent can be seen as a strong signal for help and a request for family change.

Immaturity is a relational modality that can be easily learned within the family and, as Bowen (1978) said, these processes of imma-turity can be transmitted from one generation to the next. Therefore, if two persons are scarcely differentiated from their families of origin, it is possible that their child will follow the same limited path in his/her differentiation process. However, children who grow up with immature parents can also react in the opposite way, becoming extremely mature and responsible, often assuming the role of "parentified" child.

Following Bowlby (1984) and De Leo (1989) it was suggested that violent behavior can often be unconsciously transmitted from one generation to the next. Sometimes this is not easily recognizable, as violence can be expressed in different ways, which may be implicit and subtle but no less damaging and dramatic than the visible ones.

Practice illustration: From miracle child to monster

We would now like to support these theoretical statements with the presentation of a clinical example in which a family begins therapy to deal with the extreme violence of their eighteen-year-old son, Andrea, described by his parents as a monster.

What follows is part of the description of the son's violence given by the father:

As years went by, almost suddenly, about two years ago, Andrea's problem emerged: he modeled his behavior on brutal, absolute violence, without rules, without respect for himself or others, still less for his mother, father, or older brother. My family has lived these past two years in a climate of terror and fear; there have been innumerable epi-sodes of brutality towards myself and towards the mother, together with an increased distancing from the world, from life, from friends. His only panacea was food: yes, eating until he reached a monstrous weight: over 136 kilos. A monster!

The first session is attended by Andolfi (the therapist), the father, the mother, Andrea, and Giampiero, Andrea's older brother.

The following dialogue shows the subtle game of provocation that immediately begins between the therapist and the boy. The latter scrutinizes the therapist to see what he's made of, and more importantly, if he can deal with him without fear. The therapist provokes him with absurd questions, beginning a kind of dance to earn himself the role of guide during the session. The boy "dances with him" and follows him. We quote the original text: the boy uses Roman slang and the therapist imitates him.

Why did you bring your family here today?

Therapist: So, why did you bring this family here today?
Andrea: Dunno!
Mother: Don't say that all the time!
Andrea: Hey, dunno, they brought me here!
Mother: Well, go on... tell him!
Andrea: They brought me here!
Therapist: Wasn't it your body that brought them here?
Andrea: I came myself!
Therapist: I mean, didn't they come because of your body?
Andrea: Which body?
Therapist: Yours! Dad is talking about your body. They're worried about your body.
Andrea: They aren't worried about my body!
Therapist: What would I know! It's the first time I see you!
Andrea: But... I know!
Therapist: So, what would you like me to do with them?
Andrea: Dunno!
Father: Don't think about the camera. (*referring to the filming of the session*) Don't think about anything! That is not important, it isn't a problem. I've already explained that, otherwise we'll be here for days... clearly Professor Andolfi...
Andrea: Dad, I don't get it!

Mother (attentive and considerate, as if she were dealing with a small child; she will keep this attitude during the entire session): He actually didn't understand the question!

Therapist: Sure?

Mother: Yes.

Therapist: I'm sorry, wasn't it your body that brought the three of them here?

Andrea: No, we came all together!

Mother: No, it isn't that! He hasn't understood yet, he's trying to find the right words for...

Therapist: It seems to me that the only thing that does not appear in the case history is that you, somehow, are not very smart.

Andrea: No! I think it's you who is not very smart! *(The mother touches his arm as if to calm him.)*

Therapist: I don't believe you are not very smart, I'm just telling your mom that I think you understood the question perfectly.

Mother (stroking her son's shoulder): He doesn't mean that.

Therapist: I don't think it's a problem of intelligence!

Andrea (gesturing towards his father): He's the one who brought the family here!

Therapist: On paper, in theory! But you were the one who brought the family here, in practice!

Andrea: Okay, I brought it here!

Therapist: And what would you like me to do, since you brought them here?

Andrea: How should I know? You're the one who should know!

Therapist: Well, actually I should know, but since I hardly know this family, you can help me to understand!

Apocalypse Now

Therapist: Did you come willingly or did they force you?

Andrea: They forced me!

Therapist: Ah! Now I get it! *(The therapist is holding a rubber ball. He throws it at the boy who immediately throws it back. Then he throws it at his brother, who also throws it back.)* There was some kind of problem!

Andrea (smiling amused): What are we doing here? A football game? *(Everybody smiles.)*

Therapist: How can we do this? Why did they force you to come? Did they think you wouldn't come?

Andrea: Of course I wouldn't have!

Therapist (throws him the ball again; the boy immediately throws it back): Why?

Andrea: Dunno!

Therapist: You're a big boy, why do you let them make you come here?

Andrea: I come...

Therapist: Who pushed you the most?

Andrea: Everyone!

Therapist (gesturing towards the brother): Him too?

Andrea: Him too... no! Not him! They made him come as well!

Therapist: They made you come, too?

Giampiero: Yes, but then I work, so....

Therapist: You were working?

Giampiero: Yes.

Therapist: While you were at home watching a good war movie...

Andrea: No, I was sleeping!

Therapist: Japanese?

Andrea: I don't watch Japanese movies.

Father: American ones.

Andrea: What?

Therapist: American movies, cowboys?

Andrea: No, the ones with killing.

Therapist: There are movies by Sergio Leone with killing.

Andrea: I don't like those!

Therapist: Dario Argento's movies, where there's blood and stuff rolling around...

Andrea: I don't like those! I like the ones with executioners, who kill everyone...

Therapist: Ah! Like *Apocalypse Now*?

Andrea: I have that at home!

The provocations continue, while the therapist adds non-verbal behavior, which the boy wasn't expecting at all, with the precise intention of building a therapeutic alliance with Andrea. It's the ball game, which will later also involve the older brother. This produces a rather unexpected experience between the brothers: that of playing together. The boy responds to the therapist with his own provocations, even seeming to soften when the therapist smiles. He has this huge body with a round smiling face, which gives him the aspect of a angry large puppy... He looks like he is about to growl, but his violence seems more a mask to cover up deep feelings. Yet he doubtlessly feeds on violence. He spends entire nights watching gory movies filled with massacres and playing violent video games, even though his brother sleeps in the same room. He collects weapons but, most of all, he embodies the role of the executioner, the one who eliminates all villains from the world.

When did you decide to become a giant?

The therapist, once he has broken the ice and begins to amplify the symptom, to uncover its relational functions. It's a complex symptom: the violent behavior is associated to considerable obesity which was wrongly diagnosed in a local hospital and confused with an endocrine disease, Froelich's Syndrome.

Therapist (addressing the mother): When did he decide to become a giant, how old was he?
Mother: I brought some photos for that purpose, to show them to you.
Therapist: At what age?
Mother: Fifteen.
Therapist: So when he was fourteen he was still a normal boy?
Mother: Yes, he was always taller than average, but still normal, all in all...
Father: He never wants to see those photos!
Therapist: Which photos?
Father: Whenever we take those photos out to show him how handsome and different he was, he doesn't want to see them, he even tore one up!
Mother: He ripped it up, the one of his first communion.
Therapist (addressing Andrea): How were you?
Andrea: How was I? I was a little boy, how were you when you were small?
Therapist: I was very skinny. I had an old-fashioned communion outfit, you know?
Andrea: I don't know what old-fashioned outfits were like!
Therapist: Well, they were white with...
Andrea: How do I know what I was wearing!
Mother: You wore black pants!
Andrea: I wore a jacket, a pair of pants and a shirt, like everyone else!
Therapist: And an undershirt!
Andrea: I think so!
Therapist: Everyone wore undershirts!
Andrea: I think so!
Therapist: Did you throw it away because it was a communion photo or because you didn't like yourself?

Andrea: What?
Therapist: I mean: did you throw the photo away because it was from the communion or because you were small and didn't want to look small?
Andrea (smiling): Well, I didn't want to look small!
Therapist: You like being the mean giant of the house, then?
Andrea: Of course I do!

Who is most afraid of you?

Now the focus is the violent symptom. The therapist, with his provocations, touches deeply and directly the theme of fear as a relational effect of the boy's violent behavior.

Therapist (gesturing towards the other three family members and addressing the boy): Can you tell me who's the most afraid of you?
Andrea: How do I know? They ain't afraid of me!
Therapist: Say they do something wrong, do you smack them on the head?
Andrea (irritated): But I don't smack them!
Therapist: But why? You could!
Andrea (getting angry): No! You too could smack your father then!
Mother (stopping him by touching his arm): Hey!!
Therapist: Eh! But… I am not strong as you are!
Andrea: That doesn't mean anything! I don't hit them!
Therapist: I understand that, but maybe they are still afraid of you!
Mother: Tell the truth!
Andrea: Well… That doesn't mean anything! Just because I'm this big, I have to smack someone?
Therapist: No, I'm just saying that maybe they are afraid; *(addressing the three other family members)* is anybody afraid?
Andrea (looking at the rest of the family): No, this ain't true!

Dad's worries

Father: Personally, I'm not physically afraid of him. I'm just… I have very high expectations for this therapy, I don't know if this line of reasoning… I think… it's our last chance. We tried everything.
Therapist: So it's crucially important! What are you worried about? What can happen?
Father: His future, clearly he thinks his father will live forever. Obviously I think about the future and what I'll need to do…

Therapist: Are you worried that he won't find a job, or get married, or have children? What are you worried about?

Father: I've often tried to speak about why a boy... He was always in the spotlight, he was a reference point for all of his friends, he had many interests, then all of a sudden he became lethargic, apathetic, he didn't care about school anymore, now he only cares about weapons, he always talks about those damned guns: COP .45, Beretta .45S, he's becoming a gun encyclopedia!

The brother's fear and Andrea's threats

(The therapist sits the two brothers next to each other.)

Therapist (addressing Giampiero): You were talking about your fear, are you afraid of your brother Andrea?

Giampiero: Yes, every evening when I come back home, and before going to sleep.

Therapist: Since when?

Giampiero: Since he became so big! Everyone's afraid!

Therapist (gesturing towards the parents): Are they worried you might assault people?!

Andrea: They ain't! They're worried about other people's throats, the others might die!

Therapist: So they're worried that you might attack other people!

Andrea: That's it! But I don't attack people as the whim takes me, like that!

Therapist: So?

Andrea: There has to be a reason!

Therapist: Tell me how many throats you cut!

Andrea: I haven't cut any, I'd be in jail!

Therapist: So, what are they worried about?

Andrea: That I might hurt someone, when there's a fight I might go too far!

Therapist: Ah! This means they're happy when you stay at home, because that means you won't cut anyone's throat.

Andrea: Okay, but that isn't the only way to kill someone!

Therapist: Okay, you can kick someone in the balls and break them!

Andrea: Well, to break the balls... I can take you by the neck and twist it in two seconds, right here!

(He makes the gesture of choking someone.)

Therapist: Ah!

Andrea: If not, I can break your nose, an arm; killing seems too much!

The therapist keeps talking about the same subject, he amplifies the symptom; he asks who might be afraid, inside and outside the family, and the boy uses very strong images, not so much to threaten directly, but as if to say: "If you raise the stakes, I'll raise them higher!" Nonetheless, Andrea feels that the therapist isn't afraid; how can he keep being the terrorist? He has to keep threatening and raising the stakes: cutting throats, twisting necks, and so on! In the room, the destructive energy is palpable.

Giampiero is four years older than Andrea and seems to live with a "Martian" by his side; there is no understanding between the two brothers and there never was: from the first session it is clear that Giampiero—small, unattractive and insecure—has always been less than Andrea within the family, and that all expectations have been directed towards the second child. As the session progresses, we discover that there was another brother between the two, who died a few days after birth. This death heavily influenced the family's affective balance. Several sessions later, the mother reveals that she still goes regularly to the tomb of her dead child, all these years later. So Andrea, who was born beautiful and healthy, became the miracle child!

The father is visibly worried about the situation, even though a strong bond with Andrea is still evident, while the mother—not at all worried about her giant son, at least from a physical point of view—keeps him at bay as if he were a puppy. A particular sentence strikes the therapist as significant: the mother states, towards the end of the session, that her mother-in-law and Andrea are "the same as far as violence goes!"

Did anyone help dad to grow up?

Let's now look at how all this energy, once it has been contained by the therapist, gains a different meaning. It is no longer compressed and negative, but can be connected to the history of the family in a constructive way.

Therapist (addressing Andrea): Do you think that dad had a family that helped him grow?
Andrea: Well, no.
Therapist: What happened?
Andrea: What do I know? He went to boarding school.
Therapist: Have you ever been there?
Andrea: Have you?

Therapist: I haven't.

Andrea: So? Why should I go there?

Therapist: Why did he go there?

Andrea: Because they sent him!

Therapist: So no one sent you there! Why did they send him there?

Andrea: Because his father had died!

Therapist: Couldn't his mother keep him?

Andrea: Dunno.

Therapist: Instead of a father he had a boarding school then. Which boarding school?

Andrea: What do I know? It's far away from here.

Therapist: Where is it?

Andrea: Close to Perugia.

Therapist: Have you ever been there?

Andrea: Yes, once I went past it.

Therapist: Does it look like a prison or like a hotel?

Andrea: I don't remember, it was a square building...

Therapist: A building similar to a prison, or...?

Andrea: No, it was a normal building... It must be closed by now!

Therapist: How long was dad there?

Andrea: Dunno, some ten years.

Therapist: Ten years!

Andrea: Ten, eleven.

Therapist: That's a lot! Eleven years in a boarding school, all the time! Why? There wasn't enough money to keep him at home?

Andrea: Dunno. He stayed there! Hey, what should I know about him? I wasn't there!

Therapist (smiling): You're a wise guy. Yet I think you actually know a lot of things. Did his mom love your dad?

Andrea: Not if she left him there, she didn't!

Therapist: Did she visit him often?

Andrea: No.

Therapist: So she didn't love him very much!

Andrea: Yeah.

Therapist: So he had a difficult childhood!

Andrea: Huh.

Therapist: He never had a dad who comforted him when he was afraid?

Andrea: No, he was dead!

Therapist: Nor a mom who cared for him when he was small, there wasn't even a mother.

Andrea: No.

Therapist: Nor a sister?

Andrea: Nooo, there wasn't! She was smaller than him, and was dumb too! *(The parents and brother laugh.)*

Therapist: So he practically grew up with no one to help him to feel safe. Was he able to make you feel safe?

Andrea: What should I know?

Therapist: Well, this you do know!

Andrea: Safe from what?

Therapist: Everything, fear of the dark, fear of death...

Andrea: I ain't afraid of dying!

Therapist: Of sickness...

Andrea: I ain't afraid of getting sick...

Therapist: ...Fear of being abandoned.

Andrea (talking over him): I ain't afraid!

Therapist: There are many fears!

Andrea: I ain't afraid of dying!

Therapist: What are you afraid of?

Andrea: Nothing!

Therapist: You've never been afraid of the dark?

Andrea: No!

Therapist: Weren't you afraid that, maybe, your parents might abandon you and you wouldn't have anyone to help you?

Andrea: No, I ain't the kind of guy who thinks about that!

Therapist: No fears, ever?

Mother: No, not when he was a small child.

Therapist (addressing Giampiero): What about you, did you have any fears when you were small?

Giampiero: I'm still afraid of being home by myself. If I'm home alone at night, I turn on all the lights!

Therapist (raising the tone of his voice): So you took all the fears for the entire family, while he took all the strength!

The purpose of therapy

During this session the story focuses on the death of the grandfather on the mother's side, who was an important presence in the family, nevertheless it seems that this loss didn't leave any marks on the mother; the death of the child born before Andrea seems the only event that activates her emotions: she looks in her purse for the photo of the child she liked so much, who was so beautiful and died after birth. Andrea was the miracle child, the one who had to fill an enormous void and failed. Today's anger and violence is a cry of despair, from an adolescent strongly parentified since birth. All expectations were put on him and he responded well till the age of fourteen; now, two years later, the result is a monster-child.

The father seems more available and understanding, but his starting point is an extremely cautious position, his function is that of peacemaker. He denies his own individuality, his needs and parental skills. Everything revolves around his giant son, and the more he growls the less he can be kept at bay.

Andrea's story is the story of a family that carries great inter-generational distortions. His parents, Paola and Gianni, married very young, when Paola was pregnant with Giampiero. Gianni's mother strenuously opposed this marriage, and never forgave Paola for taking her son away from her. For this reason the relationship between mother-in-law and daughter-in-law developed under continuous tensions and moments of truce, until the definitive break two years ago. (Is it a coincidence that Andrea's problems started at that same time, and that the mother described him as violent as the mother-in-law?)

So what direction should the therapy take and how should Andrea's violence be used as a guide to understand the family's violent relationships? How to restore trust and self esteem to the orphaned father, whose only guide towards personal growth was boarding school, and whose mother was as possessive as she was unavailable on an emotional level? How do we help Paola to close the tomb of her beloved child and to rediscover a more authentic and direct relationship with her two sons, freeing Andrea from the heavy responsibility of filling an enor-mous emotional void? If all these goals become possible through ther-apy, then the extreme violence of this adolescent will disappear, and will assume greater value and meaning by helping the family to find new paths in life.

After two years of intense family psychotherapy Andrea is not a monster anymore: he is a handsome young adult and there have also been many changes in the family. After a few sessions attended by the father's mother, the couple was finally able to set clear boundaries with her; at the some time, the grand-mother had the opportunity to describe in the sessions the difficulty of raising two children alone and her per-sonal suffering in sending her son Gianni to a boarding school for most of his childhood. She burst into tears when she remembered her Sunday visit to the school and the cakes she used to bake for the little boy. Andrea appreciated this shift in family dynamics and he spent a few

week-ends with grandma during the summer and their anger transformed into positive connections. As soon as Andrea started giving progressive signs of change especially in language and behavior, the father
also transformed himself into a more assertive and caring person, becoming a good model for the children. His career as a lawyer improved
and the wife became a competent secretary in his office. Paola was also
able to close the sad chapter on the lost baby and to enjoy her present life
more. In the meantime, Giampiero married and after some difficulties
finally had a baby and moved into his own place. Andrea, who watched
hundreds of English movies at night for several years, learnt to speaks
English very fluently and two years after our follow up session in Rome
moved to California where he lives with his girl-friend, and has set up
his own business.

         While this therapy was reaching its conclusion, Andolfi was in-
vited to a National Conference on Adolescents and Family Therapy and,
as he had done several times on other occasions, he proposed that Andrea should participate and give a joint presentation: Andolfi as a professional expert on the topic and Andrea as the real expert from his own
personal experience. To hear Andrea's description of the nightmares he
and his family went through and the incredible resources they found
within themselves to transform their life was a very moving and learning
experience for everybody.

         The parents wanted to be at the conference too, not only as
listeners: they recorded their family experience before, during and after
therapy and their recording was broadcast to the Conference participants. The long applause Andrea received at the end of his talk was the
best medicine of his entire life and a great sign of appreciation for what
the parents had done during those very difficult years. Other informal
and unscheduled encounters by the therapist with Paola and Gianni happened by chance at the Paris Airport a few years later and reinforced the
deep bond this family had with Andolfi, confirming once more the family's progress and the couple's pleasure in spending week-ends together.

ADOLESCENT VIOLENCE IN COUPLE CRISIS AND SEPARATION

         Children and adolescents are often witnesses or active partici-
pants in marital crises and family fragmentation, when "triangulated" by
parents who are not able to deal with their unresolved marital conflicts.
Violent behavior in adolescents can emerge in these situations and have
a different function and meaning in the family context, as now described.

Deflecting couple conflict

When marital tension explodes, both the child and the adolescent might be actively involved and become very protective towards the parents, and will attempt to re-focus the tension upon themselves: a child might do so by regressive behavior or by psychosomatic disorders, while the adolescent might enact the hostility in the couple through destructive behavior directed at self or at others.

Self-harm as a response to contempt in the couple

When silence or contempt becomes the preferred way of relating in the couple, the adolescent may move his center of gravity outside the family, using his peer group as support. In adolescents, we frequently observe depression, self-harm, and drug use when attachment figures aren't available in the family.

Affective blackmail in hostile couple separation

If parents during or after divorce force young persons to take sides, an adolescent especially might take revenge and make the daily life of parents difficult, especially in newly formed step-families. This is common in hostile marital separations and divorces, when the logic of "winners and losers" takes over, often enhanced by court processes and adversarial legal positions. The adolescent, in normal situations, grows up with a feeling of systemic justice, but he/she can't tolerate parents overstepping generational boundaries. When these healthy principles are put aside and injustice prevails, they will tend to side with one parent, (sometimes the "loser"), often enacting violent and destructive behavior. For example, this can happen when the biological father "loses" and has to leave home and the children. Some adolescents, especially males, can avenge what they see as an injustice and make life impossible for the mother's new family.

If the adolescent isn't considered as a competent and respected party in the family splitting and is treated more as "baggage" that has to move from one house to the other, the emotional blackmail will be even greater, with incredible emotional pain for everyone.

When children are forced to take sides

The natural alliance between siblings is often threatened by adult triangulations, when parents tend to split them in the battle of one partner against the other. This is a most dangerous and painful distortion in a teenager's developmental growth, as he will have to side not only against one parent, but also against one or more siblings. Emotional distance or open hostility among siblings could be the long term results of such dysfunctional family breakdowns.

Practice illustration: My son is my tumor

The dramatic sentence *My son is my tumor* was spoken during a phone conversation by a senior hospital physician having great difficulties with his fifteen-year-old only son. Requesting a family session the father showed up elegantly dressed as befitting his role and was visibly upset. Anna, the mother, who had delegated all preliminary contacts to the husband (phone call, intake forms, and so on) was present in the session but "without being there." She sat on the side as if what was happening did not concern her. Mario, wearing a black leather jacket and black boots, was "completely studded." He wore sharply angular studs on every garment and on visible parts of his body (face, hands). He was also visibly upset. The father, an old-fashioned man, described Mario's wickedness: he doesn't study, keeps bad company, fills the house with other "metal-heads," and does not listen to anything he says. While speaking of his son, the father repeated: "He's my malignant tumor!"

Mario didn't express hostility, possibly because he knew he had his father on a leash and could make his life a nightmare. He couldn't see that this "emotional revenge" was wasting his own life as well. The son described his father as a "doctor 24/7," a man who "wears the white coat" even when he's sleeping. Father and son seemed two desperate people, both very lonely, forced to face diametrically opposed lifestyles and representations of themselves. While the father was a workaholic, the son wasted his time; while the father dressed elegantly, the son was unkempt. Maybe the only thing they shared was Anna, the wife-mother of the family.

At first sight, the conflict between father and son was the dramatic focal-point of the family. In fact, more disturbing was the presence-absence of Anna during the session. She didn't speak and or participate emotionally in the dialogue between father and son. Later in the session, she revealed that she detests her husband, who never gave her anything apart from economic wealth with marriage to "Medicine," and considers her a nobody because she abandoned her studies when young.

It seems Mario has always been the mother's affective partner; he filled her solitude from a young age and grew up to embody the mother's deep contempt for her husband, paying a very high price for this: that of growing up within a distorted environment, where roles are completely reversed. His "porcupine syndrome," with its sharp studs that "keep people away," acquires a new meaning in the family context. The father masks his desperation as a husband and father through his professional role, which for males often represents a "depressive equivalent." So where is the tumor and how can it be eradicated?

FROM FATHER ABSENCE TO CO-PARENTING

Today in the transition to a new gender- and co-parenting-balance, some men have difficulty defining themselves as husbands and as fathers.

As described by several authors (Pietropolli Charmet, 2000; Cigoli and Giuliani, 1997; Lamb, Pleck, Charnov and Levine, 1987; Marsiglio, 1995; Hawkins, Christiansen, Sargent and Hill, 1995; Lamb, 1981; Sullivan, 2000; Parke, 2002) and confirmed by the author with over 40 years of clinical work with families in many different parts of the globe, expectations about the paternal role have changed.

In contemporary industrialized society, the absence of fathers in the family seems to be a very significant structural void and even when present they lack ways of being authoritative and self-confident with their children. How can a man of our times find a more adequate father role, distancing himself from the role model of his own father, who was often harsh, authoritarian and distant from his children? What this concerns is how parenting can evolve as a joint process, where the responsibility for children is equally shared by mothers and fathers in a new family dance.

Here the challenge for therapists dealing with severe family distortions is to provide a special opportunity for family transformation and growth. A systemic-developmental perspective including the main actors of the family scenario in the therapeutic process can be helpful. It is possible that fathers are less present in family therapy either because they are not engaged, because therapists work more easily with mothers and children, whether in intact, single-parent or step-families, or both.

This is illustrated in the following clinical segment.

A single-mother comes to therapy because of her son Juan's aggressive behavior, but the father has never attended a session because he has never been asked to participate by the therapist. The father's absence in the family as well as in therapy increases the void of a relevant identity figure especially for a male adolescent.

Practice illustration: Juan's despairing violence

This fragment of therapy shows some of the dilemmas in single-parent families, when the father is distant and not included in child custody, the mother has been overwhelmed by duties and responsibilities over several years, and the children are over-involved and confused by the mother's despair and the unresolved conflict between the parents.

Carmela (16 years old) is the mirror image of her mother, with whom she shares pain and sacrifice; while Juan (18 years old) is the one who enacts everyone's desperation through violent behavior towards the mother and the sister, following the prevailing South-American cultural male model.

The "macho" culture is still very much present in Latin countries: an authoritarian male with a submissive, self-sacrificing female partner who has limited freedom outside the house. Shouting and occasional slaps are very common in child education and generally accepted in the social context and are rarely considered domestic violence. Only when an "acceptable" limit is exceeded, might it be considered and treated as physical abuse.

Therefore, when Isabel describes her husband's behavior, she is referring to some form of verbal and physical abuse (especially with Juan), which is relatively "normal" and generally accepted in the community. Juan has been playing a "parental role" in a very dysfunctional manner as soon as the couple split and the father left home. He shouts and uses coarse language with Carmela, only occasionally does he slap her, but he feels he has the right to interfere in her social life: he controls whom she goes out with, when she comes home; he orders her to go to her room against her will, etc. Carmela complains all the time to the mother and uses tears as a way of making the brother feel guilty. The mother is overwhelmed by this situation.

The mother, Isabel, and the two teenage children are in therapy and the father has never been present.

Unfortunately, the father isn't even present in the minds of the female therapists who treated this family at the Psychiatric Department of Medellín, Colombia: they never requested his presence and describe him as absent and unavailable.

The following dialogues have been transcribed from a live family consultation the author conducted in 2003 in Medellín. Present at the session were the mother, the two children, the local therapists, and the author as consultant.

The history of the family: when only tears unite

The session has been running for only a few minutes and the consultant, already aware of the distance between siblings, asks Juan to do an "experiment": to move his chair from near the door and sit close to his sister. Juan agrees.

Consultant (reaching towards them while holding a piece of chalk in his hand and inviting them to draw a family genogram together): Thank you. Another experiment: can I ask the two of you *(the siblings)* to help me understand who makes up your family?
(Both simultaneously saying "no" with their head.)
Consultant: So it's possible to try the experiment of sitting close to Carmela but not that of collaborating? How often have you been able to collaborate as brother and sister?
Carmela and Juan: Never!
Consultant: When you were born?
(Children and mother are visibly moved)
Consultant: The only thing you have in common is that the three of you start crying when we speak of births. Let me understand, who was born first?
(Juan points to himself.)
Consultant: How many years later did Carmela arrive?
Carmela: Two years.
Consultant: I will ask you some questions you may find a little strange today.
Consultant (addressing Juan): What happened in the family when mom was pregnant with you?
Juan: How can I know, if I was inside...?
Consultant: That's true, but this is an experiment... you can imagine it. What do you think? Who was at home while you were inside?
Juan: Only mom!
Consultant: So when you were inside her belly, mom was home alone. And where was dad?

Juan: I don't know.
Consultant: Was he just an occasional dad?
Juan and Carmela: Yes!
Consultant: So... a dad who left mom pregnant and then went away?
Juan and Carmela (laughing): No!

* Here the therapist introduces humor in order to deal with tough issues and the kids laugh. The consultant's statement "So was he an occasional dad!" could paint a very harsh image but, when delivered in a particular way, can sound like an absurdity that makes one smile. At the same time bringing back the siblings to the time of their birth, together with the beginning of their emotional distance moves everybody to tears. Not only are the adults split, but the children are, too, and this is the wound in the relationship between Juan and Carmela that is still very painful. As we will see later, Juan's aggressive behavior towards his sister is only a more recent event which increases the distance further. Carmela has always been close to mom's long-term despair and Juan has always been excluded from their bond.

Does the birth of a child unite or divide?

We will now look at the pain, deep and well hidden in Juan. The consultant, calmly and gently, but with great determination, invites the boy to allow his implicit vulnerability to emerge through a description of the family history.

Juan and Carmela, in spite of the strong distance between them, answer the questions simultaneously. They are two siblings whose relationship has constantly been triangulated. Nevertheless, apart from the obvious distance, it's possible to perceive a strong implicit bond which unites them, but is totally denied at the conscious level.

Consultant: Have you been a son that kept parents together or separated them?
Juan: I separated them.
Consultant: Are you sure, or do you imagine so?
Juan: I imagine.
Consultant: Shall we ask mom if it is so?
Juan: Yes.
Consultant: Would you like to ask her yourself?
Mother: If we separated it's only my fault!
Consultant: How did fault get into this room? From the window? From the door?... I didn't speak about fault. I was speaking about union and

separation. The question was whether he imagines he kept you together or separated you.

Mother: He united us, then we separated after Carmela was born.

Consultant: So it is only what he *imagined* that is wrong!

Juan: I've never asked myself this and I'm not interested in knowing the answer!

Consultant (addressing Carmela): What was happening in your family when you were inside mom's belly?

Carmela: When I was inside my mom there were many problems, physical aggressions between mom and dad, a bad economic situation...

Consultant: And do you think you've been a daughter who kept them together or separated them?

Carmela: Separated!

Consultant: Are you sure?

Carmela: They separated two years after I was born.

Consultant: So you suppose that you helped them to separate?

Carmela: Yes.

Consultant: A question for both of you. Did dad want you? Don't you know? Did you ever ask him? Is he the kind of dad you can talk to?

Juan: Yes.

Carmela: Sometimes he gets upset because of us.

Consultant: Does he become violent?

Carmela: He hit me only once, for something I did, but he always shouts.

Consultant (addressing Juan): What about you? Does he ever hit you?

Juan: Phew...! Many times!

Consultant: Why did he hit her just a little, and you a lot?

Juan: Because I lived with him longer!

Consultant: Did mom want you?

Juan: No!

Consultant: Sure? Mom's here, you can ask her, if you want!

Juan: I don't want to ask because she'll say yes.

Consultant: Do you think it's a lie?

Juan: Or a fantasy!

Consultant: Is a fantasy better than a lie?

Juan: Yes.

Consultant: But you have never been sure mom wanted you?

Juan: No!

Consultant: That's hard!

Juan: Yes!

Many years of clinical experiences have showed the importance of "temporal jumps," as described by Whitaker (1989) during a session. Going back to the origins, through the use of imagination, through clear and direct questions asked by the therapist, allows us to re-visit the foundations of each child's personal growth and the family dynamics in having children. These truths, like the question: "Did my parents want me?" are often camouflaged or confused, sometimes wrapped in prejudice and secrets constructed by parents and family members in the course of time.

In this exploration, it becomes possible to replace incomplete or "politically correct" answers with more authentic responses; it is preferable for children to feel today the pain of past rejections, as this will help to construct one's identity, than to continue to doubt one's origins. This is also useful for adults, who will have the chance of making things clearer for themselves and for their children within a safe environment such as the therapeutic one.

Inviting the father to the session

Consultant: What is dad's name?
Juan: Raul.
Consultant: Why didn't you think about bringing him here today?
Juan: I don't know, I don't think he wants to.
Consultant: Maybe, but have you asked him?
Juan: No.
Consultant (addressing Carmela): Have you thought about inviting him?
Carmela: Not today.
Consultant: Has the therapist thought about inviting him?
Therapist: We think he doesn't want to come. We've thought about calling him, maybe in the future on his own or with the children.
Consultant: What about today?
Therapist: Not today.
Consultant (addressing the mother): Did you consider whether it might be useful for me to meet the father today?
Mother: For therapy?
Consultant: For me, not for the therapy.
Mother: For me he is separate in everything...
Juan (very concerned): They're not able to be together.
Consultant: Would you like to call him now and invite him to come? Could we do an experiment?
Juan (positively): Yes!
Consultant: What do we want to tell him?

Juan: To come immediately!

Consultant: Let's tell him that there's a doctor from Italy who would like to meet him, because he's still your and Carmela's dad. Does he still have parental authority or not?

Mother: No.

Consultant (addressing the mother): Have you got custody of the children?

Mother: Yes.

Consultant (addressing the children): Is he still worthy of being your father?

Juan: Yes.

Consultant: Carmela, do you agree to Juan calling him?

Carmela: Yes.

Consultant: Is this the first time you agree! Do you see that, mom? Maybe it is a good idea to invite him.

Mother: If it can help.

Juan and Carmela (laughing): Yes.

Consultant: Call him then, and tell him to come immediately!

Juan calls several phone numbers: house, work, secretary, etc... finally he manages to speak to his father. He strongly encourages him to come to the session, bearing in mind that the father needs to come from the other side of the city, and the father accepts.

Making a contract in the session

I have used this method — inviting a family member to call an absent family member during a session — many times over the years. Impromptu requests represent a strong and specific invitation to action, as they activate the people interested in his or her presence in therapy and have the power of motivating the absent person, especially when it's a father who is absent or is "kept on the outside," as is often the case in divorced families. A male parent often feels that he can be motivated and take a personal risk — especially when invited by a child — to move beyond the wall of marital grudges and hostilities. If the caller is an adolescent brought into therapy because he's violent, one can easily see how his role can be transformed during the session, from one who brings discomfort and damage, to one who suggests a positive action, eliciting a greater responsibility from the father.

Moreover, from the moment Juan sees the realistic possibility of his father coming to therapy, he can return to a more appropriate behavior. In fact, if his father participates and takes back his role of being a father for his kids, Juan might stop playing the role of "the head of the family," a role he plays in a rather clumsy and aggressive way, and go back to being a son and a brother to his sister. For instance, he could try to stop controlling Carmela's daily life, as when she leaves and comes back home, her friends, or shouting at her as an authoritarian father would do.

While we are waiting for the father's arrival, the mother's desperation is explored: Carmela recalls her mother crying for many years because she felt too fragile and incapable of dealing with two children alone, facing economic difficulties. Even though the mother describes the husband as always shouting at her and the kids, she affirms that Raul was not a bad person, but they were not able to live together. She is afraid of Juan's aggressive behavior, but even with him she is very ambivalent: he is bad, but sometimes is a good, kid and she worries about his future. Juan seems to be an adolescent who acts aggressively and impulsively, but who is acting out old family conflicts and is suffering from a lack of family direction, carrying a deep feeling of abandonment.

The arrival of the father to the session allows for a greater understanding of the family history. As often happens in many families after separation, the affective balance of the group is lost and the father, for different reasons, has distanced himself from the family. The mother and children bond in a very fused triad where roles as well as generational boundaries are totally confused. Carmela becomes the confidante and the emotional support for her desperate mother. Juan plays the role of man of the house, at first supported by the female subsystem and later, when he becomes an adolescent, rejected because he is too aggressive.

In this way there is a marked stereotyped division between the "weeping and losing" female team on the one side and the violent son–father dyad on the other. Juan's violence therefore represents the tip of an iceberg of unresolved and distorted problems at the level of martial conflict and separation, as well as long-term sibling rivalry for attention and care.

The fact that the father accepted the children's invitation and came immediately and the positive reaction of both children to his presence created a good starting point. His ex-wife Isabel seemed more animated by Raul's presence too. We learnt that it was Raul who suggested family therapy because of Juan's aggressive behavior and Isabel's low self-esteem, but he never thought to include himself in this project and at the same time he was never invited. His active participation and the positive context which emerged gave the consultant the strength to propose a change in the therapeutic plan, by including the father in future therapeutic work.

The consultant first asked the therapist and then proposed to the family that they sign a contract in the session, which would guarantee the presence and commitment of both parents and children. Everybody seemed ready and positive about the agreement. Raul wrote the content of the contract which aimed to get each person's collaboration in order to re-create harmony in the family and stop Juan's aggressive behavior. At the same time everybody committed to avoid recrimination of past disagreements and conflicts. Isabel for the first time during the session seemed relieved, as if the father's presence and his commitment represented a new chance of hope for her too. Her agreement to have the father present and to accept his collaboration with them in the future was a great sign of hope.

The session ended with everyone signing the contract, including the therapist and then shaking hands. The general feeling was very positive. The father embraced Juan, the mother embraced Carmela, but the children refused to shake hands; then the consultant took their hands in his own, saying that that was the real problem, referring to their hands, for only that moment joined them together, that distance and lack of positive connection between two siblings are signs of the profound discomfort and pain this family had experienced.

Sharing competence between professionals and families

The following day, I was invited to give a workshop at the University of Medellín for a large audience of professionals. At the end of the family session, I asked the family's permission to show the video of the session and invited them to join the meeting, noting professionals need to hear more from families about what is effective. The family agreed and to our great surprise came, stayed all day, and listened to the discussions and comments from therapists. Before the workshop closed, I asked the family if they wanted to say something about the day and the father came down to the platform of the amphitheater, thanked the professionals for their authentic interest in his family's events and pain and ended by suggesting to therapists: "Listen more to the family's voice!"

Much has been written about the use of reflecting teams starting with Andersen's (1991) chapter on different ways to obtain feed-back from families on therapeutic work, in order to empower them. These days, families in treatment are rarely invited to professional meetings, small or large, because of fear of the risk of exposing them in a professional context. However, I believe that we can learn a lot from family feedback especially when we examine segments of our work with them, and families can feel very empowered in the role of a consultant or expert. The presence of Juan's family at the workshop also allowed the therapists present to talk from their hearts and bodies more than from their heads, with the great advantage of reducing distance between those who help and those who are helped.

Working with divorced families

I would like to conclude with some comments about the best setting for working with divorced families. When there is a serious problem like violence presented by an adolescent in a separated or divorced family, I try to engage not only mothers and young persons in therapy, but also, where possible, fathers. Unless, that is, there is evidence of risk or danger, as in the case of sexual or physical abuse and/or when the Juvenile Court system is involved in working with these families where fathers are often already absent and uninvolved, I challenge the stereotype and try as hard as possible to have them present and active in therapy. I might ask children or ex-partners to invite them or sometimes make the invitation directly. For example, I may give a note to be passed on to the father to a son or a daughter in the session or, as in Juan's family, ask the boy to call the father and invite him in.

I strongly believe in family resources and in what fathers can contribute. As for Juan's family, I like everybody to be committed and be willing to sign a therapeutic contract together. This is a concrete way to collaborate towards a shared goal. Of course, if the family is divorced, I don't work with the entire family as if they are still living together. In these cases after the first meeting, I will see mother with children, alternating sessions with father and children and sometimes seeing the siblings alone. This is important in order to recreate sibling bonds and address long-term rivalry. In the middle of therapy, and at the end, I propose joint meetings with the whole family to discuss improvements and to compliment everyone for the great job they have done together.

At the end of the workshop, the therapist felt very empowered and reassured by the many positive comments of the professional audience and by the active presence of the family. She understood that not talking about the father during the sessions and not exploring the concrete possibility of inviting him was a form of prejudice. She liked the idea of engaging the children in this request (as happened in consultation) for two reasons: first, a request coming from the child is always very powerful and, second, because it was the only moment in which brother and sister showed real collaboration.

A few months later I received a letter from the therapist: she was following the contract we signed in the session, meeting alternatively mother/children and father/children. The therapist decided to ask a male co-therapist to join her in the sessions in order to provide a positive male role-model for the family. As outlined at the very end of the consultation, the lack of sibling alliance is a real problem and it needs time and dedication to "de-triangulate" children from their dysfunctional roles: the aggressive pseudo-father and the mother's confidante. The therapist also decided to provide individual counseling to support the mother, who had been very depressed and sad for a long time.

To conclude, a positive therapeutic result is not only the resolution of a presenting problem (for example, Juan's aggressive behavior), but the transformation of the family in terms of personal and relational well-being. This is described further in *The Myth of Atlas* (Andolfi, Angelo, de Nichilo, 1987) and *La terapia narrata dalla famiglia* (Andolfi, Angelo, D'Atena, 2001).

ADOLESCENT VIOLENT BEHAVIOR IN ADOPTIVE FAMILIES

The adoptive adolescent is as busy as his non-adoptive peers in the complex process of building his/her identity and in the hard task of redefining where he belongs. Nevertheless, it often happens that parents ask for professional help to deal with the adoptive child's violent behavior. With the arrival of adolescence, those critical aspects specifically connected to adoptive processes cannot remain hidden.

The adoptive story is closely linked to the story of the child's origins, to his early experiences of institutionalization, to the adoptive couple's lack of fertility, and to the first encounter of the parents with the adoptive child. It is also connected to the interface between public and private in which the adoptive process takes place. This includes different social entities: the social services, the tribunal, the organizations for international adoptions, and so on. The reconstruction of these phases represents, in clinical work, an important moment, often a breakthrough in the therapeutic process.

These painful and complex experiences, for both the child and the adopting couple, usually take place during a long period of time, even over several years. These same experiences are often denied and removed when the adoptive family is born. It's as if during the first encounter between adoptive parents and child, magical thinking freezes whatever happened before. Some authors called this phase of the adoptive family's life cycle the "honeymoon," emphasizing its idealizing and often mystifying aspects.

Adoptive adolescence often opens a space to what was submerged. The adolescent, who normally builds his identity by dealing with the *inside* of his relationships within the family and the *outside* of his relationships with peers and significant others, in the case of adoption, will also have to deal with the story of his origins or, in other terms, with what he remembers or was told of the period from his birth to the encounter with his adoptive parents.

In clinical work, anger and aggressive behavior are often desperate requests for reconstruction and integration of past experiences, which have been lived in a fragmented way even from an emotional point of view. The need to understand becomes concrete, as the adopted adolescent often fails to understand.

Apart from the knowledge of facts connected to their origins, what seems to matter most to these teenagers is the existence of an emotional space within the relational experience of the family. This space is reserved only for the acceptance of the many adoption-related experiences we spoke about earlier. How well is the experience of abandonment of these children understood by all family members? What was and is the possibility of accepting the pain without trying to go on a saving mission that often says "as a parent I will erase every trace of your pain; if I don't manage to do so, I fail"? Will the couple be able to share the sense of loss, often associated to anger, connected to the absence of biological children? Can this aspect enter into the emotional heritage of the family, easing the redistribution of emotional charges? Often children's anger gives voice to the unspoken anger of parents.

Anger itself is not necessarily a negative emotion. Often the anger expressed by the adolescent, in several non-destructive forms, can be an emotion that helps the individuation of the adolescent from his parents.

In the clinical work with families of adolescent children we often witness manifestations of anger in a child towards one or both parents. These manifestations evoke an ancient anger and express the often unspoken pain of abandonment experienced in the past. This isn't always a conscious process. On the contrary: often anger gets mixed with the parents' sense of guilt, who feel they disappointed their child or damaged him even more, or with the latter's fears of disappointing his parents or "destroying" them, evoking fantasies of loss and abandonment even for the adoptive parents.

The most complex situations seem those in which the anger enacted towards parents and in contexts outside the family is reconfigured as an attack on connection, on the capacity of the adolescent to imagine himself in a relationship. Maybe this can be explained through early relational experiences of abandonment and trauma.

We refer to learned relational models in the early stages of the life of adoptive children, borrowing from studies on various attachment styles, where the idea of bonding itself seems to be compromised.

Practice illustration: Sergio the bully

The story of Sergio and his family is an extreme one, and as such it dramatically describes some of the themes we have dealt with.

Sergio attends the first session with the arrogant and careless attitude typical of bullies. He was adopted in Brazil when he was four, together with his twin sister Rosalinda, by a couple from a city in central Italy. He's seventeen and was referred to us, together with his family, by the local social service, where his parents had gone to seek help.

The parents asked social workers for help to deal with their son's aggressive behavior, enacted mostly at home and towards the mother. For the past two years, Sergio has refused to follow the rules of the family. He does not only refuse to acknowledge the parental function of both parents, but even their identity as mother and father. Here his attack on the bond becomes increasingly dramatic, because the adoptive parents also fail to recognize him as a son, thus enacting a rejecting behavior towards Sergio.

Sergio is actually "out": out of the house, out of school, out of important relationships, out of his mind. An emotional and relational short-circuit where the theme of loss and abandonment is re-enacted through the rejection of the other: "You are not my father!," "You are not my son!," "You are not able to be a father!," "You are not able to be a son!" Father and son interact this way in day-to-day life as well as in therapy. It seems there is no room for the pain and depression that goes with the memory of an early experience of abandonment and institution-alization. It seems there is only room for its translation into aggressive acts, angry retaliations, and attacks on the Self. The only references to the past, to the story of its origins, are evoked by Sergio through a memory of his biological father, an image as vague as it is mythologized.

Sergio speaks of his biological father only in juxtaposition to the adoptive one, creating a virtual competition, in which the adoptive father lives constantly with feelings of frustration, disappointment and powerlessness conveyed by the fateful sentence: "Go back to Brazil then!" On Sergio's part it is also a dramatic attempt to feel a connection and live it through his black skin, so different from that of his adoptive parents and the majority of people who live in the country that adopted him. It's difficult for him to identify visually with a father he perceives as very different from himself.

The capacity to relate visually is a key theme in adoptive adolescents, especially in those adopted abroad, where somatic and cultural differences between adoptive parents and adoptive children are more evident. If we start from the assumption that this capacity is the emotional and relational experience which most directly gives a sense of belonging, through the acknowledgment of similarities, somatic or otherwise, we can easily understand that this is a complex experience in adoptive families. This becomes a problem if, at the moment of encounter between the adoptive parents and child—when the foundations of belonging are constructed—a piece of the child's history connected to his origin and to his cultural and somatic particulars is mystified, denied, or not welcomed. It is placed "elsewhere." It is exactly to this "elsewhere" that the adopted adolescent returns to reconnect with, understand, and recognize himself. Often this is not a painless operation.

If parents have from the very beginning kept an open door to the adoptive child's specificity, this will be the place where they can meet again for another phase in the developmental journey. Otherwise there will be fears and threats, connected especially to family loyalties. The attitude of Sergio's twin sister, Rosalinda, is emblematic for this reason.

Rosalinda seems to be in perfect harmony with her parents, facilitated by a lighter skin color and a severe chronic disease that needs her mother's—a professional nurse—constant attention. The mother herself has a long and tragic history of caring for her own mother and two sisters, one of whom is schizophrenic and the other disabled. Nevertheless, the relationship between Rosalinda and her parents appears to be emotionally poor and dependent, and does not facilitate her psychological differentiation even in regard to her thoughts. In fact, she seems to be cognitively immature. Unfortunately, the relationship between the siblings and their desirable complicity are blocked by their diverging needs and the family dynamics, which do not favor the encounter and integration of different emotional aspects: Sergio operates within juxtaposition and Rosalinda within complacency towards family loyalties; both of these are frequent mechanisms in clinical work with adoptive families.

Clinical experience—of which Sergio's story is a particularly significant example—teaches us that one of the most significant variables is the possibility that, from the very beginning, the adoptive family welcomes completely all emotional experiences that converge into the adoptive history. We can thus consider this aspect as a risk or protective factor in the developmental process of the whole family. Of course a great deal can be attributed to all the social and/or institutional workers who contribute to the writing of the initial pages in the history of all adoptive families.

Chapter 3
The pathology of dependence
and the tri-generational dimension

THE MYTH OF INDEPENDENCE

In the last forty years, individualism has gained a central role in influencing our daily life. If the positive value of this social evolution has to do with the affirmation of individual rights and with the dignity of human beings, the critical consequences of this attitude has produced an increased juxtaposition between the rights and duties of the individual and those of the community, causing a greater disequilibrium between the two.

The historical roots which brought us the emphasis on the value of the individual against those of the community go back even further, to the age of Enlightenment. However, it is interesting to note how what could be called the "myth of independence" gradually gained a foothold in western society during the latter part of the twentieth century. Economic independence, for instance, is fascinating; the needs of the individual come first in today's consumer society which produces, prepares and serves him up everything he needs, as long as he pays. You can buy everything without ever leaving your home: pizza, personal trainers, friendship, even love. Or so they say.

Science has also started to focus research towards fascinating objectives: plastic surgery, the use of stem cells, artificial insemination. The interest and experiments in cloning are the greatest incarnation of the myth of independence.

As if the individual could really stand alone! We should perhaps ask ourselves whether we are not confusing autonomy and subjectivity with self-sufficiency.

The Polish sociologist Zygmunt Bauman (2000) has given an interesting definition of our society. According to him, today's individualism is a weak one, where egotistical interests, uncertainty and fear of failure prevail. Bauman speaks about a *liquid society*, a term which describes the boundless present which pervades us, where we yearn, men and women, for the feeling of security provided by the group and for someone to count on in time of need. Yet we also fear becoming trapped in stable relationships and dread that a tight bond — whether with a community or a person — will entail obligations we do not want, or do not feel we can bear. The feeling of emptiness and existential meaninglessness, generated by these juxtaposed tendencies, can explain how dependence on others can easily be mistaken for a limit to one's own freedom and as some sort of personal failure.

From a developmental point of view dependence, as Melanie Klein (1959) puts it, is a very important *position*, necessary for the growth of healthy individuals. Someone who has never experienced healthy dependencies will have to construct pathological ones. As we will see in the final chapter, an adolescent cannot live without a sense of personal identity: if he cannot build a positive one, he will be forced to build a negative one through his family and social environment. We cannot affirm that a young person who commits crimes has no identity: indeed, he has one and it is absolutely complete — but it is highly destructive, both towards the Self and others.

THE SYSTEMIC-RELATIONAL MODEL OF DEPENDENCE: THE BALANCE OF AFFECTION

In the systemic-relational model healthy dependence is the necessary ingredient to experience a sense of belonging, because it allows us to feel loved and understood.

Murray Bowen (1978) — in line with his developmental model based on the differentiation of the Self from the family of origin, whose aim is to integrate the Self through a progressive transformation of inter-generational dependence — emphasizes the balance of affection, which should always maintain a dynamic equilibrium between belonging and separation. "You cannot separate if you don't first belong" affirms Carl Whitaker (1989), because we need to experience a series of healthy dependencies during our life cycle in order to feel that we belong to a specific group or system. "Belonging is carrying others within yourself" sang Giorgio Gaber (an Italian singer-songwriter), to explain that only when we have learned to internalize significant others can we distance and separate ourselves from them without feeling we are losing them.

The healthy dependencies needed by an individual during the course of his life assume different forms and unfold throughout life. These include: the attachment and care given to the growing child by the parents; the affective and relational containment of the adolescent; the dependence on peer-groups in times of stress and conflict; couple mutuality, formed by the bond of romantic attachment (Santona, Zavattini, 2007; Whitaker, 1958) and care-giving; the adult's ability to ask the family of origin for help when in need; and lastly, the care of elderly parents given by adult children in time of need, which represents a role reversal.

As for adolescents, they often compensate for the lack of healthy dependencies within the family through important experiences of healthy dependence within the peer group. Unfortunately, this is rarely understood by parents, especially mothers, who are often frightened by the potentially negative effects the peer group might have on their children. According to this view, we could postulate that even those pathological dependencies which influence the lives of many adolescents are actually *substitute dependencies.*

Pathological dependence happens when it becomes necessary to contain potential psychological breakdowns, in subjects at high risk of anxiety, panic or depression, through dulling or exciting experiences. Generally, the most important pathological dependencies in adolescence arise when the individual wants to escape unpleasant or negative emotional states, to get rid of his own feelings, to feel rapid pleasure and well-being, to self-medicate, or to protect against any kind of psychic tension, whether produced by internal or external causes.

In adolescence, the absence of positive dependencies in the family can cause a series of pathological ones to arise.

Aside from the well-known substance addictions, whether caused by drugs or alcohol, we now witness a drastic increase in those that are defined as *object addictions* or *new addictions.* These types of dependencies are rather new and characterized by the rapidity of their appearance in our society, where human relationships are ever more rarefied, while the relationship to objects increases frantically. And this is why these types of addiction are often not even perceived as dangerous. They are all dependencies where no chemical substance is involved: the object of the addiction is, in these cases, a totally legal and socially accepted behavior or activity.

Among the new addictions we can find: the addiction to gambling, the Internet, shopping, work, sex, and food.

The most characteristic dependencies during adolescence remain, unfortunately, alcohol and drug addictions; whereas, when it

comes to new addictions, teenagers seem to be divided according to gender: eating disorders are more common among girls, while the dependence on technological products seems more consistent among boys.

PATHOLOGICAL DEPENDENCIES DURING ADOLESCENCE: DRUG
ADDICTION

The use of drugs has always been an unfortunate and desperate
attempt at self-medication. Research into the manipulation of consciousness, mind-altering experiments, and behavioral control has been a
constant in the history of humanity. It has taken place, though using
different methods and routes, in all periods and at all geographical and
social latitudes. Through drugs, man has always tried to cure illness, to
escape worries, preoccupations and sadness, to break the limitations of
drudgery, to acquire a mystical perception, and to experience the sacred.

According to a UN report presented at the twenty-second International World Day against Drugs in the spring of 2009, the markets for
cocaine, heroin, and marijuana were stable or, in some cases, in decline,
whilst the market for synthetic drugs was on the increase, especially in
developing countries. Aside from the use of traditional drugs, which
cause a strong physical and psychic dependence and are always predom-
inantly targeted towards the young by international drug traffickers, this
particular time in history seems to be strongly characterized by a constant increase in the use, by the young and very young, of soft drugs or
dance drugs: amphetamines, methamphetamines, and ecstasy. These are
drugs that are easy to take, they are mostly pills, they do not carry a risk
of infections such as HIV or hepatitis, and do not cause the same dependency as heroin, while rapidly making the user feel bright, adequate, full
of energy, and uninhibited.

This "clean" image of synthetic drugs (ecstasy, amphetamines,
LSD, ketamine, poppers, and others) is actually false and rather
superficial: the active principles they contain affect certain parts of the
central nervous system and can, therefore, damage it; moreover, they are
made in clandestine laboratories using imprecise methods and are often
cut with potentially dangerous substances. They are illegal substances. In
Italy, the confiscation of new drugs by the forces of law and order has
exponentially increased, highlighting a shift from small individual production to the prerogative of criminal organizations of a higher level.

New drugs or, as some like to call them, context drugs, are con-
sumed by young people in well-defined times and spaces: they are used
during the weekend (which is seen as a free zone where the daily routine

of study or work is interrupted) and mainly in discos, at rave parties, or other events where techno music and its variants are dominant. Raves originated in England during the Eighties. They are big parties which are organized in isolated places, derelict buildings, or alternative nightclubs, where you listen to loud music all night long, if not for days, in the company of many other people, and where using stimulants seems the only option for increasing your stamina. House parties and raves are also well loved in the United States, and are ideal events to distribute ecstasy.

During parties you can "drop" several ecstasy pills—of various shapes and colors, sometimes personalized with zodiac signs or classic comic characters, white, sky blue, pink or light green—to get ready for the fun and, at least for four or five hours, be able to dance without tiring. There are some users who only take ecstasy, but some also take other drugs during the night: "half a strip" of LSD to increase the hallucinogenic effect of MDMA (the active principle of ecstasy), or else amphetamines or cocaine to be able to dance longer, thus increasing the side effects and danger. Deaths caused by drugs are almost always due to mixes. Many, if not all, drink alcohol, especially beer and cocktails. Naturally, hashish is not missing. It is generally used towards the end of the party, to decrease the excitement caused by the pills. Ecstasy users who decide to use heroin are few and they are mostly connected to extreme and deviant environments. They take it at the end of the night, if they realize they cannot sedate the hyper-arousal caused by the use and abuse of these substances, thus risking becoming addicted to heroin. This is also why most people take sedatives, perhaps stolen from the medicine cabinet at home.

The use of psychotropic substances seems to involve new rituals; for the younger generation taking pills, smoking and drinking are a prelude to entertainment. It is the culture of the "total high," the culture of fun confused with stupefaction and loss of consciousness, the culture of "it is forbidden to forbid," in a society where everything is possible and obtainable without limitations.

But how did we get there?

Practice illustration: Angelo's battle with heroin

From our point of view, clinical intervention for drug addiction, especially in young people, cannot happen without considering the environment in which the drug addict lives. The principal environment in which he lives is the family. It is fundamental to evaluate each case carefully and take into consideration the young person's social and family contexts, because drug abuse is often linked to difficult situation from the evolutionary perspective.

Family therapy is often insufficient to help a young person end a severe addiction, especially when it involves criminality. Nothing can change unless adequate protective measures are activated simultaneously, and these cannot consist of only a therapeutic session once a week, for one hour, in an office. Often these are families with several problems, who do not want or cannot seek professional help. These users often seek help from public services, where they are treated through every available instrument, from specifically set up local services to therapeutic communities.

Actually, when the addiction is characterized by a compulsive need for massive and protracted drug abuse, the most adequate intervention is found within the therapeutic community. Integrated and intensive treatment on a residential basis offers the possibility of containing not only the damage of the abuse or addictive behavior, but also of simultaneously working on rebuilding the personality and stabilizing the psychic symptomatology, possibly derived from primary disorders and those induced by drugs (Addazi, Marini, Rago, 2009).

When writing this book, Andolfi thought it might be appropriate to get in touch with a family he had treated years earlier to ask whether they would be willing to give a brief account of their history before, during and after their son's drug addiction. The father, on behalf of the family, answered with the following e-mail.

Dear Professor,

It was a great pleasure to hear your voice on the phone, it was like a call from an old friend with whom I had lost contact, or a family member from far away.

The feelings of connection you aroused in us have remained the same, and the respect we had for you from the beginning, has grown.

I won't deny that we often feel the need to have a meeting with you, and maybe one day I will call you for this reason.

I send you the account you requested in the hope it arrives in time and that we have done a little something that helps us to say an endless thank you!!

With affection and enormous respect, from me and my whole family.

[Email is signed here by the father.]

P.S. If you ever come to our town I hope we'll be able to meet and spend some time together.

[Here follows the account by the father.]

We married in 1977, in a small city in Central Italy. We were young (I was twenty-seven and my wife was twenty-six) and full of expectations. I was a freelance professional, my wife was a secondary school teacher.

My mother's interference in our married life had already caused some problems in our family. I was optimistic and naive, I had underestimated them, and did not confront them; in so doing I gave my wife messages that—I now understand—were very negative.

After about a year our first child, Leonardo, was born. Some problems during the pregnancy caused him to weigh only a kilo and a half, even though he was healthy. This made us, and especially my parents-in-law, extremely anxious, maybe excessively so, as Leonardo was perfectly healthy and normal, aside from the weight.

Two years after Leonardo's birth, Angelo, our second child, was born. He was a beautiful and strong child.

We were normally attentive towards Angelo, but this caused some problems in Leonardo, who started to lose appetite and became almost anorexic. This increased my in-laws' anxiety, who began paying more and more attention to Leonardo.

Because of my wife's job and my absences, our children spent much time with their grandparents.

A few years after we got married some serious problems began.

My father, who was a businessman in the construction industry, suffered an economic collapse due to some ill-chosen investments. This involved both me and my brother, for different reasons. This unfortunately lasted several years, until we all lost everything, including personal real estate properties.

Unfortunately our children didn't have a serene childhood, due to these events. My chronic absence from family events, my excessive attachment to my family of origin, and my lack of firm boundaries with the children led to more serious problems during adolescence.

During the summer of 1998 we began to understand that our son Angelo gave signals of deep distress so, at the suggestion of a psychiatrist friend, we turned to Professor Andolfi to begin family therapy. Angelo did not want to join us in therapy, saying he didn't want to be "shrunk," so only the three of us started at first. During one of the following sessions, Angelo showed up and, after saying in a rather rebellious and rude way that he no longer wanted any kind of relationship with us, he stated that he wouldn't be coming again.

Later, after a series of messages we either neglected or misinterpreted, Angelo confessed to using heroin. For a while we tried to figure out what measures to take and what attitudes to have, in order to face this extremely serious situation.

A few months later, after a long fight with our son to bring him to a drug rehabilitation center, we decided to move to a nearby city, where Angelo started attending a semi-residential drug rehabilitation program. (He was at the center from 9 a.m. to 5 p.m., and spent the rest of the day at home.) Those were very difficult times, full of anxiety and hope, while Angelo continuously threatened to leave the center, but my wife and I, in all of this, managed to raise a wall our son wasn't able to break.

After a few months the operators of the center told us we had to start family therapy, and that was how we went back to Professor Andolfi.

Finally, after the rather negative beginning of the previous time, the real therapy started. Although there were many difficulties, especially due to my reserved nature which made it difficult to open up and talk freely about my problems and those of the family, after a while communication started to flow once again, and this helped us to accompany Angelo on his difficult path to recovery. We understood the reason for our son's issues: we had always thought him very strong, without truly understanding that the excessive attentions given to Leonardo by us and by the grandparents had caused him to feel very fragile, this was made worse by the lack of communication in the family and by the serious problems I already mentioned. During the therapeutic sessions it also came to light that my wife and I were not "acting as a couple."

Unfortunately, due to a series of misunderstandings with the rehab center operators, Angelo didn't conclude his treatment. After a year and a half we returned to our normal life, in our city.

In the meantime Angelo, who had graduated from high school, decided to live away from his family: he moved to Rome first, then to Florence and finally to the province of Bologna. During those years we were very anxious because Angelo didn't want to continue his studies after high school and because we knew he might go back to using drugs. Sure enough, what we feared could happen did, in fact, happen.

While Angelo was in Rome we occasionally attended the Accademia di Terapia Familiare [the Academy of Family Therapy], but stopped after the relapse, also because we had already learned through therapy how to deal with situations that had previously occurred.

The anguish continued for quite a while, between highs and lows. Angelo relapsed more than once but in the end he understood that his future and his destiny could not be linked to drugs.

One day he returned home with an official document of dismissal which stated he had to return to his own town, and that was probably when he understood the severity of the situation.

For a while he stayed at home with us, and when he turned twenty-five he decided to resume studying and applied to University. In an extreme act of faith we let him go to Bologna to start university, where he remained for only one year.

He later chose not to attend classes and stayed with us for a while. Nonetheless he continued to take his exams. At the moment he has gone back to Bologna for an obligatory internship, and he has a short way to go to achieve his three-year degree.

Leonardo graduated several years ago, and has a provisional job in a ministry in Rome.

Today we have reached an acceptable family balance, in spite of a thousand difficulties.

We have a good relationship with our children, especially with Angelo, who, with time, has become very attached to us.

We talk a lot, even on the phone, and we're constantly up to date with all his problems. Sometimes we have robust discussions and even argue, nonetheless there are many moments of affection and frequent manifestations of reciprocal respect.

For my part, I appreciate my children very much: one of them struggles to keep a steady job and manages to support himself in Rome, hoping for better times, while the other has fought a very hard battle against heroin.

In all this, family therapy has played a very important role.

We had reached the point that Angelo detested all of us, including his brother. Now things have changed. Angelo often reminds us that he demands his share of consideration and respect from all the members of the family. Sometimes we fall back into the usual mistakes that all anxious parents make, especially excessive protectiveness. Communication continues to help us a great deal and remains the most important tool to keep us going.

We take this opportunity to say a heartfelt thank you to the S. family for their letter. It surely wasn't easy to write without reopening ancient wounds which are probably not yet healed.

ALCOHOL DEPENDENCY

The issue of alcohol abuse in adolescents is a constantly increasing phenomenon on a global scale. Our Ministry of Health has also noticed an increase in alcohol consumption, especially between the ages of twelve and twenty-nine, and reports that alcohol and alcohol-related accidents are the main causes of death among young people. Unfortunately, this data is on a par with similar statistics from EU and non-EU countries.

Alcohol has several functions in our culture: it is at once an instrument of socialization, bonding, ritual, and escapism, and a way to disqualify, self-harm, and damage both the individual's health and those who suffer from its consequences: the family and society.

The latest data on alcohol consumption reveals that many adolescents are in a state of inebriation for an average of one day in four, but what is particularly worrying is that these young people drink just to get a "buzz," and the meaning of this alcohol abuse is better understood when we free ourselves from the idea that it is connected to the pleasure of drinking. The latter, in fact, is totally secondary to the need of reaching, through a substance, that state of euphoria and well-being needed to produce a loss of inhibition. For too many adolescents, the quality of what they drink is not as important as the alcohol level being high enough to reach the desired effect. In this sense, we can see why alcohol is considered by many to be a substitute for drugs: it is a substance that can cause a state of profound psycho-physical change, but, at the same time, it is legal and socially accepted.

The decrease in health and social damage caused by alcohol use in young people has become one of the main goals of public health care, and is pursued by most nations, according to guidelines set out by the World Health Organization, and particularly by the European Union after the approval of the *WHO Declaration on Alcohol and Young People*. Drawn up in 2001 in Stockholm, this strategic agreement between the European nations proposes clear guidelines for the prevention and reduction of the consumption of alcohol among adolescents and gives special attention to the promotion of autonomy of thought in young people regarding the messages coming from the media and society.[2]

The policies of protection and prevention, in relation to the pressure exerted on young people by society and their own peer groups, recognize the need to demystify increasingly ambiguous and dangerous messages. On the one side, the consumption of alcohol is presented to young people through normalizing messages, which promote it as part of the adult and juvenile culture (think, for instance, about ads for beer or beverages like alcohol pops or "alcopops"): in this way alcohol consumption becomes part of the culture of entertainment and of getting "high," it is both a way of feeling like young people who have fun and, at the same time, as adults who break the rules. On the other hand, we have a highly critical and pathologizing response from adults to alcohol consumption among adolescents, when the consequences of these behaviors become evident: car crashes, brawls, and group rapes.

This cultural ambiguity, sometimes allows phenomena of actual adolescent addiction or abuse to be disguised and read, even by parents, as an expression of their particular evolutionary stage. Also, the majority of young people first consume alcohol at home, with their parents at first and then alone because of its availability in the home environment. In many families, permission to start drinking is considered a kind of rite of passage from childhood into adulthood. Unfortunately, though, the scientific community has not yet identified clear limits within which drinking does not negatively affect the psychological and physical health of adolescents.

When thinking about strategies of prevention and treatment for reducing alcohol consumption among young people, one of the first problems we encounter is identifying what kind of adolescent should be considered a problematic consumer.

Given their age, adolescents do not present to the clinician as someone with the typical development of a dependent personality. The pattern of alcohol consumption varies, in fact, both in its frequency and quantity, going from abusive or occasional explorations linked to a social context, such as weekend binge drinking, to real conditions of psychological and physical addiction.

The alcoholic behavior of young people can often be read as a symptom of the need to grow up, which, when still not clearly understood, is enacted through adult behavior that is socially and legally unacceptable. For many adolescents alcohol consumption, even when

2   Ministry of Labor, Health and Social Policies, 2009.

exaggerated, remains one of the easiest and culturally accepted ways of doing something that is both experimental and rule-breaking, breaching socially accepted limits.

In other cases, when the normal processes of transition and autonomy that characterize the passage into adulthood are particularly blocked, and when the conflict between the need for dependence and separation is expressed through high anxiety, frustration, angst and discomfort, alcohol can become the preferred solution for that teenager.

Excessive alcohol consumption is also a way of escaping and evading difficulties and responsibilities, a tendency that is becoming more and more common these days. In the long run, though, for some people, getting drunk is a losing strategy that amplifies relational difficulties instead of solving problems. Its outcome is a gradual and potentially dangerous loss of self-esteem and of a sense of personal power. The only way out, again, is an escape from the self and from negative emotions, with an ever more desperate search for altered states of consciousness and escape from the real world, not only through alcohol, but also through psychoactive drugs, video-games, and deafening music.

We also need to make a distinction between the various alcoholic behaviors: the ones associated with psychological disorders of various kinds, like anxiety, depression or mood instability, and psychiatric disorders, often manifesting themselves at a very young age, like schizophrenia and manic-depressive psychosis.

With alcohol, as with drugs, attention to each case and to the social and family context is fundamental, precisely because drug abuse is often related to a context where evolutionary risks are already present, either individual, socioeconomic, cultural or familial. For instance, psychological difficulties in the parents are often associated with problems regarding affect regulation in children, just as unemployment, poverty, and a lack of attention to the needs of the children can be associated with a problematic and inadequate parent-child relationship. The adolescent can respond to these difficulties in a reactive way, accepting or becoming more sensitive to peer-pressure, feeling rebellious, and choosing belonging to the group as a priority over belonging to the family. Often he will manifest increasing aggressiveness towards the parents, triggering in them a reaction of helplessness and defeat; feeling incapable, the parents will frequently renounce their control over the child. It is not unusual to find different or similar forms of dependence, like alcohol, gambling, drug addiction, and eating disorders in the histories of these families.

The correlation between early onset of drinking and a higher risk of developing a real form of alcoholism, or other conduct and personality disorders in adult life, has been ascertained by a great deal of research.

At the same time, the prognostic risk of onset at a young age can become a resource and a guarantee of more flexibility and possibility of prevention and recovery; early intervention can ensure that precocious abusive behavior doesn't translate into personality disorders and/or addictions in adult life.

The aforementioned areas of risk are the ones we should focus on to intervene and develop protective factors: a high quality of affective relationship with the parents, a feeling of being in control and supported through the difficulties that the adolescent encounters during his growth, a healthy set of values and family models, encouragement towards the development of decision-making autonomy in relation to the risks the adolescent wants to take, and better capacity to resist giving in to peer pressure.

Family therapy in the treatment of alcoholism

Research and clinical practice widely attest to the importance of family factors in determining etiology and treating alcoholism (Deas, Thomas, 2001; Becker, Curry, 2008). Likewise, research in the study of psycho-pathological development confirmed the central role of family dynamics in the onset of drug and alcohol addiction in young adolescents. The efficacy of treatment and/or involvement of the family has been further demonstrated in the case of addiction to drugs and alcohol (Liddle, 2004) in three dimensions: it promotes the engagement of the adolescent and his motivation for treatment, it increases the probability that the family will continue treatment, and it produces good outcomes and maintains them in the long run.

Nevertheless, families of adolescents with alcohol issues can be very difficult to engage in therapy, both due to poor motivation and poor confidence in the teenager in the adults' support system, and to the intrinsic characteristics of the family's relational dynamics. It is therefore important for the clinician, during this initial phase of treatment, to bring every resource available into the therapeutic system: this means teachers, friends, and even those who suggested therapy in the first place, to be able to understand the context that favored and supported the emergence of the problem and to verify the likelihood of change.

The relational reframing of individual problems offered by the family therapist, if shared with the family, builds and supports the motivation of each member towards the therapeutic work, decreasing the risk of resistance and sabotage.

Unlike traditional intervention modalities based upon symptom-reduction and abstinence, family therapy seems to best answer the need of the young person to be contained, to communicate, and to acquire new meanings.

TECHNOLOGY ADDICTION

In 1995, the psychiatrist Ivan Goldberg ironically suggested the inclusion of a new syndrome in the DSM, *Internet Addiction Disorder*, and identified a varied and complex symptomatic picture that could assist in recognizing this new disorder. This gesture was at first interpreted as a simple provocation, but later produced an interesting impact on the clinical world: the scientific community began to seriously consider the possibility that Goldberg might be right, and that it may really be possible to develop an addiction to the Internet as it is with drugs or alcohol. Since then a continuous debate has been triggered and it has not yet been concluded: several authors, though they recognize that Internet addiction can have quite negative consequences, are still reluctant to accept the existence of an addiction syndrome without substances; others, instead, affirm that these are simply behavioral addictions (Alonso-Fernandez, 1999).

One author who has been particularly busy doing research in this field since the mid-nineties is Mark Griffiths (Griffiths, Hunt, 1995). He calls *Technological Addictions* all those behavioral addictions that have to do with the interaction between man and machine, whether mostly active, as in the case of computers, or passive, as in that of television.

Griffiths states that addictions to technology, such as the Internet, share certain essential characteristics with drug addictions. These are: *dominance* (the activity dominates the subject's thoughts and behavior, gaining primary importance over other interests), *mood alterations* (beginning the activity produces excitement or relaxation), *tolerance* (the need to progressively increase the activity to obtain the desired effect), *withdrawal symptoms* (the psychic or physical sickness which appears when the behavior is either interrupted or reduced), *conflict* (both interpersonal between the subject and those who are close to him, and intra-psychic due to his addiction), and *relapse* (the tendency to restart the activity after interruption).

In more recent times, academics have used the synthetic definition of *Tech Abuse* to refer to a broader spectrum of consequences generated by the excessive and compulsive use of media technology, resulting in marked subjective discomfort, socio-relational and affective difficulties resulting in the deterioration of academic and work performance and even reaching situations of almost total detachment from external relationships (Caretti, La Barbera, 2001). More specifically, the negative effects of tech abuse go from physical issues (being sedentary and therefore becoming overweight, back pain, visual problems, etc.) to actual video obsession, that is: the prolonged and totally absorbing exposure to video, in silence and often in a dimly lit room.

In children and teenagers tech abuse is characterized by a number of specific behaviors linked to an increase in aggression (more fights within the family and with peers to spend more time in front of the video); in adults, on the other hand, it manifests through a progressive tendency to neglect family responsibilities, with a consequent increase in couple problems. There have been cases of mothers who forgot to pick up their children from school and prepare their meals (Young, Rogers, 1998).

The great variety of activities which can be accessed online ensures that *Internet Addiction Disorder* is not a homogeneous category of disorders, rather it manifests itself in various forms, clearly distinct from one another. They include *cyber-sexual addiction* (the compulsive use of websites dedicated to virtual sex and pornography), *cyber-relational addiction* (the tendency to build friendships and romantic relationships with people met online), *net compulsions* (compulsive gambling and shopping online), *information overload* (compulsive web surfing), and *computer addiction* (the tendency to get involved in virtual games, such as MUDs, interactive role games in which the subjects participates by building a fictitious identity). So-called video mania belongs to this last category, and consists in an unbridled and quantitatively uncontrolled use of videogames.

The excessive involvement of many young people in net activities distracts attention from work and school. The exaggerated amount of time spent online, even at nighttime, disrupts the sleep-wake rhythm and causes excessive tiredness, which negatively affects scholastic and/or professional performance. What is even more serious is that, gradually increasing on-line time decreases the time available to relate to significant others, above all, to real, live people. Certain fundamental characteristics of the Internet, such as its anonymity and the lack of space-time limits, offer the opportunity of living a peculiar experience akin to a dream-like state, and the Net can therefore become a psychological space in which to project emotions and fantasies. This space can easily prevail over real life, from which the tendency is to abstract oneself increasingly, causing the development of an addiction on the virtual world.

Addiction to videogames is now considered a real pathology of adolescence, to be treated like drug addiction and alcoholism. From a three-year study concluded at the beginning of 2009 by the Smith and Jones Center of Amsterdam, relating to "console addictions," it emerges that 93% of those affected are males under twenty-three years of age. Following the United States, China, and South Korea, a center for the detoxification from videogames was finally also opened in Europe, in Amsterdam. They offer therapy, lasting two months, to detoxify and rehabilitate young people affected by strong addictions of this kind.

As often happens when technological innovations arise, the Internet also allows, in many ways, an improvement in people's lives, but at the same time it represents a danger for those who cannot make appropriate use of it. If, on the one hand the Net can be an opportunity to gain social support, especially for those who have more relational issues and perhaps a low self-esteem, we cannot underestimate the fact that this very medium offers anyone the opportunity of inventing parallel identities to the real one is a risk factor for the development of full blown Internet addiction, especially in adolescents, who have not yet developed their own identity.

EATING DISORDERS: ANOREXIA AND BULIMIA

The spread of eating disorders in female adolescents has, in the last thirty years, assumed epidemic dimensions. We can state with almost total certainty that they constitute the principal indicator of female psychic distress, particularly during adolescence.

The tendency to express through the body and through actions issues that cannot be easily expressed mentally is a typical characteristic of adolescence. Eating disorders, like other behavior disorders such as deviance, drug addiction, and attempted suicide, are also symptoms of obstacles in the normal evolution of the adolescent and can be part of a turbulent adolescent crisis or may become a component in a psycho-pathological profile. In any case, the adolescent, through the eating disorder, avoids the emotional expression of what cannot be expressed, as it is too painful. Those who, like adolescents, cannot put their needs into words can release an unbearable emotional tension through the language of behavior.

We have heard a great deal about anorexia nervosa and bulimia, and a lot has been written and studied during the past thirty years, both in the field of medicine and that of psychology.

Anorexia and bulimia, while they are still described as two different forms of eating disorders, are actually two sides of the same coin, different manifestations of the same disorder. In the past, restrictive anorexia nervosa was more common than bulimia, but now it is the other way around. Restrictive anorexia and bulimia tend, in any case, to alternate at different times in the person's life, although the restrictive phase often precedes bulimic or anorexic/bulimic phases (Cuzzolaro, 2002).

In this book we'll treat these two forms as different expressions of the same syndrome.

The term anorexia derives from the Greek *an-orexis* and means "loss of appetite." This term is etymologically inappropriate for this pathology: loss of appetite is not present at all in this disorder, as the anorexic is starving, but the desperate search for thinness condemns her to extreme sacrifices to contain her terror of gaining weight.

The average age of onset for anorexia is seventeen, and the highest percentage of onsets is between fourteen and eighteen years of age. The number of cases in adulthood, at around forty years of age and after marriage, seems to be increasing.

Even though this eating disorder is the one with the highest death rate, anorexia rarely leads to death; registered fatal cases include those caused by suicide and reach a maximum level of 5% (Harrison, Fauci, 1998). The anorexic, rather than wishing to die, plays with death in order to exercise control over her life.

The male to female ratio, according to some researchers, is 1 to 10, while according to others it is 1 to 8. The percentage of male anorexics seems to be on the increase, though this could be due to an increase in requests for help. Nowadays, though, the main problem linked to body image in males is that of being as muscular as possible, rather than appearing slimmer. In this case we speak of *muscle dysmorphia*, which is considered by professionals to be the male form of anorexia.

Body image and the construction of gender identity are the main elements in the onset of anorexia nervosa. Individual factors, such as being adolescent and female, and psychosocial factors, like cultural and relational models within the family and in society, intertwine in delineating its spread.

A correct categorization of eating disorders within psychopathology is unlikely; they can rather be considered as ethnic disorders, or cultural syndromes (Devereux, 1980; Gordon, 1990), or pathological expressions of the human psyche, which the culture of belonging uses in a bizarre way to reveal its most hidden and paradoxical aspects.

Anorexics and bulimics express, through their bodies, the distress of today's female adolescence, and embody a totally intellectualized femininity where the body must be tamed. As in the 1800s during Victorian times hysterical women affirmed through their bodies their refusal to assume the maternal role, characterized by the dependency and passivity imposed upon bourgeois girls in those days, today's anorexics, with their dietary restrictions, seem to pursue a distancing from the shape of adult women.

During the Middle Ages, the mortification of the body through fasts was considered by religion as the gateway to the divine. Saint Theresa of Avila, in the 1500s, used an olive twig to induce vomit and liberate the stomach in order to receive the consecrated host. The religious mystical ideal and spiritual asceticism conferred a culturally acceptable meaning to the prolonged fast of anorexic saints. Nowadays, similar behaviors are justified through the aesthetic ideal. Whether anorexic persons are considered saints or neurotics depends only on the type of culture in which they strive to gain control over their lives (Bell, 1980).

Cultural models are not intrinsic to the psychopathology of the eating disorder, but are a rationalization of the latter which is compliant to the dominant culture. In today's culture, the commandments of aesthetics reinforce anorexic behaviors: the value of a slim, efficient, and athletic female body is juxtaposed to the "flaccidity" of the soft and cozy body that was, in other times, the standard of beauty and ideal model of femininity. All this happens together with a loss of the social value of motherhood, which is considered by many women as an option they can give small and residual space to in their lives and is, in any case, secondary to other priorities. In this overview we shouldn't underestimate the separation between sexuality and maternity that is afforded by contraceptives: although favoring an increase in individual freedom, safe sex has promoted a devaluation of maternal values, which is confirmed by the drop in birth rates in Western societies.

Whether they are medieval saints, Victorian hysterical adolescents, or modern anorexic adolescents, these teenagers seem to have in common the need to reject the adult female body. They all express, each with the language of their times, the difficulty of reconciling within themselves the dominant female role models of their culture or, more simply, the difficulty of growing up.

The medical model and behavior modification interventions

Eating disorders are psychosomatic diseases: long-term hospital-ization and antidepressant medications are considered necessary for treating adolescents with severe manifestations, often associated with daily programs of behavior modification. Anorexia can be considered as an eating phobia and treated accordingly, according to Crisp, Joughin, Halek, Boywer (1996).

Psychotherapy is also common as an individual type of support to assist in changing the distorted body image of anorexic adolescents and their fears of gaining weight, or sexuality and interpersonal relation-ships within the family and in the peer groups.

There is a long tradition of using family therapy, especially with very early eating disorders in adolescents, starting with the early work of Minuchin in Philadelphia and Mara Palazzoli Selvini in Milan, as we will soon discuss.

The idea of actively engaging families in the treatment of anorexic adolescents is still very much opposed by the medical-psychi-atric establishment, which concentrates the intervention on the patient's symptomatology rather than on the adolescent as a person and his/her family history. At best, families are involved in different form of psycho-educational techniques, in order to control and monitor the adolescent's problematic eating habits.

If we hope to support interdisciplinary team work, the rigid and standardized medical models need to welcome other treatment modali-ties which are more interested in helping the adolescent's healthy devel-opment using their family's resources.

An example in this direction is the Maudsley Hospital's (Wood-side, Shekter-Wolfson, 1991) approach in London, which is a family based treatment of anorexia nervosa in three phases.

The first focuses on "weight restoration" with intensive out-patient treatment, where the parents take an active role and no blame is placed on families.

The second phase is based on "returning control over eating" to the adolescent and parents assist their children with the help of a professional guide.

The goal of the third stage is "establishing healthy adolescent identity" by supporting autonomy and parental boundaries.

**The systemic-relational model of Salvador Minuchin with adolescents
affected by psycho-somatic disturbances**

Minuchin, starting from the premise that the symptom must be
considered within its context in order to understand its relational
meanings, includes anorexia in the psychosomatic disorders (Minuchin,
Rosman, Baker, 1978). He clearly defines the characteristics of psychosomatic and anorexic families.

They are enmeshed families, characterized by extreme proximity
and intensity in family interactions, with diffuse subsystem boundaries
and poor differentiation on an individual level. They are families where
strong hyper-protectiveness is present, both from parents towards children and vice versa. The result of this is a high level of rigidity, with a
tendency to maintain a static organization. Enmeshment and rigidity
considerably lower the tolerance threshold to conflict, which is regularly
avoided through negative triangulation.

In anorexic families enmeshment is particularly oriented
towards the daughter and her well-being, with a specific attention to her
psycho-biological needs and with poor extra-familial orientation. With
the arrival of adolescence the need to reconcile the external world with
that internal to the family also arises, and therefore so does the need to
negotiate the conflict between these two realities. This requires the kind
of flexibility this type of family does not possess: its external boundaries
are as rigid and defined as the internal ones are weak and diffuse,
favoring the creation of inter-generational and trans-generational
coalitions.

The family's attention towards the body is characteristic: "The
preoccupation about somatic issues is an important element for the
family culture" (*ibidem*). This can cause the manifestation of psychosomatic symptoms in the child, with the goal of distracting from the
family conflict. While on an individual level, the illness represents for the
daughter an identity increasingly based upon implicit definitions of
incompetence, which become even more dramatic when the adolescent is
required to express her own personal capabilities, so that "for a subject
who has painfully experienced his or her inadequacy, going on a diet is
to gain a sense of empowerment and independence" (Gordon, 1990).

Family dynamics in anorexic families: Mara Selvini Palazzoli

Selvini Palazzoli absorbed the ideas of Bruch (1973) and treated
with clinical intuition many anorexic patients individually until she

began practicing family therapy. We owe Selvini Palazzoli the most original and in-depth studies on the family models which produce and support anorexia (Selvini Palazzoli, 1977). The author defines a specific and well-structured model of the family dynamics in families with anorexic children, and speaks of an *anorexic process in the family*. The basis of her theory is the concept of *relational fraud*, that is: "a behavioral strategy which is characterized by the acting out of an inter-generational dyadic relationship (parent-child) as if it were privileged when, in fact, it is not" (Selvini Palazzoli et al., 1989), and whose implicit aim is to set the child against the other parent.

Without entering into the details of the different phases of this process, we can say that at its base is *couple stalemate*, a couple crisis which has become chronic and static and which maintains the status quo through a negative triangulation of the daughter. Apart from couple stalemate, the author identifies and highlights several general aspects in the anorexia presentations she treated during the Eighties. Among these we can find the parents' unresolved bonds in the family of origin, intolerance towards social disapproval, the anorexic's sacrificial tendency and inclination to be humiliated, and her siblings' willingness to suffer in silence for the love of their mother, which provokes rage and envy in the anorexic.

Later, in 1998, Mara Selvini Palazzoli et al. expanded previous theories by widening and refining their frame of reference in the book *Ragazze anoressiche e bulimiche*, which was the result of important follow-up research of clinical cases spanning a period of twenty years. Here they hypothesized not only about different kinds of anorexia, but also about different family models based upon each disorder.

We need to recognize Selvini Palazzoli's great contribution to changing the diagnostic approach and therefore the therapy of anorexia over the course of her career. Over time, the individual and family aspects not only of the anorexic patients, but also of their family members have been increasingly recognized, giving particular attention to the way the various layers intertwine. The interpretation moves between three interrelated polarities: the family, the individual, and the symptom, so that a distinction is made between primary and secondary anorexia on the basis of its various symptomatic functions. The symptoms of primary anorexia have a defensive function in relation to a historical problem since a feeling of inadequacy is a universal dimension found in feminine experiences across the centuries, but the defense from such inadequacy is culturally determined (Andolfi, Angelo, D'Atena, 2001).

The Andolfi developmental model for treating adolescent eating disorders

For almost forty years the clinical interventions of Maurizio Andolfi and his team with anorexic patients have taken place within their family context.

During the Seventies family psychotherapy for anorexic girls was very rare, first of all because this psycho-pathological profile was less common than it is today, and also because of social prejudice towards a disquieting disease, akin to severe mental pathologies such as psychosis; it's no coincidence it was defined *anorexia nervosa*, to stress that it had to do with the nervous system rather than with the relationship to food.

When he returned from the United States, in line with the clinical work of Salvador Minuchin he had witnessed in the Child Guidance Clinic of Philadelphia, Andolfi introduced *lunch sessions* in his own group at the Institute of Family Therapy in Rome where the families of anorexic patients and their therapists had lunch together (Andolfi, 1979).

The initial purpose of these session was to force the anorexic to eat, supporting the parents' decision as a useful resource, although a very authoritarian one, to convince the girl to eat. This was in line with an intervention procedure that was both active and coercive (perhaps this resonated with the historical reality of that time), and whose only positive aspect was to build an agreement of joint responsibility between the parents, who were otherwise divided and subject to easy triangulations. Very quickly, though, this technique was replaced by something that was almost its opposite, the paradox, based upon the injunction (verbalized by the therapist during the session) that the anorexic girl should not eat anything, while the rest of the family and the therapist conversed freely while eating, almost ignoring her. The implicit goal was obviously that of encouraging the anorexic to transgress, hoping she would end up eating to maintain a position of power in which "no one can tell me what to do!"

This language and approach have been extensively superseded and have generated much self-criticism in time. It is sufficient to read the books *Behind the Family Mask* (Andolfi et al., 1983) and *Paradox and Counterparadox* (Selvini Palazzoli et al., 1975) to understand the cultural climate and clinical thoughts of that time.

During the past thirty years, the understanding and treatment of the anorexic phenomenon within the family context has progressively changed, and the focus of our work at the Family Therapy Academy has shifted decisively from the theme of food and eating to that of the nature of evolution and identity, as described in various works (Andolfi, Angelo, De Nichilo, 1987; Andolfi, Angelo, D'Atena, 2001), in a search for the historical and relational meanings within which to locate this extreme form of rebellion against one's own position as an adolescent and against the world of emotional family ties.

Below we synthesize some key aspects useful in understanding and treating anorexia according to the tri-generational approach.

Disturbance in self-image and body-image

It is beyond doubt that the anorexic adolescent suffers from a great distortion in the way she experiences her self-image and her body.

We have met some girls, who often had gorgeous and harmonious bodies, who "vivisected" themselves when looking in the mirror, finding imperceptible or non-existent physical defects and obsessed about these imperfections to the point of exhaustion. Breasts, buttocks, nose, ears, belly, knees, and armpits can become intolerable parts of the Self and lead to family dramas, while parents and siblings become quite powerless, incapable of providing any kind of solution.

Refusal of food, use of laxatives, binge-eating, and recurrent vomiting all seem daily rituals of self-punishment and a confirmation of the impossibility of entering adolescence in a positive way.

Disturbance in the way death is perceived

We have been able to verify more and more frequently through our clinical experience that the anorexic patient rarely wants to kill herself (we obviously speak about adolescent girls, while the development of anorexia in chronically ill adult women is much more severe. We do not refer to the latter in this work). If anything, her goal is to gain even more attention; more than anything, her gesture is an exasperated expression of power and a desperate cry for independence! In the vast majority of cases, the theme and risk of eventual death due to emaciation and cachexia is present for rather long periods of time: playing with life and death is a particularly developed skill in the young anorexic patient.

We often witness more or less forced hospitalizations, always strongly traumatic, which favor a temporary biological adjustment in the girl, as she gains one or two kilos, but once she returns home things go back to normal: the game resumes unless something more extreme happens, something that has nothing to do with her ruthless control over food intake and weight increase.

These are the reflections of an anorexic girl (after recovery) concerning her hospitalization:

"I didn't want to go and, as children do, I threw myself on the ground, I held on to doorjambs while my parents, also with tears in their eyes, tried to drag me away... In that moment they saved my life. I wasn't convinced about being hospitalized, because I wasn't determined in my desire to get better!"

This is the central point of the issue, an exhausting fight and arm-wrestling between those who want to cure the girl (parents, siblings, care providers and so on), and the latter, who doesn't want to be cured!

In this sense, eating addictions are very different to those from other substances, as drug addicts have a higher risk of dying of an overdose, whether it is a voluntary or unconscious desire. Drug addicts have a much more realistic vision of the fact that they can really die of drug abuse and, in the end, some really do die by suicide.

An ethnic disorder

It seems that in poor countries, where there is a scarcity of food, it is improbable to develop anorexia. As Mara Selvini Palazzoli affirms, anorexia "is a symptom connected to opulent societies." In a culture of no shortages, people tend to play with their bodies: what significance would losing weight, gaining weight, binge eating, and so forth have in Africa where there is no food? But should those countries ever experience a boom in consumerism, there would be the preconditions to develop similar diseases.

In the clinical case we are about to describe, we find ourselves before a serious anorexic disorder in a girl from Bangladesh, who long ago migrated to Canada with her family. We will discuss this very fact with the family and friends of the parents, who have no memories of anorexic disorders in Bangladesh, where people die of famine and where social problems are profoundly different. If we then look at the Maghreb and Arabic countries in general, we can see how television ads and the mass media in general consider curvaceous bodies as the ideal of feminine beauty; in these places, skeletal and flat-chested girls would be considered unattractive.

The central role of children and prolonged dependence at home

Without a doubt, in western societies we have seen a radical change in the affective organization of the family. Rules and generational boundaries have profoundly changed, children are fewer (in Italy, we have an average of 1.2 children per family) and have assumed a more central role in the family.

We have gone from a family with a lot of children (potentially productive in an agricultural society) to a family where children, being few, are themselves "household assets"; loved, venerated, and spoiled by parents and grandparents, with a consequential loss of boundaries between those who represent authority — the parents — and those who are growing up, having to obey and respect the adults' rules.

The central role of the child, which sometimes evolves into tyrannical and omnipotent behavior, is more of a social construct than a problem created by the younger generation.

This centrality starts in childhood and continues also into adolescence, often considered the age of individuation, which, ever more frequently, takes place later on, at around twenty-five/thirty years of age, in a phase described by many authors as *prolonged adolescence* (Scabini, 1997). This phenomenon can explain the rise of addictive pathologies and desperate forms of adolescent rebellion, such as anorexia.

The "chronic child" and the Peter Pan syndrome

The anorexic's difficulty in growing up, which can be associated to the Peter Pan complex, also includes the difficulty of the entire family nucleus in confronting the evolutionary tasks of transition. We shouldn't forget that children's adolescence, particularly nowadays, coincides more and more often with having to accept the aging of parents and the possible loss of elderly grandparents. In substance, all the adjustments and reorganizations required by the family during children's adolescence are often complex, both in terms of quantity and quality. It is therefore not unusual to see a reciprocal co-dependency which compels the adolescent to begin a "career as a chronic child" (Andolfi, 2003), a child that refuses to grow up and individuate apparently because of his need to control the affective family dynamics, but in reality because of his terror of "losing himself" in the external world.

The problem is not the food, but the external world

The real problem of the adolescent anorexic is not connected to food and to tiring family battles at the table but to the external world, perceived as threatening and highly dangerous. Anorexic girls have a terrible fear of the outside world and of comparison with peers. They tyrannize the family, place of security and of predictable affective distortions, while they are hardly capable of establishing affective relationships in the outside world and so they are hardly ever part of a group of friends. They are often very good at school, they are perfectionists, but any comment which vaguely resembles a criticism becomes an immense source of frustration. Lastly, in regard to feelings, these girls are extremely sensitive towards rejections and have a terror of being undervalued. All this brings the complete avoidance of physical and sexual contact, often perceived as dirty or degrading.

Role and parental function reversal: the adolescent grandparent

We have already stated in previous chapters and will revisit the issue below (when dealing with reactive depression in adolescents), that psychological disorders during the developmental age are strongly connected to several forms of couple and family dysfunction.

The phenomenon of role reversal is very common in anorexic girls, both because of the sometimes oppressive presence of the mother during the child's development, and because of a kind of "disappearance" of the father. It is a fact that the anorexic patient controls the life of the family (this control is born and develops several years before the onset of the anorexic behavior) and she becomes the privileged witness of emotional disconnections, couple conflicts, and affective deficiencies in her parents. These young women are often substitute partners for emotionally lonely mothers and "specialize in care-giving functions towards the parents, as a kind of grandmother figure." Frequently anorexic girls identify with an emotionally important grandmother and follow her lead and her attitudes.

We remember a case in which the maternal grandmother of a young anorexic participated in a family therapy session, and showed up wearing a mink hat. During the course of the session we discovered that this girl had been very close to her while growing up, she was named after her and was put on a pedestal by her, unlike the mother, who hadn't been able to earn her own mother's esteem or admiration. The therapist suggested that the grandmother should give her hat to the granddaughter, to see if the latter would wear it in the same regal way as the elderly lady. The girl was very excited by this, and wore the hat with undeniable regality. When the therapist suggested that the hat should be passed to the mother, the latter was very embarrassed and wore it clumsily, provoking criticism from the grandmother, who thus confirmed that she preferred the granddaughter.

The regressive part and the super-adult part coexist, but are dissociated

After describing the super-adult role played by the girl within the family, we cannot forget that the anorexic behavior itself represents a strongly regressive choice, which plunges the girl back into capricious and tyrannical behavior more typical of a spoilt three-year-old. Moreover, the fact that menstruation disappears belies a biological refusal of the rite of passage into adolescent life. In this way there is a splitting, a dissociation between an adult-like and a childlike level. The aim of therapy will be to return adolescence to the girl, by playing with both her regressive and super-adult parts, and by helping the parents regain control over the family.

Anorexia as an extreme form of adolescent rebellion and search for love

Unlike men, who tend to externalize their discomforts through aggressiveness, women are generally more reflective and prefer to keep everything within themselves. Anger and pain, being negative energies, trigger adolescent rebellion by attacking the body and depriving it of vitality or passion. Anorexia is equivalent to virtual death.

We have to admit, nonetheless, that when we go beyond the pathological aspects, we often find in the anorexic a sensitive, deep, and extremely intelligent person, often superior to "normal" girls. As if being sick, the act of suffering, and making loved ones suffer, once they have been overcome, add value to one's humanity.

It is also true that the anorexic, once she has recovered, will continue to have some difficulties in regard to intimacy and sexuality; it is unlikely that she will feel secure about this, so ancient is the fear of being refused and rejected. Even after having children and a stable relationship this fear will probably remain intact. But then, who is perfect?

Practice illustration: Nita's anorexia between Bangladesh and Canada

The fragments reported below are from a counseling session Andolfi conducted several years ago in Canada with a family from Bangladesh.[3] The family consists of the father, a fifty-three-year-old marine engineer, the wife, a forty-year-old housewife and the daughters: Nita, eighteen, and Lila, fourteen.

The couple had been married for eighteen years and their marriage, according to the traditions of their country of origin, had been an arranged one. In fact, the husband had married his wife after seeing a photo of her sister, trusting they would be physically alike.

The onset of anorexia had been first noticed when Nita was fourteen and was about to enter high school. When her weight fell below critical levels, she was admitted to the local hospital, where she was force-fed, and was offered group therapy and individual therapy with a psychiatrist.

After a few months in the hospital, the entire family was sent to a well-known center in Toronto, the George Hull Centre, which specializes in families and adolescents. In this environment the parents spoke about their daughter's loss of appetite, her refusal to participate in meals and her reluctance to leave the house. Just when she was expected to become more autonomous, the opposite was happening.

Two months before Andolfi's consultation, the maternal grandmother, who lived in Bangladesh, had become severely ill, and the mother had not been able to visit her before her death because Nita's health had deteriorated precisely at the same time. We learned about this loss only during the consultation.

The family therapist, after working fourteen months with the family without achieving any notable change, decided to work only with the couple, confident that an improvement in this relationship would also have a positive effect on the girl. This work had actually been very difficult and the couple was moving towards a situation of "separation under one roof."

In the meantime, Nita's individual therapist was also becoming discouraged by the absence of change in the girl. In this context of therapeutic impasse and the persistence of Nita's anorexic symptoms, Andolfi was asked to intervene in the therapy.

---

3   This case was taken from the description by Elizabeth Ridgely in the book
Please Help Me with This Family (Andolfi, Haber, 1994), and later reviewed and
improved.

The entire family participated in this session, together with the family therapist and the individual therapist. The consultant at first remained behind the one-way mirror, and chose to come into contact with the family in an indirect way, via messages through the family therapist. Actually this position, initially meant to be temporary, was maintained for the entire first session.

This was Andolfi's first experiment of conducting a session through some kind of family supervision, with the active collaboration of the patient. This experience, which happened almost by chance, deeply changed Andolfi's way of thinking about therapy and supervision during subsequent years and, most of all, about where and how he looked for competence and resources in the family.

From counseling to supervision of the anorexic girl

What the consultant does in this case is a paradoxical experiment: he enters therapy as an external operator but does not directly intervene in the therapeutic system. Rather, he establishes a relationship with the girl from behind the mirror based upon "direct supervision." His intervention is very unusual, completely unrelated to standard procedures. However he decides that this is the only way to move freely within a situation of therapeutic impasse. Among those who participate in this encounter are all the members of staff, at least ten professionals (psychiatrists, nurses, social workers, nutritionists, individual and family psychotherapists, and so on) who had been involved with this case and who all seemed to have failed, family and therapists alike.

The consultant thus decides not to enter the session and to remain behind the one-way mirror, sending the family a rather provocative message through the therapist.

Therapist: He is behind the mirror, he has heard the therapeutic story, and may call us (*by intercom*), the message he wants me to convey is this: he wondered... since Bangladesh has failed and since Toronto has failed in terms of helping your family, he wondered how a therapist who comes from another continent could possibly be helpful this morning, and for this reason he was reluctant to come in, to begin the consultation.
Mother: What do you mean "failed"?
Therapist: Well, I sort of have to interpret for him: he meant failed in the sense of, you know, Tina (*the individual therapist*) and I started working with you about 14-15 months ago, so I imagine he means failed in the sense that nothing has changed.

Mother: Something has changed, it is changing, it's not failed, it's progressing, yes we are working on it. What do you mean? Why?
Therapist: No, failed I think in the sense that nothing has changed, for instance you came to us after the hospitalization, but our work, including the doctors' reports, have not changed a thing.
Father: I think at Brandon hospital there was a small change in her life: after being in hospital, after coming out, something did change, except she refuses to eat as much as she should.
Therapist: Isn't that why you came?
Father: And I think she's really trying... apart from that, she was used to being alone in her room at the hospital, she never went out, never met anyone. Now she is free, she goes where she wants, everything is better.

There is no hope

(The intercom rings for the first time. The therapist gets up and answers. From now on all the consultant's interventions will be "whispered" through the intercom behind the mirror.)
Consultant: What is your name?
Therapist: Jim.
Consultant: Jim, you're wonderful, try and be a good messenger for me, go up to the girl and say: you know exactly what Dr. Andolfi means when he says "no hope in Bangladesh and Toronto." Then sit down, without explaining.
Therapist (standing in front of Nita): Nita, that was Dr. Andolfi, he wanted me to give you this message: you know what he means when he says that there's no hope either in Bangladesh or Toronto!

We just described the first step in the construction of a therapeutic alliance with the girl. She knows that things haven't changed, because she doesn't want to recover, and the answers given by her parents seem to be protective ways to avoid admitting that, deep down, nothing has changed. But maybe this strange therapist who comes from afar can give voice to the lack of hope, trigger some movement, and go behind the family mask.

Mother: How can he say that there is no hope, I wonder? I don't know. There is hope, I believe.
Therapist: He feels that there is no hope, in the sense of... I mean, what's the point of him coming in? He's afraid that it won't change a thing. Do you think there is hope?

Mother: Of course, yes, I feel something is changing.

Father: Well as I said, since coming out of the hospital she has improved in every way, except for food intake. Then we noticed that she was falling back into her old habits.

Nita (with a twinkle in her eyes): I understand what he means... that I listen to him... I listen to everybody, but I don't know if I follow... I could say that I understand him... I can only do what I can. Sometimes I do, sometimes I don't, it depends. It is up to me, but I don't care and I don't listen to anyone, I only do what I want, so he's probably right in saying that nothing has changed.

Father: Well, but how do you expect to get healthy? Do you want to be healthy?

Nita: I don't know.

Father: You don't know? Don't you think that healthy people function well?

Nita: You tell me that but I don't think about it.

Father: Don't you? As I see it, your mind is changing, sometimes it stays in one place, then suddenly it changes, I feel you cannot decide what you want to do or how it should be done.

As soon as the girl hears the message of the consultant, she becomes curious: she starts moving her eyes, almost looking for the presence behind the mirror, and, at the same time, she tries to understand what turn the session might take. It is interesting to note that the first affective attunement between the consultant and the girl, which is based on his "not knowing whether to come in" and her "not knowing whether to follow him," is a fundamental connection. In other words, an implicit collaboration has begun. All this happens in contrast to the father who talks a lot without listening; the mother who is even more worried about the pessimistic description of the situation, while the younger sister, in front of the "queen," keeps her arms crossed and looks very angry.

The consultant introduces the idea that there is no hope because hope, actually, always exists, we only need the will to look for it. This is a paradox, just as it is a paradox to says he won't be able to help them, when he is really pulling the strings through the intercom, from behind the mirror. All these paradoxes shake everyone, apart from the father, who seems to be talking to himself.

Death in the family

(The intercom buzzes and the therapist answers.)

Consultant: Jim, please tell the father: you keep talking and this is the greatest sign of no hope. Can you try to keep silent for three minutes and feel the death in this family?

Therapist: Dr. Andolfi says that your talking is the greatest sign of no hope in the family. And he wants to know if you can sit in silence for three minutes to experience the death in the family.

(After a long silence the intercom buzzes again.)

Therapist (addressing the girl): Nita? Doctor Andolfi wants to talk to you.

Until this moment the consultant has always communicated through Jim, the therapist, who tried to do his best in spite of the unpredictable situation. During this interminable pause the consultant has an intuition: that this silence might be connected to an actual mourning in this family. Not many families would have tolerated such a long silence. The consultant is now ready to follow this path and feels he can directly relate to the girl. From this moment on, during the course of the session, he will only talk to her, always through the intercom behind the mirror, whispering, though the actual distance between them is only twenty centimeters and they are only separated by the one-way mirror.

Consultant: Hello Nita!

Nita: Yes.

Therapist: Do you think your father is able to feel the death in the family, now?

Nita: I don't know.

Therapist: Would you like to check? Because if he can feel it perhaps there is some hope, otherwise there is no sense in my joining you. Could you check please? Can you check with him if he's experiencing the death and the failure of this family? Can you try and then call me back?

The consultant doesn't introduce himself, he doesn't need any preliminaries but goes straight to the point, acting as if the relationship between him and the girl was already strong. He asks her to pass a very tough message to the father while reinforcing the alliance with her by inviting her to call him back as soon as the father feels something. Thus he establishes a kind of reciprocity, as Nita will also be able to trigger the consultant through her answers.

Nita (addressing her father): Do you understand what Jim said earlier? Can you now feel the death in the family?

Father (looking at his daughter in the eyes): No. I feel no death.

Nita (feeling awkward, smiling): You haven't understood... did you understand?

In spite of the verbal denial this is the first time that this man, who seemed completely detached from his emotions, reacts in a non-verbal exchange, as if he had been expecting it. What is yet to be verified is how he organizes the messages he receives. It is nonetheless very interesting to observe the looks exchanged between father and daughter, even though the girl's smile seems inappropriate for the question she is asking.

Father: I don't see why I should feel death in a family where there's no death.

Nita (addressing the therapist): What is the phone number, can I call him?

Therapist: Just pick up the receiver and he will answer on the other side.

(Nita calls on the intercom.)

Consultant: Hello?

Nita: Well, here's the answer.

Consultant: Excuse me?

Nita: Here's the answer.

Consultant: I didn't understand the real answer.

Nita: Did you not hear him?

Consultant: No, because you were laughing while talking about death, I got confused, I got a little confused, could you check if dad experiences death, without laughing? Because if you laugh, I think dad doesn't get the message, you know that? Please try again.

(Nita goes back to her seat and changes her tone completely.)

Nita: Did you feel anything?

Father: What should I feel? I don't see any death in the family.

Nita: What were you thinking about?

Father: I was thinking about you.

Nita: What about me?

Father: How things have improved.

Nita: How things have improved?

Father: I was thinking that the treatment that you've been going through was not the right treatment for anorexia. You see, if you could have stayed in hospital for six months or a year, with their help, you might have improved. Not only that. In general, where they treat anorexia, treat it properly. This is the only hospital in Toronto where they treat anorexia, with regular treatment, a year-long program. You go in at six o'clock in the morning and come back at six in the evening for between six months and a year. And if you got better and could continue for a year, I think that you would be in better shape.

It is now clear that this man is completely unable to connect to his emotions as a father, and that is why he continues with the usual theme: they just need to intensify the treatment! What is striking, once the theme of death had been introduced, is the mother's face: she really seems to be feeling something very strong that she cannot express with words. In the meantime the sister is furious. There are many important defensive structures to be overcome in order to open the heart of this engineer, but the important thing is not to give up.

Consultant: Nita, can you try to help me, seriously?
Nita: How?
Consultant: Now, if you want to help me, can you look your father in the eyes and ask him this question: "Did you die first as a husband or as a father?" Try to do it in a way that lets him know that you really would like an answer from the heart, not from the head… and you know the difference between heart and head very well. Then wait in front of him for the answer. Good luck.

While the consultant speaks with Nita on the intercom, the father, as if trying to concentrate on something, takes his glasses out of his pocket and puts them on: his senses seem to be confused, as if this man needs to put himself in focus and feel through his eyes.

Nita (addressing the father): Earlier… umm… did you feel that you died first as a husband or as a father?
Father: What do you mean?
Nita: Did you die first as a husband or as a father?
Father: I never died! I never died!
Nita: I mean, the only way that you could feel a sense of loss is if there was a death?
Father: Yeah, that's the only way.
(…)
Consultant: Hello Nita, you did very well, do you think you touched his heart or not?
Nita: It's very hard to do.
Consultant: Is it very hard to touch his heart? Or is it very difficult for you?
Nita: For me I think.

This is when co-therapy begins. From now on, when the intercom buzzes, the girl will answer directly. Nita is no longer remote-controlled: she starts acting on her own and increasingly, during the session, she will introduce her own content.

Consultant: Can you try to ask mom? Can you ask her the same question? To see if mom might be more able to open her heart? And then try also to ask your own questions, you know your parents so well. Even before you were born… I think you are the only one who can check if there is real hope in your family. So maybe today something can begin… OK? Call me only if you feel that there is any hope in your family. There is real hope only if they can feel death… real death. Not only your dying day after day but also deeper losses… much deeper, from the present but also from before your illness, some previous death, of some very important person in this family or some kind of death in the marriage… some other death. Because right now you are the only death in the family, and I think this is too much for you. Good luck.

This is a long, very intense comment, in which the consultant repeats the same themes over and over, trying to give different meanings to the suffering and helplessness in the family, that are not exclusively connected to Nita's disease. The girl understands the consultant's desire to widen the investigation (maybe for the first time) to include the family history, normalizing her anorexic disorder and confronting her, at the same time, about her control over everyone and the tyrannical way she rules the house through her symptoms. The girl at first does not understand, then she clings to the intercom, as if fascinated by the hypnotic voice on the other side of the mirror. The consultant's intercom is exactly on the other side of the mirror: only twenty centimeters of wall separate them. There is a feeling of great understanding and intensity.

Nita (addressing the mother): Have you felt any sense of loss?
Mother: No.
Nita: Nothing? And do you feel that there needs to be a real death in the family, like dad?
Mother: No. I don't.
Nita: What then?
Mother: I don't feel anything… because I'm more positive than your dad, I think.
Nita: Are you talking about your hopes?
Mother: Yes.

Nita: About dying, are you talking about that?

Mother: Yes.

Nita: Forget about hope, it's not about hope... looking back at the past, do you feel like you've lost anything in the last four years? Some part of you, or...?

Mother: Yes, I feel something, but it's not hopeless.

(The intercom buzzes, and Nita answers directly.)

Consultant: Do you want to try one last time? Can you put mom close to dad, or dad close to mom and can you ask both of them to talk about the most important losses in their life, before you started dying, day after day, of anorexia. Can you ask them to talk about which was the most important death for them besides yours?

Nita: I can.

Consultant: And try to be convincing!

Nita: I will.

Consultant: Maybe you can take off your coat... that might help too.... And try to put them very close to each other, OK?

(Nita puts the intercom down and goes to the center of the room.)

Nita (addressing the mother): OK. Can you sit here?

(The mother sits on the chair where Nita had been sitting before, close to her husband.)

Nita: What was... what has been the most important death in your life before I became caught up, you know, in this anorexia?

Father: Who are you asking this question to, both of us?

Nita: I want you to talk about it, yes!

Father: Well, in my case, my parents.

Mother: What kind of death are we talking about?

Nita: That's up to you... what has been the most important death that you felt... before... before me?

Mother: I can't tell, because there have been so many ups and downs... so I don't know which one. *(Is the mother talking about the death of the marriage?)*

Nita (addressing the father): What were you saying?

Father: As I said, the death of my parents.

Having verified the existence of these other losses, the consultant begins to look for their meanings.

(The intercom buzzes and Nita answers.)

Consultant: Ask your dad what he lost with their death, not just the facts, because if we understand what it is that he lost with the death of his parents...

Nita: Ah, what he lost because of that?

Consultant: Yes, because his heart is still locked, and your anorexia has the key to his heart, you know that. So use the key with both of them...

Nita: What is it that you lost, due to the death of your parents? You lost your parents, but what did you lose, inside?

Father: Well, I lost that feeling of belonging, the relationship between father and son... His love and attention, the ties I had with dad... but time goes by.

Nita: You never saw them again after you left home, did you? You were so far from them.

Father: Yes but I still had those feelings, when they were alive.

Nita: You carried them around with you, and when they died, you didn't anymore? So you say you no longer feel close to your parents. Because they're dead, you don't feel close to them anymore?

Father: No. That's right.

Nita: So if I died, you'd feel the same way? That you don't have a connection with me anymore...

Father: I don't know, it's a different situation, again, you are my child, I don't know...

Nita (addressing her mother): And you?

Mother: No, I don't... I don't feel that way.

Nita: Your mother died recently!

Mother (very moved, starts to weep): OK, my mother died recently, but because I didn't see her die, I don't feel the disconnection.

When her grandmother died Nita was hospitalized because she was feeling suicidal, so her mother stayed in Toronto with her instead of returning to Bangladesh to see her dead mother. Both therapists learn about this loss only at this moment and are moved by it. Yet they have been treating this family for more than a year, and this seems unexplainable, but this is unfortunately what can happen when everyone focuses on the child's illness and other life events, even the gravest, are left in the background. The pain of this woman, who was not able to mourn the death of her mother because of her daughter's illness, can now be expressed in front of everyone and assumes a value and significance which reframes the priorities of the family's difficulties.

Nita: Is she still close to you?

Mother: Yes, of course she is.
Therapist: When did she die?
Mother: Almost two months ago.
Therapist (a bit puzzled, addressing the mother): I didn't know your mother had died. You didn't go home, to Bangladesh?
Mother: No. I wanted to, but... she was sick, so I didn't go.

(The intercom buzzes, and Nita answers.)
Consultant: Nita, I think that you have now used the right key, haven't you?
Nita: I don't understand.
Consultant: I don't know...I think that you have just started to use the key to unlock your parents' feelings... do you feel there is any hope now?
Nita: I think so.
Consultant: OK.

It seems incredible, but this girl is able to unlock emotions, in session, by using her relational skills and her sensitivity as an adolescent daughter. When Nita asks her father: "If I died, wouldn't I mean anything more to you?" she also introduces the idea of a future, the possibility of a different story, of a new way of dealing with attachments. Though with difficulty, the father manages to open up about his loss, while the mother has yet to decide which death she should talk about, given that the "death of the marriage" has also crept in. The daughter gives her permission to speak about her recent loss, which represents an emotional turning point for everybody in the session. Many things begin to shift through Nita's collaboration.

The consultant feels he has to make a choice, because he cannot keep playing the phantom who orchestrates the session from behind the mirror. The long silences, the themes of death, and the emotional participation of the family in the session need to be appraised within a context that leaves some space to begin the developmental process of this family, who migrated from Bangladesh to the Western world in search of a different life. Rather than the consultant-magician from Rome, what is needed now is more Bangladesh, to return to this Indian family a sense of competence and healthy involvement in their destinies, after delegating the responsibility of dealing with their lives to Canadian hospitals and therapists.

These are the thoughts of the consultant, who decides to use Nita's collaboration once again.

In search of Bangladesh

Consultant (on the intercom to Nita): Now, can you help me again? This is the most difficult part. I think this family needs a little more Bangladesh here. Do you understand what I mean? You have been the one who was trying to keep Bangladesh connected with Toronto, but you did that in a crazy way.

Nita: Crazy?

Consultant: Crazy, a little crazy... you know your symptoms are very strange...

Nita: I don't get it.

Consultant: Your way of "being crazy," to keep your parents connected with Bangladesh, was cute but useless, it doesn't go anywhere.

Nita: I don't understand...

Consultant: You tried your hardest to keep your parents connected to Bangladesh, you know this, but you did it in a strange way. Now, my question is this: is there anybody from Bangladesh in Toronto, someone older than you, who can help me to understand your parents better? Is there anybody in town who is close to them and knows them well?

Nita: It's difficult, close to both of them?

Consultant: Because I have a crazy idea, like yours. We meet after lunch again and this time I come in, but your parents have to bring in someone from Bangladesh who knows them well and is familiar with their life over there. You represent too much of a connection to Bangladesh for them, you know? You play too many roles, sometimes you talk like you are seventy-three-year-old, you know? Sometimes you talk like a grandparent, you act and feel like a grandparent. I think this is nice but totally wrong... so probably we need some adults from Bangladesh, people that your parents trust, maybe just one for each of them. Tell your parents what I said and if they feel that there is any hope in this therapy, tell them to come back at two-thirty with two people from Bangladesh.

Nita: The whole family?

Consultant: The whole family, of course. Plus two people.

Bear in mind that the above happens at 11:30 a.m., and we have to be very convincing to persuade an Indian family that lives in Toronto to come back at 2:30 p.m. bringing along someone from Bangladesh! Nonetheless, it is worth risking when we see an opportunity and feel that some important shift has taken place.

Consultant: At the same time, when you have lunch I would like you to
eat as an eighteen-year-old.
Nita: Not as a grandmother?
Consultant: Not as a grandmother. Grandparents have problems with
their teeth, they sometimes don't even eat because they don't need it. So
eat as an eighteen-year-old Bangladeshi-Canadian girl... and try to think
that your sister is really your sister, because I don't believe that you
think you have a sister in this room.
Nita: How do you think I treat her?
Consultant: You treat her as a little pet... or as if she was your child!
Nita(laughing): Yes it's true, I do that all the time!

Nita introduces the idea of an afternoon session with clarity and
determination to her parents. Together with the mother, who also seems
immediately determined, she convinces her father and her sister to come
back in the afternoon together with two family friends. While using the
telephone to invite the friends, speaking Bengali, the parents begin to
look more animated and with hugs, kisses, and vitality they prepare to
go to lunch. The father asks his daughter to call Doctor Andolfi on the
intercom to confirm the appointment at 2:30 p.m.

Bangladesh, live

The family comes back after lunch together with two friends, a
couple from Bangladesh, Nita's godparents. Andolfi welcomes the group
in a very different atmosphere from that of the morning. Now the emotional context is more cheerful and lively, less depressed and helpless
than that of the previous encounter. Nita hands over her role of "consultant to the consultant" to the two guests. The themes that arise are very
different: memories, Bengalese traditions, difficulties with integration in
North-America. They also speak about the two families' different cultures, of their differences and similarities: the arranged marriages, the
difference between the two men's ability to show their feelings, the differences between the two women in asking their children for help, the
ways in which family members express affection and the losses in each
family. Both girls participate in the entire session and help to re-write the
history and punctuation of significant events.
A "bigger dose of Bangladesh" not only frees Nita from her central role as designated patient, but also redresses the inner equilibrium of
the family. Up to this moment, the therapists—just like Nita—have been
standing in for Bangladesh, as if the history and the trans-cultural evolu-

tion of the family had no value or weight in the present, almost completely hidden by Nita's anorexia. The more Bangladesh takes its rightful space, the more the family regains energy, vitality, and control of their lives.

Follow-up

One year after the consultation, Andolfi travels back to Toronto, and a follow-up session is organized with the family, the family therapist, the individual therapist, and the consultant. The family willingly agrees to participate, more to satisfy the curiosity of the professionals and their need to verify the effects of the counseling than for other reasons.

Nita has finished high school, she has enrolled at university, and the anorexia has disappeared. The mother is satisfied with her job, outside the home. Both husband and wife agree that their marriage has improved. The father is still somewhat rigid, but is now less of an "admiral" and more of a person. The younger daughter has improved at school and is actively involved in sports.

The most impressive effect of the consultation was to put an end to therapy. This can be interpreted in different ways: the family might have learned many things about themselves during therapy so that the effect, in the long run, is that family members can now find new paths on their own, without external help. Another interpretation has to do with the way the consultant redefined the problem: stating that "the family needs to find more Bangladesh" was a catalyst that helped them detach and separate from the therapeutic system. Moreover, it contributed to open new possibilities for a greater involvement by the family with the community, renewing, at the same time, an interest in their family history: memories, relatives, friends, and losses. The situation ceased to be a psychiatric problem and became a developmental, cultural, and family crisis.

Three years later, Andolfi visits the George Hull Centre once again, and asks to speak with the family by phone. It seems that only two weeks have passed since the last conversation. Nita is engaged to a colleague from university, a Japanese man, and is still studying. The father's marked sense of humor is now more accessible to all the family. Lila, the sister, continues to do well even in high school. The mother is happy that Doctor Andolfi remembers them, and invites him to a traditional Bangladeshi dinner next time he returns to Toronto. For the consultant, the dinner invitation is tangible proof that the family has continued the process, and that change began when therapy ended. The family does not need the presence of a therapist to witness their transformation.

Practice illustration: Frank's anorexia and the ritual of divorce

Before concluding the subject of anorexia we think it might be interesting to briefly describe a peculiar encounter, which took place several years ago in Rome, between Andolfi and a Danish family. This intervention had been requested because of Frank's anorexia. He is a fifteen-year-old adolescent who has suffered from this illness for more than two years.

As with Nita, the hospital and numerous local services have intervened to help Frank. The family therapists treating the case, who know Andolfi personally, suggest a three-day consultation-marathon to take place in Rome with the family and involving the two family therapists that treat Frank in Copenhagen.

This proposal is received quite ambivalently, as the treating hospital is against this type of intervention, while the council and local services see it as valid, and so decide to support and fund it entirely.

This is an unusual opportunity for Andolfi, and he welcomes it.

The work follows some of the processes that have already been described in this book: the consultant develops a strong alliance with Frank from the beginning and, through the boy, he explores the developmental history of the family, looking for connections between the anorexic disorder and important family life events. Among these, there emerge some basic conflicts between the couple, which continued even during the mother's pregnancy. During the session, Frank reveals that the mother kept the pregnancy hidden from the husband for six months, and that she had told him several times, when he was a child, that "dad never wanted him." In fact, the couple finally separated when the boy was four. The mother states that she never wanted any other man at home, and perhaps she forgot that Frank became her stable "partner" from that moment. Even now the boy looks at his mother as if asking for permission to speak.

Not only does the woman not desire new relationships, but she also regularly controls those of the ex-husband, offering suggestions about which woman would suit him best. The ex-husband depends on her not only for relationship advice, but also for various business suggestions.

Therefore Frank grows up in a highly enmeshed context, where the inter-generational distortions are serious and formally negated. The older sister chooses to rebel and runs away from home, while Frank continues to be the adhesive in the original triangle. His symptoms are almost inevitable in such a distorted environment, and the encounters will help to highlight everyone's level of suffering supporting the family mask.

The aim of the Rome sessions is to create an experience that will break their Nordic respectability, where everything seems in order, to facilitate concrete changes.

After getting to know the parents' families of origin, working on the genograms and establishing that they are both interested in Frank's recovery, a therapeutic ritual is devised which allows the parents to celebrate their divorce again during the session, while Frank translates for Andolfi—because a real ritual must be spoken in one's mother-tongue! In a nutshell, they all commit to make radical changes so that a real individuation will become possible, maintaining only the bond of parental functions. To allow this to happen, the father will no longer use the mother as his advisor, while she pledges to facilitate Frank's progressive emancipation, and the father undertakes to perform paternal functions directly, without delegating everything to the mother.

This ritual is celebrated and a final contract is signed by both parents and by Frank, who also commits to encourage the couple's detachment by living the life of an adolescent who socializes outside the family, without the emotional blackmail hiding behind his regressive and childish behavior.

Moreover, Frank undertakes to work on building an affective relationship with his sister, described by everyone as indifferent to the family, but actually neglected and disregarded by the parents who are too busy with Frank's hospitalizations and with their need to fill too many voids through the boy's illness.

Maybe these encounters seem to be more focused on reaching an agreement between the ex-spouses, as happens during family mediation sessions, than on exploring the suffering, as in psychotherapy. Nonetheless, we must not forget that sessions taking place in a different country acquire an almost magical value, as they inherently imply change: the fact that two adults and a problematic boy are highly motivated and go to another country, together with their therapists, to think over their difficulties with the help of an external consultant, all of them speaking another language (English) is, of itself, extraordinary medicine. Also the fact that we "use anorexia without talking about it," considering Frank as a competent subject instead of a patient, modifies expectations, and the intervention on family distortions becomes the final objective, allowing Frank to enter adolescence with fewer fears and worries, both personal and relational.

Two years later Andolfi, while in Copenhagen for a family therapy seminar, meets the two therapists together with Frank and his father, in a kind of follow-up session. Frank's anorexic symptom have disappeared (anorexia is almost always curable if we intervene during adolescence by engaging the family in therapy), even if Frank seems to be a clumsy adolescent. What is more surprising is the change in the father's attitude towards his son. It is as if he has finally allowed himself (with a few years' delay) to rediscover his son, while the latter seems happy that his father really wants him now and spends much more time with him. They are both very happy to see Andolfi again and to report the changes that have taken place.

The mother's absence can be interpreted in two different ways: on the one hand, it can be interpreted as a form of altruism, allowing the father-son dyad to find its space without the intrusive influence of a third person, while on the other, it might be connected to the void she has to bear within herself, if Frank's umbilical cord really has been cut, and to the difficulty of accepting and showing her own loneliness.

OBESITY: A LARGELY NEGLECTED DISEASE

While anorexia nervosa and bulimia have been widely studied in their individual and relational dimensions within the realm of eating disorders, obesity has been treated more for its medical complications than for the individual, family and social components of a complex medical/psychological condition.

Obesity today is a real epidemic : there are over a billion overweight adults in the world, of which at least three hundred million are obese. The phenomenon is constantly increasing in developed as well as developing countries. The largest number of obese people can be found in Anglo-Saxon countries, where this phenomenon is mostly due to an unhealthy diet, but it is a fact that *trash food* travels quickly around the entire planet.

In spite of these dramatic figures, there are still strong prejudices and social stereotypes toward body sizes. It isn't difficult to understand that being overweight in a world which promotes fitness as a religious value can result in a big problem, especially during adolescence. Excess weight can be a serious obstacle in building social, affecttive, and professional relationships, not only because of the psychological fragility of an obese person, but also because society easily labels obese people as weak, lazy, lacking a strong will, insensitive, spoilt, and, therefore, responsible for their own condition. In reality excess weight, especially when it is considerable, is not only a problem of personal responsibility and tenaciousness as the diet industry would have us believe. Besides, recent studies have confirmed that diets, especially at a young age, can be a risk factor for obesity in adults (Ostuzzi, Luxardi, 2007).

The embarrassment of people when facing obesity has to do with blame-laden stereotypes and this is probably the reason why *political correctness* as a communication modality has been adopted in most developed societies: you cannot tell someone that they are fat or overweight, because this term is considered offensive, neither can you enter into its real causes. The issue has to be ignored, and perhaps the language of denial is not necessarily for the benefit of those who suffer from obesity: it might rather be a kind of defense for thin people, who, in denying the problem, don't have to deal with their own embarrassment. Moreover, protectiveness, as we frequently stated in previous chapters, is just a way of hiding, even if it is well-meaning, and can easily be misinterpreted as lack of interest.

Furthermore, Western culture promotes an ideal of extremely skinny men and women, by excluding from the fashion industry those who are not thin, by building small elevators, small armchairs in public places, and the same goes for airplane seats, and so on. Fat is not fashionable, and therefore we act as if it does not exist!

In this climate of complete disinterest in the deep individual reasons of a complex disease, the media bombards those who are overweight with the serious threats they will face if they don't do anything about their weight: diabetes, cardio-vascular diseases, pulmonary emphysemas, arthritis, cancer, and so on. Above all, this is done by strongly blaming obese people.

In recent decades, Western societies have given little attention to creating healthy living conditions, because of the emphasis on what we produce and own rather than on our psycho-physical equilibrium. Essentially, our lifestyle is not organized in a way that allows us to take care of ourselves and our health.

Children are the alarm bell for this rapidly expanding phenomenon: today, in Europe, one child in three is overweight and the reason for this is generally connected to lifestyle: they eat badly and too much and, most of all, they are not sufficiently physically active.

Experts in the field talk about *puer condominialis*, a neologism that indicates, in a frighteningly concrete way, the latest product of the consumerist society: a child who lives in the city spends little time outdoors, uses the elevator instead of the stairs and spends his days in front of the television or at the Play-station.

A bio-psychosocial model of intervention for obese adolescents

With the exponential growth of problems connected to obesity, medical/psychological modalities of interventions started to flourish; nonetheless, management of childhood and adolescent obesity is commonly based on low calories, low fat diets, on lifestyle interventions where physical activity and behavior modification are the main targets, as written by several authors (Dietz, Robinson, 2005; Edwards et al., 2004, Epstein, Valoski, Wing, McCurley, 1994) together with cognitive-behavior therapy (Braet, 1999). Anti-obesity drugs facilitate weight-loss and weight-maintenance according some relevant endocrinologists (Hainer, Toplak, Mitrakon, 2008).

Endocrinologists, pediatricians, dietologists, psychiatrists, and nurses are very involved in the evaluation and treatment of obese adolescents, according to a medical model, centered on hospitalization and appropriate nutrition. In this sense, the main treatment modalities are very similar to those used with anorectic/bulimic adolescents. The treatment is focused on the disease, but where is the person of the problematic adolescent with his/her needs and fears?

We return again to the question of what the role of the family is and what to do with peer pressure in dealing with obese adolescents.

Do we really care to know and explore the person and the symbolic implications as they involve the body as a mean of relating, expressing, and communicating?

Empty and full

The obese adolescent experiences great difficulty in tolerating frustrating situations and the anxiety caused by the perception of a void which needs to be filled. The frustration threshold is very low in obese teens, especially in social situations, in peer groups, and in work contexts. In this sense there are many similarities with the emotional fragility of anorexic girls who, however, cope better with their distress through intellectualization and rigorous behavior.

Stress acts directly on the metabolism, as it can induce to eat more. This is not always a pathological phenomenon, but can become one if any external agent breaches the defenses of the obese person, or reduces them and threatens his/her psycho-physical integrity. Moreover, it has been verified that while stress might not make people overeat in normal situations, it can have the opposite effect when they are on a diet.

The search for identity

Nutritional abuse in adolescence can also represent an extreme way of searching for one's identity. In fact, all pathological behavior in adolescents, whether they have psychological, psychosomatic or relational problems, can be seen as an attempt at finding their identity through a difficult obstacle course.

In follow-up sessions with various families long after the end of therapy, adolescents that had been brought to therapy for different issues, including severe eating disorders, after overcoming their difficulties recognized that suffering and bearing large weights on their shoulders, as well as making loved ones suffer, had allowed them to feel they had heroically reached a resolution. In short, they had gained a lot of self-esteem by overcoming a great obstacle in their lives. At the same time, family members remembered the suffering, but more so the strength they had acquired as a group through the painful process of change.

Excess weight is determined by the interaction of genetics, behavioral, psychological, and social factors: the body speaks louder than many words and signals deep suffering, sometimes denied by the obese adolescent and by family members and always comprises a strong relational component, as we will see in the following case illustration.

Family therapy as a model for treating childhood and adolescent obesity

Family therapy as a model for treating childhood and adolescence obesity has been introduces by many systemic-relational therapists. Minuchin et al. (1978) often spoke about *enmeshed families* to indicate family structures based on fusion and lack of clear intergenerational boundaries. Thus the body of the obese adolescent is used as a protection from relational contact and as a necessary safe distance: on one hand this is due to the fear of losing the other, and also to the fear of losing oneself in the other. Selvini Palazzoli (1977), Ugazio (Ugazio, Dixon, 2013), Aveny, Caputo, Cuzzolaro (1998), Ostuzzi, Luxardi (2007), and Andolfi et al. (2001) describe the need to better define a relational scheme for psychosomatic disorders, and Ardovini et al. (1998) outline the need of a new discipline called *obesiology* to integrate bio-psycho-social dimensions of this disturbance.

In Malmö, Sweden, Nowicka and Flodmark (2011) have developed and described their work in a Childhood Obesity Unit in a hospital setting. They present a treatment modality called SOFT (Standardized Obesity Family Therapy) based on systemic and solution-focused theories, combining Selvini's et al. main ideas (*Paradox and Counterparadox*, 1975) together with de Shazer principles (1985). They state that family interactions are an important source for implementing and maintaining lifestyle changes and in their approach they combine normative interaction and collaborative family support.

The framework of obesity in adolescence is always the family, together with the social environment

It is very difficult for us, as family therapists to isolate the personal fears and inner conflicts of an obese adolescent from family functioning and social dimension.

In our clinical work we have often considered obesity as a metaphor for relational "weights" in the family which, when inadequately shared on an inter-generational level, oppress the problematic adolescent. Lack of rules, inter-generational confusion about care-giving and parental responsibility, couple hostility together with strong affective triangulation of the children, inability to deal with chronic or psychiatric disorders in a child are some of the reasons leading to the onset and establishment of obesity in young people, sometimes associated with other types of dependence such as drug or alcohol addictions.

We often witness a progressive isolation of the obese person from his/her social contexts, which can also be related to peer discrimination. Obviously the fat that envelops his body only appears to defend him, while, inside, there is great emotional fragility and a strong preoccupation with feeling really accepted and appreciated, often hidden by gregarious and engaging behavior. Not infrequently very friendly, obese young people, once they have gone back to an appropriate weight, feel as if they are lacking an identity, feel more socially inadequate, and say they have lost their congeniality.

All this makes us believe that, as in the extreme opposite which is anorexia, the real problem is not the body weight itself, but rather the distorted body image and, more importantly, their having been at the center of severe affective distortions in their families for a long time.

Practice illustration: Luisa and the redistribution of weight in the family

Luisa is twenty years old, and comes to therapy with her parents and her younger brother Emilio, who is fifteen years old. The mother calls because of some depressive symptoms in the girl and her bulimic behavior: Luisa has gained weight during the last four years and has exceeded 100 kilos. She is also worried that Luisa is unable to find a stable job, because of her relational difficulties outside the family.

At the time of the first appointment we were given very little information, as though the woman didn't want to let us know too much about her family over the phone.

During the first session we learn that Luisa is an adopted child. She was brought home when she was a few months old, after seven years of marriage and three failed pregnancies, which resulted in abortions. Five years after Luisa's arrival, Emilio, a biological child, was born much to everyone's surprise and joy.

At the moment, Luisa weighs over 100 kilos and suffers from deep insecurity, which seems to mirror that of her parents, who had started couple therapy some years earlier to deal with some misunderstandings and strong depression on both sides.

Mother, father, and daughter participate in the first session. The brother is not present and, on this absence, the therapist begins to build an alliance with the patient: he asks her the reason why Emilio is not present and what leads her to bring her family to therapy. As always, he places the patient in the middle, recognizing her competence in the family history. The therapist does not hesitate to talk about the girl's obesity from the first moment.

From visible fat to unpredictable news

Therapist: I'd like to know something: did you already feel you had a different body from the time you were small?
Luisa: Yes, I've been on a diet since I was eight!
Therapist: How much did you weigh when you were inside the belly? Do you know?

Luisa: What do you mean, inside the belly?

Therapist: Were you big?

Luisa: Yes, I was big.

Therapist: Even inside your mom's belly?

Luisa: Ah! Inside the belly, I don't know, anyway I've always been big. Even in baby photos I was nice and chubby. They always told me that when they put diapers on me they had to buy those with ribbons, as the ones with the tape wouldn't fit.

Therapist: How much did you weigh when you were born?

Luisa: Three kilos point one.

Mother: So they told us, around three kilos.

Therapist: Three kilos is normal, neither under nor overweight.

Luisa: I remember the photos of when I was a baby, I didn't fit into the high-chair.

Therapist: Did your mom have milk?

Luisa: No, mom didn't breastfeed me, because *I was adopted*!

Therapist: Ah! I didn't know that!

In the face of this very important piece of information, which the therapist could not predict, the question is how to keep working without spoiling the pleasant atmosphere, with this girl who goes back to childhood and narrates her story within what she feels is her family. This sudden change of scenario could have blocked the therapist, making him go in other directions.

Therapist: When?

Luisa: When I was three months old.

Mother: Four, to be precise.

Luisa: What I remember, more or less, is after my brother's birth... and something before that.

Therapist: Help me understand something before we get to the adoption. Before you adopt a child you go through different phases, do you know anything about this?

Luisa: Yes, I know that my mother couldn't have any children, that she had three abortions, so they (*the parents*) wanted...

Therapist: Do you know what the problem was?

Luisa: Why she had the abortions?

Therapist: Yes.

Luisa: No.

Therapist: Did you ever ask her?

Luisa: Maybe she told me, but she only told me that she aborted after she had been pregnant for three or four months.

Father: We don't know either.

Luisa: At that time you weren't told much.

Mother: The doctors did some tests, but couldn't find the cause...

Therapist: So they married?

Luisa: They married and seven years later they adopted me.

Therapist: So, these abortions happened in the seven years after they got married?

Luisa: These three abortions.

Therapist: And what do you think happened at home before you arrived?

Luisa: I think it must have been very unpleasant, well, two people get married and want to be together and build a family... An abortion... well, it happens…

Therapist: Two, maybe. Three is bad luck?

Luisa: Especially for mom, it can't have been a very positive, pleasant thing!

Therapist: So you think mom was very upset by these events?

Luisa: Yes.

Therapist: So the depression started from that?

Luisa: Yes, I think so, but I also think that in the end she was happy that she could have a baby anyway.

Therapist: Of course. Do you think that they ever thought about separating during those years?

Luisa: No.

Therapist: You don't know or you're sure they didn't?

Luisa: No, they never told me whether they thought about separating, but I think not.

Therapist: You know, sometimes even parents tell lies... You know?

Luisa: Yes. We never spoke about this, but I think not.

Therapist: You think not. Do you want to ask them, just to...

Luisa: Well! I think these negative things can also create a connection between people.

Clearly, if we manage not to get caught in own prejudice, we can keep working with calm and the necessary curiosity. The therapist is not diverted by the fact that no one had informed him about the adoption: he accepts the facts, collects information, but does not deviate from his path.

Asking the girl what she thinks about a hypothetical separation between her parents is an appropriate question since she had stated that her parents had gone to couple therapy for a few years. It is extremely important to listen to the voice of children, whether small or grown-up, and to what they have to say on any developmental theme. Separation is a quite-familiar but not necessary family event, and, even when it does not happen, a child might have his own ideas about it.

The therapist entered into the theme of adoption and into the parents' losses with authentic naivety, without previous information and, most of all, without taking anything for granted. As we learnt from Whitaker, it is very useful to ask questions during the first encounter in a naive way, because when you know little you can give yourself greater freedom to explore, without thinking twice about what is a suitable question. In subsequent encounters this freedom decreases, because you might substitute the naivety with some sort of *double thinking* ("Should I ask this or that?...") and the family members can answer this in a similarly ambiguous manner.

The first encounter is like starting a puzzle: first you need to find the pieces that give a relational meaning to Luisa's symptoms. In theory, we know that all that pertains to a family member is also part of the relational life of the others, however, we must try to find the meaning of the symptoms in that specific situation. It is field research: the more the therapist widens his perspective, the more the search is enriched by further elements.

The therapist asked the girl information about her weight. He actually started from there; nevertheless, he did not dwell on it for long; he will return to it later, when the puzzle is more complete and further pieces will help him understand better. These telltale pieces are: the relational life of the parents before the arrival of the daughter, the three abortions, and finally the principal aspects of the dynamics in the couple relationship. This girl is very extroverted and available: she willingly tells the story of the two families of origin, demonstrating her competence, sensitivity and capacity for reflection.

It is not the first time in our experience with girls with eating disorders, that we discover their great ability as privileged witnesses to the developmental history of their parents, as though playing the role of "competent grandmothers of the family."

Who owns the fat?

Therapist: Have you ever thought that you might be able to divide your weight into sections and redistribute it? Could you find a "fat weight" that belongs to you and one that belongs to the others?
Luisa: I think so.

Therapist: According to you, how many kilos are yours and how many belong to the others?

Luisa: Let's work it out, now I weigh 102 kilos and I believe that 50 kilos are mine, for sure, then I'd say that the rest belongs to the family...

Therapist: That would mean the grandparents too?

Luisa: Both the relatives on one side and on the other, all the relatives.

Therapist: How many kilos do we give them altogether?

Luisa: I'd give 5 kilos each, and that makes 10 for both families.

Therapist: 10.

Luisa: This way we have 60!

Therapist: We have 60.

Luisa: Then I'd give 10 kilos each to the two of them (meaning the parents) and we arrive at 60... 80!

Therapist: 80.

Luisa: Then 2 kilos to my brother, earlier I would have given more kilos to my brother, now I don't have any kind of problem with him anymore, at least apparently... 2 or 3 kilos, 5 maximum, not that many, a lot less than to my relatives, but I'd give more to the relatives in Rome than to those in Messina.

Therapist: Let's do something, go to the blackboard, divide the space into two parts, on one side write "maternal family," on the other "paternal family" — this way it's more precise.

Luisa: Yes, otherwise I will forget.

(Luisa goes to the blackboard, thinks for a while and starts to write, while Andolfi and the family sit in front of the blackboard in a semicircle, as if they were attending a math class.)

Luisa: 50 kilos are for me, that's clear, isn't it?

Therapist: Of course!

Luisa: 2 kilos for my brother. 10 kilos for the relatives in Messina. 18 kilos for dad's relatives. 6 kilos for dad. 11 kilos for mom!

Therapist: Now it seems that the sums are almost right. Who knows, maybe one day you'll become a top model. All you need to do is give back the weight to the rightful owners! This could be the goal of this therapy... And then the depression will also disappear, you'll see.

After using a good deal of humor and translating the affective dysfunction of the family into concrete metaphors, we can begin to sketch a therapeutic path designed to retrace the developmental history of the parents, to allow us to return to the present with new perspectives for change, ...

Therapist: When dad was your age, did he feel the weight of his parents?
Luisa: I think he felt it a lot!

... to proceed with our search for the histories of loss and tri-generational voids, present in both families, and to connect the past to the present through the value and meaning of fat.

Role reversal: who mothered whom?

Therapist: Has mom ever worried about the adult way in which you think?
Luisa: She's worse than I am, she thinks all the time too, she tries to examine things in depth.
Therapist: Has she always been this serious?
Luisa: Yes.
Therapist: How much did mom weigh when she was 20 years old?
Luisa: I don't know how much, 80, 85 kilos, she was chubby like me, she also went on a lot of diets.
Therapist: Did she tell you?
Luisa: Yes.
Therapist: Even now?
Luisa: Now she's careful, because we went on a diet together... With acupuncture I fasted for a month; she fasted for three weeks. I kept fasting and had a nervous breakdown, because I didn't recognize my body anymore... after a month I was completely different from before, and I felt as if the wind could make me fly and blow me away, I felt completely defenseless compared to before.
Therapist: So now you're telling me something else... that this fat is like a blanket, like a sweater, a Norwegian sweater!
Luisa: Yes, it is. I went on diets very often and I put on weight again because I was afraid of being so exposed, apart from the fact that when I'm thinner I'm a lot cuter and, maybe, this is why I'm a lot more visible. When I'm fat, instead, I'm also visible, but when someone sees me he says "Look at that fatty!," and then he turns around and looks away.

This girl's awareness is incredible. She knows her fat has a protective function and offers the therapist the opportunity of getting inside the family, because this doesn't make her afraid, as this is the place where she feels safest.

Therapist: Have you been more your mother's or your father's mom, when they felt lonely?

Luisa: Dad rarely asks for help.

Therapist: Well! We can ask for help even in less obvious ways...

Luisa: Yes, yes, you can see it more when my mom needs it.

Therapist: How was your maternal grandmother? Was she more of a mother or a daughter with her children?

Luisa: The problem with my grandmother is that she had completely different relationships with everyone.

Therapist: With her *(pointing at the mother)*?

Luisa: Maybe she acted more as a daughter with her, I don't know, I don't remember very well.

Therapist: Ask her *(the mother)*.

Luisa: What should I ask her?

Therapist: With your own words.

Luisa: What kind of relationship did you have with your mom? Did you feel you were a daughter or a mother with her?

Mother: No, I neither felt I was a daughter nor a mother... I felt as a daughter to her until I was ten years old, maybe.

Therapist: Do you understand? So mom was an orphan at ten, can you imagine? Did you know?

Luisa: Maybe this is why she has always wanted to solve other people's problems: because she was never able to solve her own!

Therapist: This is strange, because this happens even with biological children: you expect from a child what you haven't been given by a parent, did you know?

Luisa: Yes, I know this.

Therapist: Of course, I can't imagine the work you've done... when do you retire?

Luisa: In August.

Therapist: Meaning what?

Luisa: Because I work in a supermarket, so in effect they give us a kind of pension... and then they can take us back.

Therapist: But I'm talking about another kind of retirement... do you know what I mean?

Luisa: Because I won't be a mother anymore?

Therapist: Good! You don't trust that your mother will be able to do it by herself...

Luisa: But I think I've already retired.

Therapist: Do you know when you'll retire? When you start losing those extra 30-40 kilos and you give them back...

Luisa: To the families?

Therapist: To the families, to the grandparents, to mom, to whom you gave 11 kilos... mom weighs more than dad, almost twice as much.

Therapist (addressing the mother): Did you know, mom?

Mother: Yes, yes.

Therapist: But are you sure that now, through your fat, they won't continue with couple therapy? Whom should I work with?

Luisa: I hope it'll be useful for them too!

Therapist: But this is the problem! Because you seem to me like a charitable lady, like someone from the Salvation Army... what do you call them...

Luisa: Why? If we solve everyone's problems it's better for all, isn't it?

Therapist: Yes, just so long as it doesn't cause confusion!

Luisa: Excuse me, why? If we solve my problem we also solve their problems! If my problem has nothing to do with their problem, if we manage to demonstrate this... that there are no problems between us! Because they say they have problems with me and that's not true, because those are normal problems, everyone has them! We can obviously solve them, it's not as if they are insurmountable...

Therapist: Do you know what surprises me?

Luisa: What?

Therapist: That you are too sure with them and too frightened outside!

Luisa: Hmm...

Therapist: Do you understand?

Luisa: I feel sure with the people who know me!

Therapist: I understand, but the world isn't made only of people who know you!

Luisa: In fact, when I'm with people who don't know me, whom I don't know, I feel insecure...

As the session proceeds, it is interesting to note that the importance of a tri-generational approach to Luisa's problems becomes more and more evident. At the same time we realize the importance of working on the outside, on the peer group and on the work context, which seem threatening to a girl who is as much an expert within the family as she is insecure outside of it. The fat was always a useful cover, but Luisa will have to confront progressively all her insecurities and her poor self-esteem in order to individuate.

The therapy will include both territories, family and society, and Luisa will lose her weight and reach a stable 60 kilos, returning the excess weight to both the maternal and the paternal sides, and, most of all, she will manage to forge a more solid identity.

A year after the end of therapy, Luisa calls Andolfi and expresses the desire to watch the videotape of the "session on the weight that needed to be redistributed," saying that she could not believe she "had weighed more than 100 kilos." To the session are also invited the principal protagonists of this therapy: the mother, the father, and Emilio. They will be able, after the playback, to see how they were before and to remember the difficulties they overcame together, further reinforcing the changes they achieved.

Chapter 4
Depression and attempted suicide in adolescence

DEPRESSION OR EXISTENTIAL SADNESS?

It is a fact that depression has greatly increased during the past decades, both as a psychiatric syndrome in psychopathologies and within the collective imagination, earning the definition of illness of the century. The term depression is so abused and over-used that any kind of psychological issue connected to unfavorable life events risks being labeled as *depression*. We could all define ourselves as depressed, in one way or another. Sadness has disappeared and even the word itself does not seem to exist any longer, deleted from use, along with others such as apprehension and desperation. All kinds of psychological disorders are easily classified as depression, and the term depression is necessarily coupled with antidepressant.

This confusion is anything but accidental, and is sustained by the proliferation of antidepressants available on the market, which are increasingly sophisticated and in need of more patients. Prozac and other serotonin inhibitors have been presented to the general public as miraculous drugs. In fact, the last ten years of the past millennium have been defined as the "brain decade," with enormous American funding dedicated to research in genetics and neuropsychology.

Blazer (2005) states, in a very critical voice, that "contemporary psychiatry has found the brain but lost the person, together with his family and his community," and the consequence of this marketing cam-paign was the transformation of normal sadness into psychopathology. Everything is anxiety and depression, everything is anti-depressive and anxiolytic. Feelings have been impoverished and now, if we want to be sure not to be given a prescription for psychopharmacologic drugs, we must not feel anything, we must be emotionally empty. Thus, we witness the spread of social alarm: even though its cause is not yet clear, depression is commonly considered an obscure, contagious disease which should be avoided (according to recent research at the National Monitoring Unit of Women's Health, women fear it even more than breast cancer); a disease that, once contracted, provokes feelings of shame and at times even deep guilt. Depression is dreaded to the point that the modern individual is willing to do anything to avoid it, even though he does not really understand it; should he ever suffer from it, he will be able to buy a "pill to feel better."

Feeling sad or dejected is not sufficient to declare that you suffer from depression. What is wrong with feeling down when life is hurting you? Sadness is an intrinsic feeling in human nature, it can be found in animals too, and has nothing to do with the pathological phenomenon of depression. It is an important psycho-physiological resource in life, as its weight can counterbalance euphoria which can, at times, put us at risk (Horowitz, Wakefield, 2007). Sadness is a noble and positive feeling: it allows us to reflect on our limits, our mistakes, and to correct them, it gives us the time needed to stay with pain until we can overcome it, it helps us to learn and re-frame grandiosity and egotism, which separate us from our own interior world and from real and authentic relationships with others. The fact that sadness allows us to get in touch with our real essence explains, perhaps, why periods of deep sadness also produce many important creative expressions, artistic or musical.

Depression is a completely different thing. It is a disturbed affective condition which can manifest in several forms, greatly differing, one from the other, in severity and persistence: it can be represented by a symptom, an altered emotional state, a significant illness, as a response to trauma, or as an actual endogenous disorder, such as *major depression* or as *manic-depressive syndrome.*

The most common and widespread type of depression is *reactive depression*. It can appear at any time in our existence, to fill the void caused by a loss, by a failure or by a severe wound brought about by life events. This type of depression can be ascribed to a specific external factor, which can be defined as a traumatic event: for instance the death of a loved one, the end of a romantic relationship or adverse circumstances producing a deeply negative change in the life of a person.

However, if it is true that feeling sad as a consequence of negative events is normal and sometimes useful, what distinguishes common sadness from reactive depression?

Psychiatry indicates three different ways in which a person can emotionally react to an adverse and painful event: with a normal affective reaction, with a disproportionate one, or by falling into a depressive state.

The first case includes the common transitory feelings of frustration or sadness we were referring to earlier. It is a temporary sadness, appropriate in relation to its trigger, and does not particularly affect the somatic field, professional, or scholastic performance, or family relationships and friendships.

The disproportionate affective reaction includes exaggerated, intense and persistent emotional responses, which interfere with the subject's capacity to control the stress from which they originate. It is, in any case, a transitory reaction from which the subject recovers in a relatively short period.

While the depressive state, in all its forms, is a truly psycho-pathological condition, in which one loses the love for life, the ability to act and the hope of getting well. It is heralded by a set of symptoms which tend to emerge at the same time and cannot be underestimated.

Reactive depression is the type of depression which best responds to psychotherapy, because the latter considers and includes the contextual elements of the individual's malaise; he can therefore be helped to work through possible losses or ongoing conflicts which triggered the depression. The relational nature of this disorder is the reason why we favor family therapy as a treatment.

There are also those forms of depression which the DSM-IV calls endogenous depressive syndromes: *major depression*, *bipolar disorder*, and *manic-depressive psychosis*. These are pathologies in which the typical symptoms of depression are organized within well-structured clinical frameworks, which are often severe and prone to chronicity. The picture becomes gloomier and includes the complete loss of one's love of life, mood disorders, often accompanied by a severe debasement of the sense of one's value as a person, limitless anguish, patently exaggerated self-accusations, the loss of decision-making abilities, and the alternation of depression and euphoria.

All of these forms involve severe relational difficulties within the family and often in the working environment and in friendships. They are particularly debilitating conditions, comparable to organic diseases and characterized by strong biological components and a considerable familial incidence. They are endogenous syndromes which require prompt and prolonged interventions, both on the psychotherapeutic and pharmaceutical level, as well as the rehabilitation of social competences.

Although there have been great breakthroughs in the research on the origins of depression, the majority of its causal mechanisms is still unknown. Depression is doubtlessly the result of a continuous and inter-active dialogue between biological, personal, psychological and environ-mental factors. Each of its presenting forms has its own clinical physiognomy, its own evolution and therefore needs a specific psycho-therapeutic and pharmacological strategy. In this book, we will not deal with these types of pathology. Instead, we will discuss reactive depres-sive states arising during adolescence.

THE CHARACTERISTICS OF DEPRESSION IN ADOLESCENCE

Adolescence is a phase of the life cycle in which every individual, at different times and in different ways, goes through periods of sadness, boredom, shyness, fear, and anguish. Apart from being the time of first loves, friendships, and ideals, adolescence is also often associated to recurrent depressive states. In daily life, an adolescent can spend long hours doing nothing, followed by sudden moments of passion and interest for something that strongly inspires him, though maintaining a touch of boredom or profound apathy difficult to remove.

The mood swings which characterize adolescence are quite frequent, and there are many adolescents who display steady depressive traits, connected to the physical and psychological metamorphosis we spoke of in the first chapter of this book. But then, the developmental task of adolescence is a painful one: entering adulthood progressively implies a strong sense of losing and surrendering childhood—that magical developmental phase when we grow under the protection of parents—and the realization that, from now on, we have to rely on ourselves.

If this depressive state seems to be a physiological passage in the growth process of the adolescent, it is also unfortunately true that more recent epidemiological studies show that, during adolescence, these forms of depression are increasingly structured, often accompanied by suicide attempts.

Young people are also victims of pathological depressive states which can manifest in various forms. Sadness, melancholy and nervous-ness are common symptoms. The adolescent might lose interest in his favorite activities and progressively withdraw into his own small private space. Low self-esteem is common, as are negative thoughts about him-self or his future. He can feel confused, indecisive, lacking energy to fulfill his daily duties, and his work and academic performance can sud-denly deteriorate. There can be an increase in phobias: fears associated to specific situations such as going to school or work. As depression becomes more and more acute, due to feelings of low self-esteem and desperation, self-destructive thoughts such as self-harm and suicide arise.

As in adulthood, in adolescence the symptoms of the illness can be hidden or disguised by other conditions that do not appear to have anything to do with feeling down. Drug and alcohol abuse often accompany juvenile depression and worsen its outcome. There can be concentration problems, as well as unrest or hyperactivity, together with other disorders such as anorexia, bulimia, insomnia, and anxiety. Depressed adolescents can manifest antisocial behavior, such as hostility, aggressiveness, and reckless and defiant behavior towards rules and authority. All this can make depression more difficult to recognize for parents, teachers and, sometimes, professionals.

Before beginning clinical interventions, it is important to discriminate accurately between the depression which is a normal developmental phenomenon of adolescence and a real depressive disorder. This is not always an easy distinction to make, especially in a period as malleable as adolescence. In any case, the outcome of a depressive episode during adolescence is generally less severe and more predictable than depression during adulthood because, at any moment, there could be a developmental push towards other goals and other existential scenarios favoring the growth of psychic energies and new and unforeseen resources.

A NEW FORM OF DEPRESSION: THE PATHOLOGY OF ACTION

If we look into the literature and on the Internet for information about the two words depression and adolescence, we find various works by scholars and/or research centers in different fields of study. They are mainly doctors, psychiatrists, psychologists, neurobiologists, and high school teachers. The Association for Research on Depression in Turin refers those who wish to get information on the theme of juvenile depression to specific websites dedicated to depression-anxiety or to academic publications concerning "panic attacks and youth disorders" and so on. But, we could ask ourselves, how are panic attacks connected to depression? Isn't depression a disorder manifesting in mood swings, sadness, and wanting to die? What kind of depression are we talking about?

Alain Ehrenberg, a French sociologist, in his beautiful book of a few years ago (Ehrenberg 2000), considers the depressive condition common nowadays as a *pathology of action*. That means that in our globalized, consumerist, and frenetic society where time is money and the value of performance is paramount, depression represents the tomb, the failure to reach our goals. When do we become depressed? When, for some strange and unfathomable reason, we feel blocked and cannot realize our objectives, our plans, and the goals we set for ourselves.

According to Ehrenberg, the symptomatology of depression, in our time, has progressively moved from *sadness* to *inhibition*, to a loss of initiative in the social context where "reaching goals" is the only decisive criterion through which we judge the value of a person. The nucleus of depression has shifted from guilt and moral suffering to inadequacy and lack of satisfaction (*ibidem*). Even treatment has been gradually adjusted to the dominant cultural standards, both in the case of clinical treatment and self-help: it needs to be effective and quick. We have become reliant on the use of psycho-pharmacological drugs, as well performance-enhancing drugs, such as cocaine or dance drugs. In the United States the prescription of antidepressants to children and adolescents has increased by over 60% in the past decade, a tendency also evident in Europe. These drugs are generally used to treat major depression in adults, but their effectiveness and safety in children and adolescents has yet to be adequately ascertained. In Italy, an evaluation by the National Project ARNO (Pharmacological Prescription Monitoring Unit) shows that 22,000 minors were treated with SSRI antidepressants in 2002. These drugs are more frequently used by girls between 14 and 17 years of age (the male/female rate is 8.4/4.8). However, depression is not just a female problem. The information produced by the Third Report on Childhood Conditions, prepared by Eurispes and Telefono Azzurro, indicates that, in 2002, 7% of the Italian population between the ages of 6 and 19 suffered from depressive issues (this reached 8% in the United States): 5.3% of young people between 11 and 14 years of age and 13.8% of those between 15 and 19 years suffered from depression.

In the past few years, in our clinical work, we have witnessed a constant increase in Panic Attacks in adolescents and young adults. What is a panic attack if not the apotheosis of inhibition and block? In line with what Ehrenberg states, could we also define panic attack as a cultural syndrome? On the other hand, the world in which we live is becoming more and more complex and many young people do not feel adequately prepared to take on daily challenges, principally their relationships with peers and with the opposite sex, experienced in terms of performance and, therefore, as steps towards success.

But then, why do some adolescents become depressed, while others seem to deal with the transition towards adulthood effortlessly?

Evidently, the culture of belonging, per se, is not enough to cause pathologies in people. If anything, cultural models may become a rationalization of the pathological expression of the human mind that conforms to the dominant culture, and may reveal, in a recognizable form, one's most hidden and paradoxical aspects.

DEPRESSION, THE ADOLESCENT AND HIS FAMILY

If, as stated by Bowlby (1980), the most likely causes of the onset of a pathological depressive state during adolescence are experiences of loss which cannot be accepted and are therefore denied, then the litmus test of a young person's capacity to face the difficulties of adult life seems to be determined by his level of tolerance to frustration and loss of security. Understanding the way in which an adolescent reacts to negative events can help parents to evaluate those reactions correctly, which can otherwise be under or overestimated in regard to the risk of depression. Let's remember that the adolescent not only does not voice his distress: often, as happens with children, he can give somatic expression to his issues or, with the ambivalence typical of this time of life, he can hide them behind behavior that is contradictory or diametrically opposed to his real feelings.

We have often stated that it is extremely important to distinguish between transitory depression, connected to processes of growth, and more severe and potentially riskier situations. This is not always easy for today's parents, who live in "child-centric families" and are more inclined to favor dependence and protectiveness than to listen to the voice of the adolescent or his despairing cry.

What is harder to admit is that, sometimes, we need to give children permission to be unhappy (Zattoni, 2009). It is not the duty of parents to make their children happy, even though, as mentioned in the first chapter, at times their worthiness as parents is measured by how well they fulfill this expectation. The child has to be the creator of his own happiness, joy, and success, as he can only achieve them if he is able to suffer and conquer his autonomy. If we tell an adolescent or child "I'm only happy if you are," we put an excessive and unfair weight upon his shoulders, a responsibility he should not carry, and deny him the opportunity of working through his pain autonomously. The adolescent, as we have seen, always has some pain to work through. Moreover, the parent is not setting a good example by clinging to his child's future happiness in order to avoid looking at his own developmental gaps.

Parents and children often risk becoming accomplices by denying the sadness of a child, simply because the parents are the ones who cannot tolerate it. They get stuck in enmeshment and dysfunctional relational dynamics which are difficult to leave behind. The only outcome will be that the adolescents will feel deeply useless and lonely, since they are not being recognized for what they have become, but are still considered and treated by their parents as if they were small children, born only to receive and think about themselves as recipients, without needing to give anything back (*ibidem*).

It seems that families have the very important function of accepting the suffering and frustration that the adolescent has to tolerate. Moreover, there are many cases in which the family itself generates a fear of loss, whether the latter is real or fantasized.

The clinical experience gained through many years spent in contact with distressed adolescents and their families clearly shows that different reactive forms of depression can arise when one or more of the following conditions are present in the life of the adolescent and his family: loss of a significant family member, divorce or severe couple conflict, often aggravated by inter-generational components, academic failure and strong loss of status in the peer system, or abuse or physical and psychological deprivation, often linked to social marginalization.

THE LOSS OF A FAMILY MEMBER DURING ADOLESCENCE

Adolescents frequently come in contact with death through the loss of a grandparent. Several authors, especially Vegetti Finzi (2008), have described the value and centrality of grandparents in today's families. The latter often have crucial functions: economic support of young couples, organizational support that makes up for institutional absence, and most of all—when we think of adolescents and modern broken families—they are fundamental for emotional development, guarantors of continuity and security, and the historical memory of the family. Having said this, we can readily understand the sense of loss felt by adolescents when a particularly significant grandparent is ill or dies. These are wounds that cannot be easily healed, but are also direct ways of experiencing the transience of the human condition. Frequently grandparents leave some sort of affective legacy for future generations, and this is sometimes passed on to the grandchildren rather than the children, especially in cases where the adults were not able to individuate and reach the "I" position described by Bowen. But if the adolescent cannot make this generational transition, the loss of security and guidance connected to the death of a grandparent, together with that typical of adolescence, might lead him into a depressive state. The outcomes are strongly influenced by his level of individual fragility and to the family's coping system, that is to say: to the capacity of the family group to act as a team to overcome negative life events.

The premature and traumatic loss of a parent or sibling is much more dramatic. We have witnessed many clinical cases where the request for therapy is motivated by a more or less hidden depressive disorder in the adolescent. On reconstructing the history of the family we often find a pre-existing dramatic event connected to the death of a parent or a sibling. This event often freezes the developmental process of the family and destroys its emotional balance. Bowen describes this process very well, and calls it an *emotional shock wave* (Bowen, 1978), a dense network of subterranean after-shocks which can show up anywhere within the family system and can last for months or years following an important loss.

In the previous chapters we gave clinical examples of what happens when a sibling dies prematurely. The case of Ciro, a young adolescent we described when speaking of family myths, helps us understand the weight carried by the choice of a name, and its meaning, in the face of traumatic life events. In this case the name was taken from the older brother, who drowned when he was only eight years old, and given to Ciro, who had been suffering from reactive depression for several years, and who we met, in therapy, together with his family. Another important fact is that both brothers had inherited this name from a heroic grandfather who sacrificed his life for the whole community! Repeated names, but especially the deep relational meanings and expectations that underlie them, become invisible networks of underground emotional shock waves going from one generation to the next, and give the parents the illusion that they can fill the void left by the loss of a child with the arrival of a new one. If the latter has such a programmed beginning, the second child is at risk of carrying this unbearable weight for many years, if not for his entire life, thus entering into a depressive spiral.

Andrea's situation, described in the second chapter, is very similar, even though his symptoms are very different from Ciro's obviously depressive state. Andrea is a second child, and never got to know his little brother, who was born two years before him and died a few days after birth. This event will nonetheless condition his life from the start and for many years. Andrea is the handsome, healthy, and special son, he is the miracle son, in contrast to the first child, who was insecure, not good-looking, and undervalued by both parents. Andrea fills the home with his smile and his vitality, but the dead baby has "never been buried": at the start of the therapy, when Andrea is eighteen years old, we learn that the mother goes regularly to the cemetery to grieve this loss.

Andrea, who has been a good and handsome child during infancy, becomes a monster in adolescence, he gains weight until he looks like a giant, becomes violent, and enacts this aggression, especially at home, towards his mother and older brother. Ciro expresses his unrest through complete denial and infinite sadness, while Andrea, on the contrary, denies his sadness and his depression and enacts his suffering in an enraged and aggressive way, impersonating a monster, after wearing the mask of "miracle child" for too many years.

With the help of the family and through therapy, both need to find — not without effort and suffering — their own true identity, finally freeing themselves from roles and functions inadequate to their growth. This also requires the adults to become able to confront their own unresolved issues and work through their losses.

The premature loss of a parent can be a devastating experience for an adolescent and undermines his sense of security and faith in life and in his own family. Often, the young person's pain is not sufficiently understood and accepted by the surviving parent and by the family at large, both because of how this is expressed, and because the adult is so caught up his own pain that he does not know how to approach and understand the deep depression that motivates the behavior of a child who has suffered such a loss.

The adolescent rarely expresses his pain in an explicit and direct way, and he communicates his suffering to his peer group rather than at home, due to the feelings of reserve or detachment which young people often manifest within the family. Reactive depression in adolescence often shows itself in an indirect way, such as through behavior (rejection, rage, verbal or physical aggression), through the body, with the appearance of various psychosomatic disorders (such as eating disorders, dermatological issues, insomnia), and through academic failure or blockage. This is why it is very important that family members learn how to interpret the different ways through which the adolescent expresses his grief, and accept his pace and his way of working through the loss.

Practice illustration: Giovanna and the death of her father

Giovanna, a fifteen-year-old, is brought to therapy by the mother because of increasing conflict between them, but mostly because of her daughter's aggressive behavior towards her new partner. Giovanna cannot stand him and does not accept any of his rules or reproaches. She always comes home late and is doing poorly at school. The mother does not understand what is happening to her and reprimands her harshly, saying that she does not understand her grief for her husband's death, which happened two years earlier, while she, a nurse, works day and night to support her. They have never spoken about this loss: in the course of one of the first sessions the mother states that "it would have been too painful for both of them," and has spoken about it even less since the arrival of the new partner who, being a man, is expected to fill the void left by Giovanna's father. There has been no time to stop and process the suffering left by such a difficult loss, for both mother and daughter. On the one hand, we have the mother's job and new partner to "give Giovanna another father figure," and, on the other, the daughter's negative and externalized answers, such as coming home late, poor academic achievements, and the aggressive refusal of a paternal substitute; all understandable and human reactions, but they are focused on moving on, rather than on stopping and entering the void left by this loss. This will be the aim of therapy: entering the void and helping mother and daughter to express themselves openly in their own different ways, allowing the suffering for this common loss to flow, in order to rediscover a deep connection between Giovanna and her mother which will give sense to everything, including new relationships.

In other cases, following the traumatic death of a father (caused by a car accident or a heart attack) we have met adolescents, in therapy, who become the "custodians of the lost parent," renouncing their relational lives, refusing to go to school and spending their entire days in their room, as if to keep alive the father's memory by an extreme act of love, for which they often pay the price of severe and persistent depression.

If the loss is that of a mother, with many adolescent girls we have often observed a total role reversal, so that they became the actual caregivers for their fathers, caring for them and supporting them in everything. But who will take care of their deep sadness for such a profound loss? Having a parental role during adolescence, in extremely stressful situations, can be very useful to both father and daughter, as long as it is a transitory and reversible condition, otherwise it can create a false Self for the adolescent, at the expense of their own psychophysical integrity. Depression will become a defensive mask with which the adolescent hides from life's dangers, even during later evolutionary phases. Unfortunately, families often continue to follow their script even after such a difficult loss: if in the developmental history of a family the man was unable to support his partner emotionally and acted as the fragile element, always in need of his wife's care, it is very likely that these mechanisms will repeat themselves, with the daughter assuming a maternal function towards her father.

A loss always has the potential to cause a crisis within the family, and represents an element of discontinuity and affective reorganization; nevertheless, this is the most productive moment for making changes within the family system and reorganizing the status quo. In this sense, the reactive depression of the adolescent and the request for family therapy are an extraordinary opportunity for change.

More generally, we can say that the loss of a loved one in the family allows the adult to see the adolescent in a different light, removed from the clichés that describe him as uninterested, insensitive and self-centered in relation to family issues. On the contrary: it is precisely during situations of loss or the severe illness of a parent or family member that adolescents show their strong emotional attachment and sense of belonging, and manifest it concretely through their sadness and depressive states.

Practice illustration: I cut my wrists... but just a little!

As we have seen, sadness is a very profound affect during adolescence, often unconscious and mostly hidden by opposite feelings, risk-taking or incomprehensible acting out. Let's not forget that depressive symptoms can potentially degenerate into a downward spiral: aggression, connected to the narcissistic rage that is typical of adolescence, can initially be silenced by a shutting down, but will later explode and be directed against others, or against oneself through more or less severe self-harm behavior, culminating in attempted suicide. This becomes even more worrying when the adolescent becomes the point of contention in the endless war between parents and their own families of origin, because even an extreme signal might not be understood by immature parents, too preoccupied with their own needs and incapable of respecting the lives of their children, as in Federica's case.

Federica is a fifteen-year-old girl who comes to therapy with her mom, dad, and seven-year-old brother, Matteo. The family has sought our help because of Federica's behavior, which her parents define as intolerable: she plays truant and her academic performance has plummeted in the past year, she smokes, she gets drunk with her friends, does not answer her phone when she's out, and several times she left the house at three in the afternoon without a word and returned late at night. A couple of times the police, alerted by the father, have found her the following dawn, skimpily dressed and on the street, in the company of ladies of doubtful repute. Moreover, hidden under the long sleeves of her sweater, small scars are visible on her wrists. "I cut my wrists... but just a little" is the answer given when the therapist asks where those marks came from.

The parents are separating after serious difficulties which began immediately after the birth of the second child and had remained totally hidden until now.

During the first session, two things are striking about this family: the very dense and heavy silence that falls immediately after every participant's brief answer. There is also an enormous difference between the very obvious worry shown by the father, and the almost non-existent concern by the mother, for this daughter who seems hell-bent on attracting their attention through all possible means.

The mother ran away from home at seventeen, as a reaction to terrible physical and psychological abuse by the father against her and her mother. As a result of threats by her father, no one in the family went looking for her, so for a long time no one knew anything about her. She managed to complete her studies, with the help of precarious jobs, and later found a stable position, always relying on her own abilities, never trusting anyone and learning to ignore her fragility to avoid breaking down. Only later, through a relative, was contact with the family re-established, but not with the father, who died shortly afterwards.

Unlike his wife, Federica's father, a well-known businessman, is excessively worried about his daughter's behavior; it gives him no peace and keeps him in an anxious state day and night, constantly distracting him from his job, which is quite demanding and under public scrutiny, placing his reputation at risk.

He leaves home with few words: the hatred and contempt he feels for his wife, who, according to him, never accepted his choices in life, leaving him alone for many years, make him cut short explanations, even with his children. He seems to be saying, "It is over and I am leaving!," even though it is not at all clear from which family members he is separating.

What strikes us immediately during the session are the heavy silence and differing levels of concern for this daughter, which seem to outline the abysmal distance between the parents, who have crystallized on the opposite sides of a mountain of hatred and contempt which has grown over the years. There is a constant war between them: they only communicate in writing, by means of emails or SMS. The mother does not answer the house phone, preventing the father from speaking with his children in the evening. He calls them directly on their mobile phones, and even tells them about his new girlfriend, seducing them with promises and projects that the mother is ignorant of.

In this situation the daughter is in the middle of a painful and unbearable loyalty conflict. The anger she feels towards both parents, who see nothing but themselves and their need for revenge, makes her want to punish her father, the "traitor," by escaping from home and from school and putting at risk his public image with blatantly scandalous behavior, and her mother, the "victim," by mortifying her with her academic failure and a strong devaluing of the female role. Meanwhile, when she is alone, Federica cuts her wrists... but just a little!

ATTEMPTED SUICIDE DURING ADOLESCENCE

The tragic truth is that suicide has become the second cause of death between fifteen- and eighteen-year-olds after car accidents. The percentage of suicides in young people has tripled during the past thirty years, not including deaths caused by risk-taking behavior verging on the suicidal. Drug abuse, as well as scooter accidents, could be considered masked suicide attempts.

Some surveys show that around 20% of high school students have, at times, considered suicide more or less seriously, but luckily they do not put it into practice or do not succeed in the same way adults do.

Girls threaten to do it more often, and their attempts are more attention-seeking than self-harming. Whereas, boys do not talk about it much, but enact it in a more definite way if subject to deep depression. The female to male ratio is 1:7.

The European country with the highest number of attempted suicides and juvenile suicides is Finland, particularly during November, when there is no sunlight and little snow, which reflects artificial light, and when darkness covers everything. It is a condition that should make us reflect: what if persistent darkness is what comes before death? If so, what are the dark areas of our beautiful and bright society, so attentive to childhood rights, where so many of our young people get lost?

PSYCHODYNAMICS OF ATTEMPTED SUICIDE IN ADOLESCENCE

Several research projects in the psychoanalytic field have looked into the psycho-dynamics of attempted suicide in adolescence, and have

encountered unusual difficulties in finding the psycho-pathological nucleus of suicidal intent. No agreement has been reached about the nature
of the principal risk factors. The debate on the effectiveness and means of
prevention and intervention is still open.

What is more surprising about attempted suicides during adolescence is that, in most cases, the teenager's family and peer group do not
suspect anything.

Pietropolli Charmet highlights the difficulty in finding—even on
careful examination of the suicidal adolescent's development—sufficiently serious evidence of mental suffering to speculate on the existence
of a psycho-pathological picture. On the other hand, it is quite easy to
find a combination of relational events amounting to a network of
possible micro-traumatic events in relation to a narcissistic weakness in
the teenager (Maggiolini, Pietropolli Charmet, 1994).

Scholars agree that attempted suicide is usually enacted by an
adolescent who cannot separate and individuate from his mother. The
mother seems to be extremely important in these processes of separation
and individuation, especially for boys. Let's remember that this dilemma
begins at birth and continues into adulthood: if we consider how many
adults are stuck in a strongly dependent position, "chronic children" as
Andolfi (2003) calls them, it becomes obvious that this imaginary umbilical cord has an extremely important value.

Several clinical reports show that adolescents attempt suicide
when they cannot invest their desires and attachment on new objects of
love. It is interesting to note that fusion between mother and son is often
accompanied by a difficulty in establishing a relationship with the opposite sex. The ability to separate and individuate from emotional bonds in
the family of origin is directly proportional to the ability to build new
ones outside of it. On the other hand, if we think about the relationship
between father and daughter, we can easily state that, usually, a girl's
first boyfriend is always her father, and he remains the best of all men
for her. Fathers are proverbially jealous of their daughters, and are cautious about giving them to another man. This is ritualized when the
father "gives away the bride" by walking the daughter down the aisle.
But if this is so, we need to ask ourselves: where is the individuality of a
person if she becomes an object passed from one hand to another?

In summary, suicide is for the adolescent a means of regression
towards the typical security of a primary symbiotic state (total fusion
with the mother) and a resolution of the phase of separation-individuation from parents. In this sense, suicide represents the adolescent's sacrificial illusion. The fantasy of one's own funeral has its roots in the need

to see, as in a movie, what happens after death, to verify the love of one's parents and siblings. One of the cases we present later is that of Elena, an eighteen-year-old girl who ended up in hospital in a comatose state, having taken a huge amount of psycho-pharmacological drugs. During one of the sessions she says that she really appreciated those who had rushed to the hospital to see her. Even at those moments, when she was struggling between life and death, she was extremely sensitive to the presence or absence of family members, especially that of the father, "who had abandoned her when she was small."

From a more relational perspective, attempting suicide is a desperate attempt to defend his identity and re-establish limits and boundaries, by an adolescent whose narcissism is fragile and vulnerable. This is a form of violence against himself, but also violence against his parents, as the body is the symbol of the bond with parental figures. If we consider eating disorders, the body of an anorexic girl, who is often enacting a slow form of attempted suicide, is a perfect example of what we stated above. We no longer know whether it is the girl's body or that of the parents which is dying.

Another disquieting observation is that adolescents who attempt suicide often do not seem to be conscious of the reality of death, but appear anchored to a sense of immortality typical of childhood naivety. In therapy with teenagers who have attempted suicide, we have often heard them recounting the event in a way that demonstrated a certain lack of awareness about what was happening to them. It sometimes seems that these young people risk dying not so much because they want to, but because they have no understanding of what it means to pass from life to death.

In fact, for adolescents, suicide is often a way of being the focus of attention even after death. It is as though they kill themselves to live forever in the memory of those who remain. Many teenagers nowadays talk about suicide candidly on Facebook: they can vent all their existential desperation on social networks, announcing extreme gestures casually. Undoubtedly the Net can exponentially increase the resonance of their gesture. Unfortunately these adolescents can sometimes be serious about it. The tragic story of Carlo is emblematic, as recently reported by the mass-media: three days before hanging himself in his bedroom he wrote on Facebook: "I'm about to arrive in the afterworld!" He had started a countdown on his virtual profile: minus three, minus two, minus one. His 107 friends thought he was waiting for a special day, perhaps his birthday. There was no birthday. Carlo was just waiting to kill himself.

RELATIONAL ASPECTS OF ATTEMPTED SUICIDE

There is no doubt that attempted suicide is an extremely complex form of non-verbal communication. It is a message that has to do with something extremely important which cannot be expressed otherwise. Perhaps it is a cry for help, to restore a broken bond with one or both parents, a tragic expression of a desire to be understood on very important issues, because unable to find the words to communicate it.

Practice illustration: Mayday, mayday!

Paros is a fourteen-year-old Greek boy who attends family therapy after a series of attempted suicides, all quite dramatic and almost infantile. The script is always the same, even if the methods change: once, he throws himself from the roof of the family's two-storey house right before his father, who is leaving in his car. Another time, he hangs himself noisily in the bathroom, only to be saved by his father whose studio adjoins the bathroom, and once he falls spectacularly from a bike which he was racing at full speed down the slope of the garage, again, with the father nearby. The father, who works full-time as a diplomat and has no time for his son, states that his son is crazy, that he needs to be hospitalized and to be given drugs. The idea that his son's gestures might be dramatic requests for attention does not even cross his mind.

A case similar to that of Paros, in that it is a request for attention from parents constantly at war, is the suicidal behavior of Giovanni, an only child, who was found lying on disused train tracks in a small town in Sicily, waiting for an improbable train to arrive.

In the next chapter, on the subject of network interventions, we will describe the case of Bianca, an anorexic girl brought to therapy in an extremely serious condition. Every day she would ask her mother to check on her during night, while she was sleeping, to make sure she was still breathing. The mother carried out this ritual every night. We all know very well that the biggest worry for all parents of a new-born baby is the child's breathing, so they constantly check that everything is OK and that he doesn't turn around in his crib. What can this mean, when an eighteen-year-old girl asks her mother to check if she is still breathing? Clearly the relational implications of this request are very strong, but so is the difficulty in expressing this bond with words, in a more adult and explicit way; therefore, we see a reversal to childish behaviors which are very regressive.

It is fundamental that a family should learn to decipher the adolescent's often complex and cryptic language, even with suicide attempts that are quite extravagant, as the ones described earlier. Unfortunately, it is too often the case that parents and relatives, very involved during the first phase of assistance to the adolescent, once he has survived the danger, end up trivializing the attempted suicide and define it as a childish action, an expression of his weakness and immaturity. Parents fail to communicate to their child the seriousness and danger of his behavior, or their dismay, because they believe, in good faith, that by saying that the event is serious or severe they might increase the risk of another suicide attempt or, in any case, make things worse. In reality, when this happens, the situation might become even more dramatic: it is as if the adults' denial colludes with the child's magical thinking (Andolfi et al., 2007), thus multiplying the risk factors.

Practice illustration: Lucia and an impossible life

We have already described family situations in which there is a risk of depressive onset in adolescent children. At times these depressive states are not recognized and therefore degenerate, leading to self-destructive behavior. Sudden losses, hostile couple separations with strong triangulation of the children, domestic violence and child abuse, intergenerational confusions and distortions, neglect and social marginality are all situations that can, in extreme cases, lead to suicidal behavior.

As the adolescent's intention is typically sacrificial, we cannot underestimate those situations where severe psychiatric pathologies are present in one or both parents (psychosis, alcoholism, bipolar disorders, addiction to drugs, and so on): when the adolescent perceives the behavior of parents as threatening, he might feel that his own attempted suicide could have a rescuing function.

Lucia, a sixteen-year-old girl, comes to family therapy following a serious suicide attempt. The father has always denied the severity of the chronic alcoholism of his wife, who has made a number of suicide attempts over the years. Alcoholism and maternal depression are the affective conditions under which the girl has been raised. The mother was abandoned by her own mother at a very young age and feels incapable of living, it is, in fact as though she has always been "dead inside." The father, accustomed to minimizing every problem, has also done so with Lucia's extreme gesture, after she threw herself from the window. Since her birth, Lucia has been the only vital element in the house; she grew up absorbing her mother's pain and, in her own way, tried everything to help her in a very responsible way, until she entered adolescence, when her self-destructive behavior began. Previous therapeutic interventions were focused on saving the girl who threw herself from the window, and on individual diagnosis and pharmacological treatment, without any attention to family components and behavior. But can we give an adolescent her life back without changing the affective context which surrounds her and informs her behavior?

Another very important risk factor is present when the person hates their own body. Often, teens who attempt suicide had demonstrated, in the previous years or months, the presence of a conflict with their own body through eating disorders, excessive concern for the aesthetics of their body or hypochondriac disorders.

Romantic disappointments, devaluation, obvious or concealed labeling in the family, at school, or in the peer group, can have destructive effects on the adolescent and precede suicidal intent. Narcissistic fragility in the adolescent exposes him/her to pain, eliciting a catastrophic shame reaction. Common wisdom says that "shame kills more people than guilt." Shame is a crucial element in suicide attempts and adolescents often attempt suicide because they feel ashamed. When adolescents suffer a romantic disappointment, the parents tend to rationalize, minimize or, on the contrary, to worry unduly. The difficulty arises because they are not able to relate to their children—who suffer because they are losing something very significant—by listening rather than by looking for improbable solutions.

As for academic failures or feeling left out or rejected by the peer group, parents generally have major difficulties in deciphering their children's idiosyncrasies and weaknesses in the social realities outside the family, especially because they do not know the language, the rules of communication, and the complexity of friendships of today's adolescent generation. We only need to think about networking, sending messages through mobile phones, and the meaning of Facebook to young people, to understand that theirs is a completely different world.

Another difficult situation is that of adolescents who have been discharged by Emergency Rooms, Intensive Therapy Units or Antipoison Units, who cannot understand why their body has been spared, even thought they had decided to kill themselves. If, on the one hand, they are happy they survived, on the other, they are displeased or surprised that their body is still alive. This is a part of the childish game we referred to earlier, where there is no perception of the value of life, in terms of not being able to resuscitate the body and, therefore, that it is not possible to get another one.

As for concealed suicide attempts, it is surely more difficult to prevent scooter accidents than drug abuse or similar behaviors. And the number of accidents is enormous. Even in this case we are dealing with the myth of immortality. Let's think about those teenagers who constantly defy death by slaloming through traffic, as if they were on a race-track, and those who refuse to wear a helmet, especially in the south of Italy! It is alarming to see how little they are conscious of the boundary between life and the risk of dying. We believe that these potentially self-destructive behaviors are underpinned by *masked depression*.

Without a doubt, the strongest risk factor for attempted suicide is a previous suicide attempt. This should make us reflect on the importance of intervening effectively and decisively when the first episode occurs. We will discuss this in the next section.

EMERGENCY THERAPEUTIC INTERVENTIONS

Emergency care as a magical waiting space

An emergency is not the place for family, psychologists, or psychotherapy. The hospital is the first port of call when there is an attempted suicide, and it becomes a magical waiting space, a specialized place where the suicidal adolescent's life can be preserved. However, we would be mistaken to imagine that this is where magic happens, although the Emergency Room, Emergency Unit, and Anti-poison Center are the inevitable first and fundamental steps. The second problem, after a life has been saved, is how to return it to its natural environment.

The normal procedure by health institutions, such as Hospitals, Emergency Rooms, and Emergency Units, is to isolate the adolescent who attempted suicide, to prevent any kind of stress to the patient. This tends to create a kind of protecting bell jar around him, removing him from all those elements that might cause tension or alarm. Anxiety, preoccupation, and disruption in the family, including strong feelings of guilt and powerlessness in the parents, are excluded from the medical intervention which only focuses on saving a life.

We are of the opinion that this approach is very medical and not in the least relational. Our point of view is radically different: the sooner and better we re-establish active and positive bonds around the adolescent, the more efficiently we can contain the problem and promote a positive outcome. When an adolescent who attempted suicide arrives in the Emergency Room, we should do our best to activate immediately a support network, but not just with the parents. The latter, by themselves, can represent the weakest unit because they are too involved, directly or indirectly, in the suicidal event. Whitaker always insisted that "the more you widen the system, the more life there is; the more you limit it, the less there is." By this we mean the extended family, from siblings to grandparents, to friendships. Naturally, this network should also include the hospital system with its various professionals.

The recovery model at the Clos Bernard Hospital in Paris

The experience of some of our colleagues in Paris, psychiatrists and family therapists, is enlightening. They have developed a very innovative, truly systemic model of intervention which supports the active participation of the family during the hospitalization of the adolescent who attempted suicide.

After a brief stay at the General Hospital for emergency treatment, admission to the clinical unit of the Clos Bernard Hospital requires three fundamental conditions: the adolescent must agree to the hospitalization, which lasts an average of 10-15 days; the family must participate in family therapy sessions once or twice a week, during and after hospitalization; and lastly, the adolescent must return to school in the shortest time possible.

The initial part is the most delicate: an entire admission team is activated from the moment the adolescent and his family arrive at the hospital. This team is composed of the person in charge of the service, a psychiatrist, an educator and a nurse. The first goal is to understand the reason for the admission, and for this reason the whole family is required to be present (parents, grandparents and so on), in order to elicit the collaboration of the entire family group. Often, the adolescent initially refuses to be admitted, while his parents insist that he should be. For this reason, there is an initial session of one, two or three hours with the family, in an attempt to reach an agreement. If this is not possible, the team suggests meeting again the following day. Sometimes, if necessary, a home visit with three generations present is scheduled. Actually, these first encounters are not focused on the suicide attempt at all. The team takes advantage of the emergency situation, and of the need to reach an agreement, to get an understanding of the family, its history, and its relational dynamics, so that the context and motivation of every family member, including the adolescent, begin to change in a positive way.

In agreement with what we previously stated, the Paris group also believes that the moment of crisis—when the family is frightened and dismayed about the child's suicide attempt—presents the best opportunities of achieving full and extraordinary collaboration with the family system as a whole, a much more difficult task under normal circumstances.

When parents are divorced, parallel work takes place, engaging alternately the family of one parent or the other to reach a common agreement. In the case of an immigrant family that does not speak any French—very common in Paris—cultural and language mediators are engaged.

It is common practice at the Clos Bernard Hospital to invite the whole family to visit the ward and the room where the adolescent will stay. Where possible, the young person will also have the opportunity of choosing the room he prefers, in a kind of hospitality process. The visiting hours are very flexible: the family can stay at the hospital the entire day, and they can eat with the adolescent at the hospital or go to a restaurant. Obviously these options need to be discussed and decided with the clinical team.

The philosophy behind this kind of intervention is that of making the family feel competent and involved with the hospital environment; this is a highly motivating factor in obtaining the agreement of the adolescent. In this way, a strong synergy is created between the family and the clinical team: a fundamental element to obtain excellent results.

Once the adolescent has been admitted, the family sessions begin. These encounters are fundamental in allaying the fear of suicide and for laying the foundations of new contexts of safety, which will allow the adolescent to overcome his experience of incompetence and powerlessness and to engage in new life projects.

After discharge, the sessions will continue outside the hospital setting—with the same team—with the aim of helping the adolescent return to school and to normal relationships as quickly as possible. It is standard procedure, when necessary, to offer individual support and medication alongside family therapy.

Post discharge: how to use the crisis to stimulate change

Even after the patient has been discharged, psychiatric and therapeutic interventions are often designed to avoid stress and to avoid involving the family—thus reducing the available resources—for fear of creating or exacerbating relational tensions. The intervention is therefore a purely individual one, often mediated by pharmaceuticals. Many other situations never come to clinical attention, as some family and social cultures tend to normalize the adolescent's act and deny its future consequences. So everyone acts as though nothing ever happened. In these cases, we cannot track how the situation evolves, unless there is a second suicide attempt with consequent hospitalization.

We generally find that many parents are so shocked by the event, once the danger has passed, that they tend to become protective about the suicidal event. This behavior, on the one hand, is due to defensive dynamics useful in avoiding thinking about the relational reasons for the gesture and their related guilt feelings, and on the other, by the need to hide this event from the extended family and wider social context, since current opinion regards this kind of behavior as reprehensible. In this context it is worth remembering that only a few decades ago, the Church would not allow funerals and burials in consecrated cemeteries for those who had committed suicide.

In contrast, in these pages we would like to highlight the familial and social advantages of examining in depth the reasons that drive a young person to put his own life at risk, and to view in a positive way the inevitable family crisis that follows, to widen the perspective without reducing the meaning of this event to that of a childish action or an adolescent mental disorder. The suicide attempt of a young person certainly carries a personal meaning, as it is his own life that has been put at risk, and it is undoubtedly the answer to existential conditions he finds unbearable; nevertheless, the interpersonal nature and relational meaning of this gesture are also undeniable. It is precisely the value that this event assumes in the dynamics of affective relationships that motivates us to work with the entire family group, in the search for new resources and new developmental paths for everyone. A suicide attempt wipes out all the certainties and habitual behavior patterns of a family, but it also offers the fearless, curious, and respectful therapist an opportunity to accompany the family in their processing of the suffering which always underlies such a dramatic gesture.

Practice illustration: When to die: before or after graduation?

Carla is twenty years old; she studies Psychology in Rome, her parents are fifty years old, and she is an only child[4]. The family lives in a

---

4   The description of this case was taken from the book *Le perdite e le risorse della famiglia* (Andolfi, D'Elia, 2007); it has been reviewed and improved.

small city in central Italy and the girl commutes every day. For a number of years, Carla has been suffering from anxiety and depression, with periodic crises leading to self-harm and suicide threats. She is being treated at her local Mental Health Clinic and by her family psychiatrist with anti-depressants.

Carla, an only child, has always been considered a miracle child, but she has also been the cause of her mother's worsening health. The latter, Angela, has been suffering from a heart condition since she was eleven years old, and for this reason the doctors had always advised her not to have children. In fact, shortly after getting married, Angela became pregnant and, feeling very guilty, had an abortion for health reasons. The following year Angela's condition seems to improve, so with much fear and trepidation, she carried to term this second pregnancy, which will lead to Carla's birth. In spite of the parents' happiness about the arrival of this much wanted child, Carla's development is not easy. The mother is constantly ill and cannot take care of the baby, so her husband, Luigi, takes her place in everything. When Carla is eleven years old the mother has two open-heart interventions to replace two cardiac valves. During this period the girl is very protective towards her mother, and becomes her father's helper in taking care of her. At sixteen, she develops a strong resentment towards her mother, which gradually intensifies until today when, concurrently, the depressive crises begin.

Carla is a pretty girl. Nonetheless, she begins to show some obvious psychological difficulties connected to acne. By the time she comes to therapy her dermatological issues have already resolved, but she passes many hours in front of the mirror, feeling ugly, hating her body, and experiencing strong feelings of emptiness and boredom. She is dating the son of her mother's cardiologist, with whom she feels very disappointed. She escapes her unrest by binge drinking at the week-end.

Carla treasures her writings and her poetry, and brings approximately eighty poems to the sessions. We have chosen one, the shortest, to give an idea of Carla's psychological state when she arrives at our office:

In the silence of the night
I'd like to feel the faint breeze of dreams
and of pale fantasies,
but I can only hear the cry of a heart
tired of beating
and of marking a time so absurd for me
and for those who live close to me.
     In the night, I would like to find peace

and tranquil rest
and not violent awakenings
filled with anguish and fearful dread for tomorrow.
        In the enchanted night
I'd like to find eternal peace,
I'd like to find myself
as if in dreams,
beyond this life.

        What follows are extracts from the second therapy session. Carla
has attempted suicide again, between the first and second session. The
participants are the mother, Carla, the father, and the therapist. Andolfi
is supervising behind the one-way mirror.

Therapist: So, let's hear the news. Who's going to tell me the news?
Carla: I don't much want to talk today, I'm in a terrible mood!
(The mother gestures to the therapist that the daughter should speak.)
Therapist: Is the daughter going to tell me the news?
Mother: Quite important news.
Therapist: Why does mom want you to talk about it?
Carla: Me?
Mother: Eh! My darling, it happened to you!

        This third suicide attempt, which took place in the interval
between the first and the second session, seems to be Carla's calling card,
her way of inducing panic and anguish in both the family and the therapeutic system. The family reacts with detachment and denial. It almost
sounds like a conversation taking place at the hairdresser's, about something that happened to someone else. We also need to remember that
this is not a family unaware of how serious a problem can be: the mother
has lived with the themes of life and death all her life! It rather seems to
be a conscious choice by the family. Carla, lucid and provocative, describes her attempted suicides in this way.

Carla: So… well, Friday night I made myself a lethal cocktail of drugs.
They were not at home. There are plenty of drugs in my house, psycho-
pharmaceutical drugs, anxiolytics, painkillers… I took a huge amount,
not because I wanted to calm myself but because I wanted to die. I mixed
them with alcohol and went to sleep. He *(the father)* found me by chance,
because I fell from my bed while I was trying to go to the bathroom,

because I needed to pee. He took me to the hospital; I was put in intensive care; they pumped my stomach. I was in hospital for three days.

Therapist: When did this happen?

Carla: The twenty-sixth.

Therapist (addressing the parents): She doesn't look like someone who just attempted suicide!

Mother: No.

Father: No, not at all. It was Monday, right?

Carla: Yeah, well, it happened the day after my exam.

Mother: It happened at home. In the morning, she was here in Rome with her father, she had to take some exams. She didn't; then, in the evening, she came back home and did that.

Therapist (addressing the mother): Were you there?

Mother: I was not. I had planned to come back the day after.

Therapist (addressing Carla and her father): So it was only the two of you, plus her family *(Carla's maternal grandparents).*

Father: Yes, but they didn't wake up, although I screamed to wake Carla up and...

Therapist: Was it by chance or did you hear her?

Father: No, I came back late and was in the kitchen, I heard some strange noises from her room, I went in, I tried to talk to her, I realized that this wasn't normal sleepiness, and I tried to understand what had happened to her. She mumbled something I didn't understand and then I made her lie down on the carpet in the kitchen, she was a dead weight, quite difficult to move, and I called the ambulance.

Therapist: Was it the first time that this happened?

Father: The first time it was this serious. There have been, in the past, at least that I know of...

Carla: It happened three times: the first time I took a lot of medicines, but not lethal, so...

Father: Pills.

Carla: No, pills and drops. I went to the Emergency Room and there they put me on an I.V. drip, but then I didn't mean...

The psychopathology exam

(The supervisor speaks to the therapist on the intercom.)

Supervisor: Tell Carla that doctor Andolfi would like her to take some sort of pre-exam. She should write on the whiteboard the different types of suicide, as if she had to take an exam on adolescent psychopathology.

This is the question: make a list of the different types of suicide in adolescence.

Therapist (addressing Carla): Doctor Andolfi is asking if you, as a future psychologist... How far away is your degree?

(Carla and her parents laugh.)

Therapist: He is asking if you could take an exam on adolescent psychopathology. Could you write down how many types of attempted suicide can take place during adolescence? Write it on the blackboard. *(Carla, interested, gets up and starts to write on the whiteboard.)*

Carla: According to me, for women, from articles I read in newspapers, and from what I know, I think that for a woman it is easier to do it with drugs.

Therapist: And how would this happen?

Carla: So, well, the easiest way is when you already see a psychiatrist, because then you have the opportunity to get all the medicines you want. You have the prescription, you go and buy them, you only need to have enough money. You can do it even if you don't have direct control over the drugs, because you pretend to lose them, but in reality you accumulate them. I did it, not because I wanted to kill myself, only because I didn't want to take any drugs, my father knows this very well, I pretended I was taking them, I collected an enormous quantity, then he *(the father)* found out...

Therapist: And how do you make this cocktail?

Carla: It's like this: if you are familiar with drugs, you read the dosage, you know very well which dose will do the trick, or maybe at first you do it by chance, then you take more and more, because you expect the giddiness and drowsiness. It doesn't happen straight away, and that makes you take more. For instance, I used Control but it was never enough, four pills were not enough, then another four, another four, another four, and sleep would never come, so I always increased the dosage.

Therapist: And where does this usually happen?

Carla: In private. Usually you wait for silence, when no one is around, generally in your room.

Therapist: In your room, in the daytime, at night?

Carla: At night.

Therapist: And what is the probability that such an attempt will succeed?

Carla: This kind of attempt, according to me, has a high probability of success, I was unlucky and failed!

Therapist: Can you write it on the blackboard?

Carla: The percentage of success? I think it also depends on the type of control one is under. Anyway, in my opinion, the risk of succeeding is 60%. I'm over-controlled, but it often happens that one is over-controlled by the family!

This girl studies Psychology, is remarkably eloquent, and seems to activate herself immediately when directly provoked to explain her issue by pretending it is a Psychology lesson: what better than to use her field of competence to build a therapeutic alliance? Carla answers thoroughly, as if giving a lecture; she gives examples of various types of suicide, of the various forms it takes according to gender, the percentages of success, demonstrating the ability to go from theory to practice. She has quite high intellectual and reflective abilities, as well as an alarming lucidity and detachment when speaking about death. Nonetheless, like the psychiatrist treating her, we too have excluded the possibility of a psychotic syndrome.

Supervisor (speaking to the therapist over the intercom): Do you mind if I talk to her?
(Carla goes over to the intercom.)
Supervisor: Hello? Good morning! I'm sorry, I know this is a therapy session, but I'd like you to think for a moment that you are at the university.
Carla: I'm already in trouble with exams!
Supervisor: How many did you take?
Carla: One, just one!
Supervisor: Which one?
Carla: The simplest one, Pedagogy.
Supervisor: Pedagogy! But I have the impression that you went faster in life than in the exams!
Carla: That's what I think as well!
Supervisor: I'd like you to answer some questions about Psychopathology, which is a third-year exam.
Carla: Umm, I don't understand, what do you mean?
Supervisor: Excuse me, doesn't the Psychopathology exam come later?
Carla: Yes, in the third year.
Supervisor: In the third year. So I'm asking you to make an effort as if you were in the third year – you know why? Because many Psychology students confuse psychology with therapy, they enroll in Psychology, but what they really want is to go to therapy, do you understand?
Carla: I don't know if...

Supervisor: Actually, you also go to therapy, so maybe you're better off than they are; you understood where to go for therapy and where for the profession, don't you think? So maybe your ideas are clearer, it is a good start. But now there is a problem, because maybe you won't be able to get your degree, because if you die before that...?

(Carla laughs.)

Supervisor: It is five years, right? So, you know, five years is a long time, and maybe it could take you longer, what if it takes you six years? So you have to think whether it's better to die before or after getting your degree. That is already a question. Have you ever thought about it?

Carla: Yes, I have, I never managed to say it, but...

Supervisor: There! I would like you to transmit all these things we are talking about to your parents and to the therapist, OK? Can you help me?

Carla: Yes, just that or...

Supervisor: Wait a second, follow the thread of the conversation. I called you because I am a fifth-year professor ...

Carla: Eh, I know! I get to follow your classes, because my surname starts with M!

Supervisor: Why, you are in the M-Z group! So there's no turning back! Maybe this will help us. If you make it to the fifth year! Maybe this therapy is a pre-exam, you see? So, the first thing we need to figure out is whether you think you'll want to live till the fifth year. So, if today we take the psychopathology exam, which is a third-year exam, you need to give us some time so you can get there with your studies too, you know?

Carla: OK.

Supervisor: By the way, this will also reassure your parents a little. In this way you'll give them a few more years, otherwise we will all be thinking about it all the time... Do you know the game they used to play with a daisy: "She loves me, she loves me not...," right? Well, they have to think, with the daisy: "She kills herself, she does not..." This is hard for two parents, you know? Speaking of which, I gather you are the second one, at least in the two generations we met. Your mom is the person who had the most fantasies of death, right? With her heart! See, I have the impression that sometimes young daughters try to find their way, to differentiate themselves from parents and manifest their needs in a weird kind of way, right? Sometimes they do it with clothes, they do it with boyfriends, and sometimes they do it with their life. As if to say: mom has always been the center of dad's life, and yours, because she was the one at risk, always in the spotlight because of her illness, and now you'd like the spotlight to be on yourself. I'd like you to explain this, with your own words, these things I said about your parents, and then wipe off what you wrote on the whiteboard, because you got a good grade for your explanation about the different ways of committing suicide... But it is easy to explain the "how." It is harder to explain the reasons that drive a young woman to take her life. You answered the first question brilliantly; now we need to talk about the deep reasons for it. People never want to commit suicide for the sake of it, it is always an interpersonal fact, you understand? So now you could explain your motivations!

Carla: Mine?

Supervisor: Of course! Good luck with your work!

Carla: Thank you.

(Carla goes back to the whiteboard.)

Carla: So, he said that I got a good grade. But now he wants to know the reasons... and this is more difficult for me, because I've never read anything about psychology, I only know how I feel. For an adolescent girl, I think a lot has to do with.... the rejection of her own image, not in the sense that she perceives herself as ugly, but that she also feels rejected, in many ways by parents, who maybe tell her: "You are too this, too that...!" I think it is easier for a boy to be a rebel, to be more independent. I think that for a girl it is more important to gain the approval of her parents about what she does. And sometimes she doesn't even feel understood by her friends, by whom she feels attacked and judged! Then, you know, in small towns people talk and gossip behind your back, and when you feel attacked from many sides, you feel judged and you find yourself alone, you cannot express yourself, you haven't even got the cultural basis to face something like this, maybe because you're young, maybe you haven't got anyone to talk to, not even a psychologist, then you realize you're isolated. For me I think it is different, more a question of my character, I'm fundamentally a pessimist and my parents were never able to mitigate this. They didn't manage to do it because, I have to say, I'm very extreme, I go from moments of euphoria for life, for things, for joy, to moments of tragedy that don't make any sense, for me life is either a tragedy or a comedy!

Therapist: Anyway, what changed after this attempt? This is the third one, right? What changed compared to the other two?

Carla: This is what I can't understand: for example, I think that the other two times I didn't really want to die. Even the second time, which maybe was the most dramatic because it happened in Rome, when I was by myself, I had that huge amount of drugs, I knew very well that I'd only get a massive stomach ache, nausea, vomit, and that I wouldn't die. I wanted to feel sick, but this was justified by the fact that I wanted to feel sick to the extreme and then feel better. It seems absurd, but it happens. This *(the third attempt)* was dramatic because I was actually very lucid, because I hadn't been drinking before-hand, I drank only to mix drugs and alcohol. I was perfectly lucid and started to take a quantity of drugs I was very familiar with, and which I already knew could be lethal in that dosage. There was this background intention, but I was unaware of it while I was doing it. What was different is that the first time, when I took those drops, and the second time in Rome, I thought: "Death, death. There, now I'm going to die, so I'll get it over with!" This time, instead, something different happened; even now I have trouble understanding. I didn't realize the seriousness of it, and even now I don't, because I wasn't thinking about suicide. That is, I wasn't thinking about dying, but I did everything right to commit suicide, as if I'd planned it for a long time, the correct quantity of drugs to die! The professor *(Andolfi)* asked me if I ever thought that it will take me another five or six years to become a psychologist, and whether I regretted that... I mean, if I kill myself I'll never become a psychologist, I'll never study things that I might like! And there was also another thing I didn't think about when I was taking those pills, he *(Andolfi)* asked me: "Did you ever think about your parents, your loved ones?" I realized I was being selfish, because I never thought about those things. I realized I always thought about different things, like my books, my CDs; I was obsessed!

Mother: Also her photos.

Carla: Yes, my photos, my stuff, my poetry, my clothes. I thought about all this material life, it is material, yes, but it is also my life. Now, I haven't thought about university, I only thought about all my things...

There couldn't be a better description of what a girl thinks when she risks dying by attempting suicide. We have witnessed this kind of situation very often in our practice. Carla speaks about a background intention that becomes more and more powerful the less it is consciously perceived. Her words seem to convey that the suicidal act has an extremely dramatic value, an urgency to be in the spotlight which, if read as a need to affirm the Self, says a great deal about how this feeling of "invisibility" in her significant relationships has reached an intolerable level for her.

What is present in her mind, in those moments, are concrete things, books, CDs, clothes, memories, and thoughts through her photographs and poems. Her family is not present in her conscious thoughts.

What she calls selfishness is a feeling that comes from a difficulty in answering the question: "Who am I?" This harrowing question, often very difficult to answer, is intimately connected with the profound metamorphosis of adolescence, as well as with the familial dimension, particularly with what Bowen calls *Family Ego Mass*, or the emotional melting pot of the family where the boundaries are very confused and everyone has a complementary function, as in a kind of interlocking puzzle. Carla's mother has always played the role of the sick person, the father's only function is firstly to look after Angela and then her elderly parents, who live in the adjoining apartment. In this dimension of emotional entanglement, Carla can only exist "if she's no longer there." To remain alive, for her, means to continue being a part of this undifferentiated mass of affections, family emotions, and complementary functions.

Let's imagine you are dead...

(The supervisor enters the room and introduces himself.)
Supervisor (addressing Carla): The grade you got in the subject is good; the one you got in life isn't! Now, we have an imbalance here between your ability to deepen your knowledge of Psychology and a great tragicomedy being played out in the family! Let's imagine you are dead, what would happen here *(pointing at the parents)*?
Carla: Should I try to get into their shoes?
Supervisor: Sure. Let's start from your mom.
Supervisor (addressing the mother): Madam, how is your heart condition? If your daughter died, would you get a heart attack?
Mother: I thought, and I also talked about it with her, I thought that facing such an event, which is the biggest tragedy for a parent, I would not have been able to bear it. But I did, I reacted like everyone else.
Supervisor: Madam, I'm talking about your daughter dying, not about her playing with death! How would you react if you came home and found your daughter dead? Forgive me if I talk about this, but we have to talk about what happens after in order to stop what might happen before...
Mother: I would feel enormously guilty. But I can't bear talking about this, unfortunately!
Supervisor: Madam, unfortunately these are the things we have to talk about. I want to understand.
Supervisor (addressing Carla): Then you tried to kill yourself at home, when only the two of you were there! *(Supervisor looks to Carla and her father.)*
Carla: No, dad had already gone out.

Father: Yes, I left because I had an appointment with some friends, and got back home at a quarter to one.
Supervisor: And when did she try to kill herself?
Carla: At ten thirty in the evening.
Supervisor: OK, let's imagine she died. You come back from playing bridge and you find her dead. What happens inside you?
Father: I don't know, maybe I refuse even to think about it.
Supervisor: You refuse to think about it, but your daughter has actually tried to kill herself three times!
Father: I can't, I don't know, in life I'm usually well prepared for all kinds of events, but this is something that, deep down, I have always avoided thinking about!

We have widely discussed the frequency of denial in parents after their child has attempted suicide. It is fundamental that the therapist does not collude with what we have defined as a "denial plot" by the family and that he should feel free to enter this entanglement. While Carla might raise the stakes on her life and sooner or later lose it, none of them is able to consider the consequences of such an event, because it is too painful and upsetting. "I can't even consider" this possibility, says the father, yet it is some kind of Russian roulette they all participate in, where no one is able to make a change in their part of the script. We wrote an article, "The therapist as director of the family drama" (Andolfi, Angelo, 1981), and this definition seems to fit this kind of situation well. It is the therapist's duty to enter the family drama and to help everyone in the session to find a new role and re-write the story of his/her life in the present moment, as Stern would say. This work requires a return to the salient points of the family's developmental history to transform its meanings, in order to mend emotional wounds which are still painful and unhealed.

Therapy can then stimulate the search for the resources, blocked in time, within the tri-generational history of this family.

There has always been a gloomy atmosphere in this house, a sense of illness everywhere: in fact, the mother is frequently hospitalized. It is also important to note that Angela's parents, whose only child she is, have always lived in the same house. The grandmother in particular played an important role for Carla, since she was a child. In the last few years, the health of both grandparents has deteriorated to the extent that they need to be cared for by a care-giver. Neither Angela nor her husband Luigi have ever left the house for more than a couple of days.

There has always existed a strong competition between mother and daughter who, unable to develop their femininity and more generally their life, have expressed it through themes of illness and death. Mother and daughter have always competed to be taken care of by Luigi, who constantly mediates between them, notwithstanding the fact that he also takes care of the sick parents-in-law. Therefore, Carla grew up knowing that the recognition of her primary needs had to be mediated through illness, and the winner is obviously the most dramatic one.

The metaphor of "walking on a tightrope, if you fall you die, if you stay on it you win" captures a fundamental element connected to both Carla and her mother. The latter is surprised by the atmosphere created by the "academic lecture": for the first time she begins to see her daughter in a different light and decides to make an effort and to participate in the family's therapy.

Little by little the family manages to express the suffering of so many painful events and to experience it without hiding it or using it as an attack or defense weapon. Luigi begins to question his "undercover life" and finally relinquishes his role as chronic caretaker and recognizes himself as a person with his own needs and desires. Angela learns not to use her illnesses and, at the same time, she gradually starts recovering both the roles of wife and mother, allowing her daughter a kind of second birth: after two years of therapy, Carla will no longer need dramatic actions to affirm herself and express her needs. She now lives in Rome, where she studies Psychology and is getting good grades. Once the roles and generational boundaries have been better defined, she seems able to face her problems as a young adult with a positive attitude, both within the family and in the outside world. She has substituted the psychiatric institutions, where she played the role of depressed patient for several years, with a group of peers.

Carla and her family describe themselves during a follow-up session that took place two years after the end of therapy. Andolfi asks Carla to comment on her parents' life at the present moment, and asks them about their daughter's life.

Carla: Since I've been living in Rome I haven't witnessed their married life much, but I can see they're much more easy-going, they go out together...
Andolfi: There's a bigger space for the couple, then...
Carla: Yes, I think so: more space for the couple; there's more complicity. They go out together on Saturdays, and there's also this, since my grand-

parents have passed away, they do the shopping together, and they had never done it before!

Andolfi: And what do you think about Carla?

Father: She is still very fragile, small things still trigger her, psychologically she is no longer behaving the same way, but she's...

Mother: Less aggressive, she's more relaxed and she faces things with more calm. Also in regard to exams, she doesn't drive us to despair. She lives her life more calmly.

Practice illustration: One hundred and fifty Tegretol pills

At the time of the first encounter with Andolfi, about ten years ago, Elena was eighteen years old; she was referred by a psychiatrist at the general hospital where Elena had been admitted as an emergency after attempting suicide. She had taken one hundred and fifty Tegretol pills, an anti-epileptic drug she was prescribed for the *petit mal* seizures she was erroneously diagnosed with four years earlier. Elena was saved in the nick of time and for a long while she remained in the intensive-care unit, hovering between life and death[5].

Her parents, Luciano and Tiziana, married young, when they were about twenty-three years old, because Tiziana was pregnant with Elena. They separated very quickly and the mother was given custody of the child, while the father took no interest in her for several years. Tiziana has a dependent and immature personality and is not able to care for her daughter, who soon learns to act as a mother to a mother who is unable to give her affection and to assume the most basic responsibilities. Tiziana lives in a socio-cultural environment more focused on production and social image than on real affective relationships, and she loses herself. She becomes a drug addict and enters a drug rehabilitation center, where she remains for about three years. Elena is about five- or six-years-old when her mother is taken away from her. The official explanation is that "she has gone far away to cure an illness." During this period, the father comes back into her life, although her maternal grandmother is the person who mostly takes care of her.

As soon as Tiziana is discharged from the rehabilitation center, the caregiving system changes once again, with deep sadness for the grandmother and, most of all, the father who, although briefly and irregularly, had felt he could assume some paternal role. The child becomes a

---

5   The description of this case was taken from the book *Le perdite e le risorse della famiglia* (Andolfi, D'Elia, 2007) later revised and improved.

kind of baggage, constantly moved from one house to the other. Tiziana and Elena now become a couple, literally absorbed by the hotel owned by Tiziana's family for more than ten years, until the moment therapy starts. Mother and child live in a suite, like guests. Though Tiziana shows remarkable creativity (she paints with passion and creativity), her family considers her unproductive work-wise, and incapable of being a mother. Furthermore, she has a series of improbable boyfriends, whom her daughter can barely tolerate but who, much to her joy, last a very short time.

Elena grows up like many children who suffer from emotional abuse, and claims everything for herself in equal measure to the degree to which she feels totally abandoned and manipulated by the adults responsible for her care. She manages to tyrannize family and hotel staff, is driven to school by the waiter on duty, and claims all sorts of privileges, shocking her uncle with the brazen clothes she wears on Saturday nights at the hotel night club and with the friends she sneaks into the disco. If you cannot have true affection, you can at least exploit the secondary advantages afforded by the lack of it, such as increasingly expensive objects and demands. What's more, her frequent fainting spells (which have been diagnosed as epileptic fits for a long time), create a climate of apprehension and excessive protectiveness, which make her even more dependent on the care-giving system. Although she is very intelligent and sensitive, Elena goes to school irregularly, with minimum effort.

The father grows more and more distant from his daughter, both due to his increasing professional duties and to the new family he has made with a partner who has already given him two daughters. Though the relationship he has with Tiziana is characterized by a polite coldness, he thinks that the hotel is a completely unhealthy environment for his daughter to live in, but does not lift a finger to change things and does not visit his daughter, or call her, for fear of having to speak to one of his ex-wife's relatives.

The sessions with Elena and her father are doubtlessly the hardest ones, because the girl is constantly blaming and vindictive towards Luciano, while he is unable to get past the cold and rational defenses he raises when his daughter accuses him. While Elena is very protective towards the mother, whom she perceives as fragile and immature, she is not willing to accept anything when it comes to her father: she has not felt wanted from the moment she was born, then she felt abandoned for many years, and finally she felt replaced by the other two daughters, even though she claims to feel very close to them. During these sessions, between insults, Elena betrays her incredible desperation and an implicit desire to find a paternal presence, especially now that she is an adolescent. But her father does not know how to get past words and recriminations and is unable to understand her feelings: he is too defended by his system of certainties. Even though the climate of the sessions is difficult for the father, he never misses one, even when extremely busy with his work, and agrees to bring along his family of origin.

The wall between Elena and her dad

The excerpt that follows is taken from one of the many sessions with Elena and her father, in an attempt to demolish the wall that has always kept them distant and separate from each other.

Elena: I have such a difficult relationship with him that... I'm not able to tell him so many things!
Therapist: I'm sorry, can I ask you something? Is it also difficult for you to look him in the eyes when you speak with him?
Elena: Yes.
Therapist: Because when you speak with him you look at me; it's like being the bank of a pool game!
Father: But she can also play with the mirror if she wants, our gazes can meet through that mirror.
Therapist: That's even worse! Even you can't look at your daughter in the eyes. How many years have you been avoiding each other?
Elena: No, no, I never look at him directly. At the moment I feel I'm going back into depression, I cry often, I can't sleep at night, sometimes I can't eat... I'm going through a tough time.
Therapist: It seems to me that you lack trust and closeness as well. This has nothing to do with age and gender: intimacy and closeness are connected to the very difficult periods you went through. Maybe if we talk about this we can make progress. Because I think that trust has been missing for a long time and I don't know who made this happen.
Father: What are you saying?
Therapist: I don't think Elena trusts you.
Father: I can say that it's true that we don't have enough intimacy and trust, because they are built by having a closer relationship than the one we had before, but I don't think that trust... that I really trust Elena.
Therapist: Do you feel that dad has trust in you?
Elena: Yes, he has trust, I think he trusts me, but I don't trust him, I feel that he's fooling around with me.

Therapist: You really don't trust him! What do you expect from him: betrayals, abandonment...?

Elena: Yes, I think he's fooling around with me a little, because he rarely calls me, he is not very interested in me... we get in touch only for material reasons, it's bad to say material... only when I need to buy something.

Therapist: So you feel fatherless?

Elena: Yes.

Therapist: As if he somehow was dead to you?

Elena: Yes, I don't feel the presence of a father, yes!

Therapist: Does he know about this? Does he feel it or does he deny it?

Elena: No, I think he has understood this a little. I mean, sometimes I call him, but only because I make an effort, or because they tell me to. At other times, if it were up to me, I wouldn't call him at all, because every time I call him I don't know what to say, or else I feel he's detached, he asks me about school, which is important to him, while it isn't so much for me. School is everything for him, it's as if he only judges me on my academic performance.

Therapist: So the only thing he's interested in is school?

Elena: And soccer!

Therapist: Why, do you play soccer?

Elena: No, I'm talking about my favorite team.

Therapist: Which is?

Elena: Lazio... because he knows I'm a big supporter, so the subjects we talk about the most are school and soccer, otherwise we've got nothing to talk about!

The problem of the telephone

Therapist: Have you ever thought that he betrayed you for another person? That he left a daughter to be with a partner?

Elena: I've never thought that a parent could betray a child for a partner, and this goes for both mom and dad, even though our relationships are different. But it seems to me that since he has been with this woman things have been different, as if she held him back. Yes, I can say this.

Therapist: What does he do to avoid being held back?

Elena: For instance, he rarely calls me from home, and he doesn't do anything about it.

Therapist: What do you mean: he's embarrassed about calling from home because his partner might think that he calls his daughter too much?

Elena: Yes. He always calls me from his car, because when he arrives home it's a mess, there are the children, there's her. So he calls me from the car. Also I call him when I know he's coming back home.

Therapist: So you never call him at home?

Elena: Well, rarely.

Therapist: And who calls more?

Elena: I do!

Therapist: Why?

Elena: Because he won't call me!

Therapist (addressing the father): Do you agree?

Father: Well personally I don't agree about a lot of these things!

Therapist: Can you tell me which ones?

Father: Well, first of all I can speak about stupid things such as phone calls. Can I speak honestly? It really gets on my nerves, because I spend my life on the phone working, obviously. I think it's ridiculous that I have to call a Residence where a dick-head porter keeps me waiting for ten minutes. Professor, I can't waste ten minutes.

Therapist: Why do you have to go through the switchboard to talk to her?

Father: Of course! You have to pass through the switchboard and you start counting, one two three, who knows where Elena will be, maybe she's with the grandmother, or with the mother, or with the aunt, and then ten minutes pass. Dear professor, let me tell you: it's not for me!

Therapist: Did you ever give her a cell phone?

Elena: I have one, I have one. My cell phone is always switched on!

Father: Okay, okay. When I call her, I'll call her directly on the cell phone.

Therapist: So you don't have to pass through the switchboard, after all?!

Father: When I need to and have the possibility I call her on the cell phone. When I haven't got my cell phone or I can't I have to go through the switchboard, because I can't remember anything, I can't remember phone numbers, so I call the Residence, that is the only easy number I remember, so then... ten minutes, fifteen minutes, the line goes dead, you have to call back...!

Therapist: Can't you keep your daughter's phone number in your wallet?

Father: I have Elena's number in my diary and on the phone, and I call her when I can. When sometimes I have to use a fixed phone and I don't remember the number...

Therapist: Ah, now I see!

Elena: Okay, it's not such a big deal to learn a phone number! I remember yours. Does it mean that when you haven't got either your diary or your phone you don't call?

Therapist: What's your daughter's phone number?

Father: I don't know, I can't remember it!

The suicide attempt

Elena, like Carla from the therapy session we mentioned earlier, is a writer. She wrote this some time after she attempted suicide:

That night I had no fear,
everything felt meaningless,
everything was different,
I saw things as I never saw them before,
and then I swallowed one hundred and fifty pills,
and I cannot even remember laying down
my heavy head, full of thoughts,
the most absurd ones,
on the pillow.

The following is an excerpt of what she told Andolfi about her suicide attempt when she woke up in the hospital:

Elena: When I woke up from the coma, I can't remember what day it was, I saw dad entering the room. I could have only one visitor at a time. Then he asked me if the following day I would rather have mom or him, and I told him: mom. From that day I always saw mom, because I believed that since mom had gone through bad moments like that, at those extreme levels...
Therapist: She could understand that about you.
Elena: Yes.

The therapy

It's hard to synthesize the therapeutic work of three years in a few pages. The most important goals, nonetheless, have been the redefinition or rather the re-construction, from scratch, of inter-generational boundaries, and the reinforcement of the parental functions, especially the maternal ones, allowing Elena to learn how to live adolescence in a healthy way, without fluctuating between being the pampered princess and her mother's nurse.

During the three years of therapy Elena has encountered, in session, members of her entire relational world who, in different configurations, accepted the invitation to therapy: her family from the hotel; her father, who was split between Elena and his new family; her mother, who was able to rehabilitate herself a second time, this time as a mother, slowly regaining her role as a parent and finding a real home where she could live with her daughter and last but not least, Elena's friends, a source of support often ignored by therapists. Finally, it was also necessary to create a collaborative climate with other professionals, such as the neurologist who disproved the diagnosis of epilepsy and modified the anti-epileptic therapy, so helping her social rehabilitation. In the final phase, there was also the important contribution of an individual therapist, who enabled the girl to imagine herself in the future, once the past had been put to rest.

The follow-up ten years later

Some months ago, about ten years after the end of therapy with this family, Andolfi had a follow-up session with Elena and her mother. Actually this encounter had been planned after Elena had asked for a consultation to address the relationship between her first child and his father, from whom she has separated, and who lives in a city in the north of Italy. The child seldom sees his father who has started a new family, and Elena is afraid that, for her son, this might be a repeat of the bad relationship she had with her father, and that a new wall may be built between parent and child.

Elena had this child, now six years old, from her first relationship, and later married a man with whom she had twins who are now two years old. She has a position of responsibility in the family hotel, but lives with her husband and children in her own apartment.

After greeting each other warmly, the group sits down to remember the therapy and retrace what has happened since then.

Elena says that her relationship with her father has improved, he has changed; they see each other more often and he respects her, both as a mother and as a worker. They seem to have overcome their resentments, due to the fact that Luciano and Tiziana have also found a new equilibrium in their relationship.

What is particularly striking is that the two women recognize how fundamentally the change in the mother has allowed Elena to grow up. Their deep bond of love, complicity and understanding has kept them close in their common invisibility and has become a resource for both, allowing them to play different, and finally adequate roles. Let's see how they tell the therapist this.

Therapist: Elena told me on the phone that you changed a lot!

Mother: She did?

Therapist: I recall that we worked with you as well as with Elena during those sessions, right?

Mother: Yes, yes.

Therapist: And when therapy ended your life was surely different compared to when we met, at the beginning of therapy.

Mother: The empty-bed syndrome, the real man, the fears...

Therapist: The fears... and something more, you felt that your family had not recognized you for such a long time, and because you were creative, they considered you worthless, correct? Do you remember?

Mother: Yes.

Therapist: You had already made the leap back then, but how are you now? On a professional level, on an emotional level...

Mother: Well, the empty-bed syndrome has disappeared, because I feel fine even when I'm alone. I mean, if I sleep by myself, I sleep well. So this is already...

Therapist: It is an enormous change!

Mother: And then, I found a real man!

Elena: They've been together for three years!

Therapist: That's a record!

Mother: Most importantly, it's been three years that I haven't cheated on him! Because I had the tendency to cheat! And I dealt with it. So, inside of me...

Therapist: How did you deal with it?

Mother: By not cheating! Being loyal towards myself, respecting myself as a woman, that means that if I decide I'm in a couple, I live the couple. The moment I feel like cheating, I question the couple and so I can let go.

Therapist: So, has your self-esteem increased?

Mother: Yes, yes, also because I haven't got this continuous need for affection from other people anymore, so...

(She also says that she has had great success on a professional level, and her works of art have been displayed in several exhibitions. Even her ex-husband bought one of her pictures and hung it in his living room.)

Therapist (addressing Elena): Do you see how good she is? And to think that your uncles used to say: "Instead of working, she paints those pictures!"

Mother: Ah, yes, and I've also won with my family: now my father wants to display my pictures and my photos in the hotel rooms. So now they're finally in their place, because I'd painted them for that place, but they took them away to the country house.

Therapist: Really?

Mother: That was the reason why I felt a bit dejected... they didn't value my effort...

Therapist: So now you've been reconsidered by everyone. Your ex-husband reconsidered you, he took one of your pictures, your father reconsidered you...

Mother: My art!

Therapist: What more can you want from life?

Elena: Well! She's also a wonderful grandmother, the children adore her, she helps us!

Therapist: Incredible!

Therapist (addressing the mother): Do you remember the difficult years?

Mother: I sure do! I remember when I felt I was falling apart... I had this feeling of deep sadness, this feeling of emptiness, I felt as if I spoke and no one answered. But I found my balance in the end!

Therapist: You've been very good! And it seems that Elena is now following in your steps.

Mother: Yes, yes.

Elena: Yes, I've broken free too, I go there to work. I mean, now I see the hotel as the place where I work, as a support, because I've always known that I didn't want to live there. I don't like the idea, not for myself or for my children.

Therapist: Now, I know that these are not nice questions... Have you ever reflected on what you were doing when you were 18 years old?

Elena: I was another person then, I mean, I can't recognize myself in that person today. It is as if I had seen a movie or had been told about it!

Therapist (addressing the mother): What about you, can you remember how you were back then, when you were another person? I mean, what do you think about it? Because you did not attempt suicide, nonetheless you came close to completely destroying your life!

Mother: Yes, in fact, I risked my life every day, with drugs, right?

Therapist: That's right. So you never got to the point where you could really have died.

Mother: Yes, but I was worse because I tried to destroy myself little by little.

Therapist: Do you remember that part of your life? Is it a part of you, or do you have the tendency to forget it as well?

Mother: No, I recognize it as my need to escape reality, to escape the fear of facing all those people who surrounded me, because I couldn't handle it, they scared me emotionally. So I sought some sort of cocoon-like environment. Drugs were a kind of cloak for me. Unfortunately I didn't understand that it was the cloak of a demon and that they were poisoning me, but I felt that they were protecting me... And then I told myself that if I had the courage to take those drugs that lead me towards death, I would also have the courage to go towards life! So when I feel vulnerable, when I'm afraid...

Therapist: You find this strength.

Mother: I tell myself: "I have to win this, precisely because I've already won so many battles!"

Therapist: So, who saved you? Was it your daughter, or was it the thought of having a daughter? What was it that...?

Mother: I thought I had to save myself for the sake of this child!

Therapist: So it was really her *(pointing at Elena)*. You were always trying to understand the reason why she was born, right? Wasn't it so?

Elena: Yes.

Therapist: So you see how important you were? And not only to yourself. Who knows where mom would be today if you hadn't been there?

Elena: In heaven!

Therapist: You have really been her anchor. And that is why you helped her so much.

Mother: Yes, very much!

Therapist (addressing the mother): She protected you! We adults always say that we protect our children, but often it is the opposite, right? Not only that, there were moments when no one recognized you in your own house, you were treated very badly. I remember the sessions as if it was yesterday. The only person who supported you was your daughter. Isn't that so?

Mother: Yes, yes, I can see that!

Therapist: You two have helped each other a lot.

Elena: Yes, a lot.

Chapter 5
Enlarging the therapeutic system

SIBLINGS DURING ADOLESCENCE AND IN THERAPY

Siblings grow up, mature and grow old together. The fraternal bond covers all phases of existence, from childhood to old age. It is the most durable bond and, because of this, its intensity varies according to circumstances. Salvador Minuchin (1974) defined the fraternal relationship as the *keeper of the family frontier*.

We have stated in previous chapters that brothers and sisters do not always carry the same value within the family. There can be *white and black knights* (Whitaker, 1989), who are considered, by the family, to possess either healthy or pathological skills, they can be healthy or vulnerable, and so on. When there is a great discrepancy between one child and another, and when there is a hypothetical first-rate as opposed to a second-rate child, this means that we are in the presence of distortions which need to be examined to identify negative triangulations, according also to gender, birth order, and other relevant events that took place within the family. These variables cause the children to take different and sometimes diverging paths, sometimes planned from the beginning (from the moment of conception), by parents and by the extended family. We just need to consider the choice of names, which often mirrors the rules, traditions, and myths of the family, and which anticipates differing and sometimes contrasting destinies. Much further along in the life of siblings, the moment of inheritance can trigger conflict and competitions, and is the litmus test of the quality of family relationships. It is precisely the allocation of assets after the parents' death, at once a concrete and emotional event, which re-configures the ways in which the family planned the children's destiny and the nature of their relationships. Often, in the face of blatant emotional injustices the result can be the building of barriers and complete emotional disconnection between siblings or, in other cases, endless fights between the new families. It is indeed possible to avoid these heavy disruptions by the older generation on the following one, but it can often happen at extremely high personal and relational costs, because it is sometimes necessary to "betray the parents" in order to reach an agreement between siblings, and escape those powerful invisible loyalties made up of family credits and debts (Boszormenyi-Nagy, Spark, 1973).

Another important element attesting to the quality of the relationship between siblings is what Bank and Kahn (1982) define as *level of access*: belonging to the same gender and age proximity determines high access, and in these cases the relationship between siblings is characterized by reciprocity, symmetry, and empathy (Dunn, Plomin, 1990), and by the sharing of emotional experiences, leading to an intimate and tight bond qualified by a high degree of loyalty. Conversely, siblings with low access often belong to different genders and act as though they belonged to different generations: the age difference is at least eight to ten years, and therefore do not have a shared history. They are characterized by a "partial dis-identification," as defined by Bank and Kahn, which can bring a sense of alienation. Moreover, nowadays the increase in step-families has caused an increase in siblings with low access, as there can be a big age difference between the children of the first marriage and the children of the new couple.

Nonetheless, we have to say that although we have often found confirmation of the above in our clinical practice, there have also been opposite situations, with children who were close in age but totally incapable of collaborating and sharing life experiences, as well as siblings of widely differing ages where the eldest became a kind of hero for the youngest, a guide to follow in times of difficulty. In short, the horizontal relationship between siblings, regardless of gender and age, depends greatly on how much the parents allow their children to become siblings, without triangulating them negatively and without involving them in their couple dynamics and in *family mandates*, which sometimes undermine the natural generational alliance between siblings.

The participation of the sibling subsystem in joint family sessions, with its specific way of functioning, is an excellent opportunity to evaluate the permeability of family boundaries (Minuchin, 1974) and to identify possible "parentification" of children (Framo, 1992) or, in any case, those considered essential to the family balance. It also represents an important therapeutic resource during critical and conflicting times within the family, as we will shortly see.

Being the siblings of children with physical or psychological problems is inherently a great challenge to the creation of a generational alliance: a child with a severe or chronic illness is generally over-protected by the parents or by the wider family, while healthy children, on the other hand, are inevitably more emotionally neglected, or given an adult role from a very young age.

We have verified in therapy that the siblings of children with severe psychiatric or physical disorders, needing constant care, can be roughly divided into three categories: those totally involved in the situation of the sick sibling, who give up their freedom in order to take care of the brother, absorbing the emotional atmosphere of the family and who, in adolescence, are likely to experience profound sadness, often neglected, as everybody's attention is focused on the other's illness. In the second group are those young people who, in time, flee and build their interests outside the problematic family: they are often accused of selfishness and are guilt-ridden for having "run away from home" and for having prioritized their needs over a series of problems of a brother. The third group includes the healthy children who constantly mediate between the needs of the sick sibling and the often critical or judgmental responses of the parents.

The volume *La terapia narrata dalla famiglia* (Andolfi, Angelo, D'Atena, 2001) describes a comprehensive longitudinal follow-up study to evaluate the results of family therapy. Interviewing siblings helped us to understand many things: first of all, we understood how difficult it is to create joint family motivation, where each member, on the one hand, makes an effort to be available for therapy for a common project while, on the other, examines what personal implications and individual benefits therapy might have. Many adolescents, who had been in therapy because of a sibling's psychological problems, told us in follow-up sessions that they had not really understood the reason for their presence in so many sessions, all focused on the problems of the sick sibling. They admitted that they participated only because the parents had pressured them to do so for the sake of the common good. In some cases, we perceived the disappointment or regret that they had not found an adequate space in therapy to talk about their own problems or unattended needs within the family.

An anorexic girl, who had begun therapy in a physically and psychologically critical condition told us, in a follow-up session three years after the end of therapy that, for a long time, she had thought that she did not actually have a sister, and only regarded her as a bother. Only once she recovered—at the age of seventeen—was she able to rediscover the pleasure of having a sister. The latter, two years younger, was able to finally admit that she had hated her for all those years, because she took her parents away from her, and they did not follow her education with the same care and attention they gave her sister.

All of this confirms, again, that illness deeply affects the family's emotional assets, often dividing siblings, and causing strong feelings of exclusion in those whose role is that of healthy children. The scope of therapy should be not only to cure the one with a severe problem, but also to redraw the boundaries between generations and strengthen the alliance and harmony between siblings.

We have often tried to encourage the discovery of emotional harmony between siblings, often holding specific sessions with only this subsystem. The fact that parents were not present during those sessions represented a clear and strong act of differentiation between the two generational levels and a rare opportunity to allow adolescents to interact without the adults' interference or mediation.

The children's evaluations and suggestions on how to change the family's highly dysfunctional relational modalities have always been very useful. On the one hand we were interested in the past: the history of the family and the children's development over the years, the most significant events in the life cycle of the family preceding the illness/disorder of the child who brought the family to therapy, the relationship between the parents, both at the care-giving and guidance level and that of couple dynamics. We often erroneously think that the marital territory is private, forgetting that children are the privileged witnesses and the interested observers of the way in which their parents form a couple, especially during adolescence, when they begin to experiment with romantic relationships. If we wish to create a strong understanding between siblings these are fundamental ways in which we can activate them. It is often surprising the maturity and balance they demonstrate when speaking of themes that are taboo at home.

It was later useful to investigate the present, where the illness/disorder of the child dominated everything: we tried to explore how the territories of illness and health were kept distinct within the family, with a net division of functions — those of the healthy child and of the sick one — and we tried to recreate a unique competence, that of siblings, using each other's different life experiences.

We have seen, within this book, how to redefine dysfunctional behavior and what is the cognitive and experiential value of many psycho-pathological symptoms. We would also like to redefine and broaden the boundaries of healthy children, who often suffer from a lack of genuine interest towards their hidden vulnerabilities and pathologies. It is surprising to see how liberating this can be for siblings, who can finally give words to the feelings and moods experienced in solitude.

After exploring the family level and building a connection of true understanding between siblings, it is possible to explore the young person's relationship with the outside world, the school and the group of peers. When we leave the family environment, we can often observe the extreme vulnerability of those who have bullied their parents with their illness (think about anorexic or psychotic patients) when facing the out- side world: the real fears are often outside the home, even though the emotional battles are fought within it. Sessions with siblings can become a privileged space where we can better understand the social openness of each member and a resource we can later use in joint family sessions.

Practice illustration: Love transforms the bond between two siblings from sickness to health

Edith is anorexic. She is still in hospital at the time of this ses- sion, although her general health is improving. Her mother, grandfather, and older brother suffer for a genetically transmitted disorder of the pan- creas. Edith's parents divorced when she was 4 and her brother, Patrick, was 7. The mother then remarried and had a little boy called Serge, who is not present at the session.

The dialogue below is taken from a live family consultation by Andolfi, in Paris, two years ago: Edith is now 18 years old, Patrick is 21, the parents and maternal grand-mother are also present at the session, together with their therapist who has been working with them for over a year.

An exchange of sickness

Consultant: So, you contacted a family therapist to help you with which problem, specifically?
Edith: I am anorexic.
Consultant: So you brought your family to therapy?
Edith: They suggested that I should have therapy.
Consultant: But, without your anorexia they would never have come here?
Edith: Well, I think that we really need it, but we would never have asked for therapy if my illness had not been so serious.

Consultant: I understand, maybe I am wrong, I think that between Patrick and Edith there has been a kind of swapping of sickness over the years... No? Do you understand what I mean? Patrick was the first who had some physical difficulties, is it true? Were they serious?

Patrick: Painful.

Consultant: Painful, can you explain it to me a little? I am a doctor.

Patrick: Well, it is linked to the pancreas, it comes from my mother and my grandfather, it is a disorder of the pancreas, it makes it destroy itself, and sometimes it brings painful crises.

Consultant: Where do you feel the pain?

Patrick: (indicating his belly) Here, it's like being stabbed with a knife.

Consultant: Since when?

Patrick: They found it when I was four.

Consultant: So maybe you had it before, but it manifested when you were four.

Patrick: Yes it is genetically transmitted.

Consultant: So you do not remember the first four years without pancreatic pain?

Patrick: No.

Consultant: So, for your whole life, till now, it is Patrick who has been fighting with his pancreas.

Patrick: As my mom did.

Consultant: And how did mom overcome the problem?

Patrick: She found out about it very late, and it is an illness that, little by little, destroys the pancreas completely.

Consultant: And it destroyed mom's pancreas?

Patrick: Yes, so now she is diabetic.

Consultant: Is that better or worse?

Patrick: It is less painful but much more complicated.

We have been in conflict all our childhood

Consultant: (To Edith): So, for many years you grew up with a brother who was a medical worry, always in crisis and needing help.

Edith: During his crises I shut down and waited for it to pass, I thought it was something he did to get attention, I think my thoughts were not right, and I was wrong about many things.

Consultant: You thought the crises were a trick.

Edith No, I knew they were real and he was suffering, but I was taking this very badly and I never asked Patrick, when he had a crisis, if he needed any help.

Consultant: So you two were not a team?

Edith: No.

Consultant: Never?

Edith: I think we were a team, the three of us, after the separation but...

Consultant: Yes, but a team made up of a brother and sister is different from a team which includes a mother.

Edith: We have been in conflict all our childhood and we finally started to accept each other during adolescence, only a few years ago.

Consultant (to Patrick): And what did her anorexia mean for you? Pancreas is a genetically transmitted illness linked to the family, but anorexia is such a weird disorder that sometimes you might think it is spoilt behavior, something strange; it is not a proper illness like the one due to the pancreas. But you can die, actually there is more risk of dying of anorexia, if it gets very bad, than with the pancreas.

Patrick: We do not run the risk of dying with this disease of the pancreas, but it is a psychological illness too. I went to see a psychologist who helped me a lot; I think that now it is definitely a painful time for Edith, painful for the family, but for me it is a good thing that she has been doing therapy which includes the family: we would never have done it, if there had not been this problem with Edith.

A Greek drama

Consultant: Dad, how do you understand the history between your kids? What would you like to see changing in their relationship?

Father: It is true that the first time Patrick went to hospital, it was a trauma for everybody. For me, who did not know anything about this illness, for my wife and for my mother-in law, it has been a catastrophe, it has been a shock for us as a couple, as well.

Consultant: Did the couple relationship start to break down because of this?

Father: No, this is not what I meant, but it has been a really hard period, we had been very strong and close together for one year and then maybe there was a release of tension and consequently a few years later... the divorce.

Consultant: So, Patrick's problem has been an earthquake for the family.

Father: Yes. The first time, the first 3 months of hospitalization were terrible.

Consultant (to Patrick): Did you know this?

Patrick: No.

Consultant: It is always important to learn things, don't you agree?

Patrick: Yes for me is important to know what happened…

Mother: The hospitalization was longer than it was supposed to be.

Consultant: How old was Edith then?

Mother: She was a year and a half old.

Father: We were going from one to the other, we had to be with Edith, too.

Consultant: So it has been a really hard period of your life.

Mother: I remember precisely when, during the hospitalization, we realized that it could be the same problem my dad had. And it was me, my dad and Patrick , the three of us… it was fate…

Father: A Greek drama.

Consultant: And your daughter has been breathing in a lot of Greek drama and she is now living her own drama, but she can heal with anorexia.

Mother: … She nearly died twice.

Consultant: Yes, but 90% of anorexics manage to heal completely, it is true that she is running a big risk with her life, we cannot minimize it, but we need to understand how to overcome it, and she has all the resources to overcome it, but something needs to happen on an emotional level.

Is magic possible? Love can conquer disease

Consultant: Can we try a magic trick? Could we reduce the distance between you two and see if it is really that hard?

Patrick: Do we have to get close?

Consultant: Yes, as close as you can.

(Patrick moves his chair closer to his sister)

Consultant: Wait, is this the best you can do?

Patrick: No, but it is true that…

Consultant: Don't speak, let the feeling be there between you, without words.

(Patrick moves his chair a little closer.)

Consultant: Is this the closest? Wait…is it embarrassing for you, because you are a man?

Patrick: Yes, it is embarrassing but not because I am a man. Maybe it is because of my illness, I often think I am selfish, I think in a selfish way.

Consultant: Are you happy to feel your sister next to you?

Patrick: Yes

Consultant: (To Edith) And you? Are you happy?

Edith: Yes

Consultant: Then stay close and feel it.

(*Both brother and sister are moved by this emotional closeness and put their arms on each other's shoulder and kiss each other very tenderly.*)

Consultant: Stay like this a little longer and experience how much you love each other. This is the kind of magic we can do, we cannot heal the pancreas, but we can heal the distance between two siblings. How long have you been waiting for this?

Edith: For a long time.

Patrick: We made some attempts at the hospital, but only because of the illness, it was not natural.

Consultant: You should meet each other in health, as brother and sister, with love, because you have shared a family who struggled together and then was separated. You shared a lot of difficult experiences, you share a little brother, you are the most relevant couple, a very solid unit which is more important than hospitals or medications. This is a special strength (*indicating their closeness*) and not so difficult to get, either. Mom, dad, and grandma have been waiting for this for a long time but they could not force it, it is something between you two. Pancreas and anorexia are relatively important, but it is your love that gives you strength.

Patrick: It is true that we are not simple people, and it is difficult for us to say nice things to each other.

Edith: Patrick has always been very emotional, and I am, too; if I show it less it is because I'm afraid to be too sensitive and I think that this is our weakness ... we created a distance in order not to suffer.

Consultant: It is not just a weakness, the fact of being sensitive, it might be difficult to accept, it might make life harder to live, but it allows us to experience difficulties and joy, too; do you understand what I mean? Can I make a suggestion? Try to feel the physical contact, the smell of proximity more, leave your head out. You use words to keep distance, maybe this is coming from higher up: maybe you learnt this from your parents?

Patrick: We are Protestants.

Consultant: What has that to do with what I was saying?

Patrick: Yes, I would say we have the tendency to keep a distance, to rationalize things and to deal with them intellectually.

Consultant: When you meet each other, could you forget that you are Protestants?

Patrick: It is part of our culture.

Edith: I just want to add something that I believe is important: I have the impression that before my illness my parents, although they have rebuilt their lives, had always been strong and had a good relationship, but since I have been sick, the situation has been deteriorating between them, there is a bit of distance and I hate that, and I am sorry for this.

Consultant: Yes, in fact their separation has been worn down because of the illness, so maybe you need to change ways to keep everyone together; through strength you can meet with each other in a better way, because in this family the joining through illnesses has been stronger than through health, you need to make a change, and love is the best medicine.

This therapeutic segment illustrates very clearly the importance of sibling bonds and how to facilitate a deep experience of closeness and love between two problematic children during a family session.

Too often psychotherapy has been described as a cognitive encounter based on verbal exchanges and therapeutic conversations. On the contrary, after many years of experience and follow up of family interventions we are convinced that the language of the body, the active use of physical space (closeness versus distance) and touch are very powerful means of encouraging deep personal/interpersonal transformations.

Getting close, putting an arm around a sibling's shoulder, kissing each other tenderly are extraordinary healing devices in an appropriate therapeutic context, as shown by Edith and Patrick; even more relevant because it happens in front of the parents and grand-mother, who are witnesses and indirect participants in this transformation. Illness might divide, but mutual love can restore harmony.

A year later, after this single consultation, Andolfi was contacted via e-mail (very unusually, through a common family friend), first by the father and then by Edith, because of that session's positive impact on every family member. They expressed the desire to have another meeting with him in Rome (!) or in Paris in the near future.

THE ADOLESCENT AND HIS FRIENDS IN SESSION

Friends carry a very important emotional value throughout life, though they have different functions at different life stages. Friends are our playmates during childhood, and become the first points of reference outside the family through which we value and measure ourselves in a social context. Moreover, they represent an emotional support at those times of life when we need to revise the process of separation-individuation, having the positive function of containing the pain caused by hardship. They help us heal the emotional wounds that life inflicts on us and compensate for the shortcomings in our other relationships, as in the case of illness, bereavement, hostile couple separation, and loneliness.

Let us consider, for example, the value of peer groups for teenagers with separated parents: the adolescents help one another and share the thoughts and emotional difficulties arising from the disintegration of their families through the contexts and rituals typical of this time of life. Friendships are places where people can develop parts of themselves that are inaccessible or unexplored within the family.

The enormous emotional value of friends resides in the fact that they represent the memory of our familial and social developmental processes, as they have shared with us a portion of our existence and with them, over the years, we have built a relationship full of confidence and deep understanding.

In some cases, friends might even embody the family: for instance, people who are very alone or troubled and suffer from constant feelings of marginalization or loneliness, might find comfort in friends who demonstrate a genuine interest in their life.

Russell Haber was the first therapist who used friendships in therapy (Andolfi, Haber, 1994), and theorized that friends had a particular function as consultants in family therapy. In reality, Haber discovered this by chance during family therapy with an aggressive adolescent. Therapy had helped with some family problems, but had not succeeded in modifying the boy's behavioral problems at school. Asking the boy's friends to participate in the session turned out to be a great resource in overcoming the impasse and from that moment Haber decided to include it as a therapeutic tool. Following his example, for many years we have conducted sessions with friends in therapy: thus, we invite to sessions the friends of teenagers, the friends of the couple, and of adults in general, those of the elderly and the friends of immigrants, who are the real and privileged witnesses of the family's uprooting and of the distance from the social and family world they came from. The objective is always the same: to explore the social context that will allow us to broaden our view of the family and of the individual's problems, and to find concrete resources in the emotional world of those who come to seek help. Asking for help from a friend, even in therapy, activates solidarity and understanding. These are very important to people who are experiencing a moment of particular weakness and need to regain faith in themselves and in their relationships.

Friends are, in fact, a group of privileged witnesses to the development of the adolescent outside the family, and can offer different and very useful descriptions of his life.

Practice illustration: Luisa's brother and friends in session

In Luisa's case, the obese girl we spoke about in the third chapter, we can appreciate the benefit of having a joint session with the subsystem made up of siblings, friends and boyfriend, all belonging to the
same generational level.

What follows was taken from a session which took place later in
therapy, when the girl had already lost several kilos. Other participants
to the session are: the brother, Emilio, who is two years younger; Luisa's
boyfriend, Gianluca, and her friend, Emanuela.

Therapist (addressing the entire group): Have you noticed any change in
Luisa lately?
Emanuela: I noticed something, and I can't really accept this thing that
makes me... well, it doesn't make me suffer, but it makes me sad. When
Luisa is chubbier she's always cheerful, she always wants to joke around.
Our friendship is solid... I really feel good when I'm with her, and I
laugh a lot. But when she loses weight, I don't know why, maybe it's be-
cause of the effort she makes... she is more restrained, she seems more
serious, more quiet, less cheerful...
Therapist: More adult?
Emanuela: Yes.
Emilio: More adult!
Emanuela: And I feel sorry, because I want her to be cheerful all the time!
Emilio: That's true, she's right!
Therapist (addressing Luisa): Did you see? Your friend really understands
this!
Emilio: I had noticed this as well, but I thought I was the only one.
Therapist: So in these two months of therapy we really created a problem
by making you lose weight!
Emanuela: No, I want her to lose weight, but I also want her to remain
cheerful!
Emilio: Sometimes she hits rock bottom, she goes over the top a little bit,
and at other times she tries her very best and... I have no idea! I don't
know what happens to her!
Therapist (addressing Luisa): What have you understood about yourself
through these encounters with your family? What would you tell them
today, in simple words?
Luisa: Yes, well... first of all, in the various sessions we had I understood
that my anxiety was not just down to me, that I looked disgusting, and

so on. I understood that things are caused by various factors, and not only by one person.

Therapist: So, we've overcome the "disgust syndrome"!

(Everyone laughs.)

Luisa: More or less! I've also thought a lot about what you told me, about the "joker," because I'm aware of certain things, but that is not enough.

Therapist: Do they know about the joker?

Luisa: No, they don't.

Therapist: Do you want to tell them yourself?

Therapist (addressing the friends): Do you play cards?

Luisa: The adoption is the joker: I use the adoption to hide myself, to justify myself, I use it as I like.

Gianluca: Like a joker!

Luisa: Yes.

Emilio: Am I wrong, or wasn't it the same with the fat?

Luisa: It's true, it's a difficult situation, because when I lose weight I feel like I have to play a different role, like I have to be good when I'm slim, I have to do certain things and in a certain way, while when I'm fat it doesn't matter!

Emanuela: You really let yourself go!

Gianluca: Anyway, the last time she lost weight, when she became thin as a rake...

Therapist: When?

Emilio: When she went on the super diet!

Luisa: Last summer I lost twenty kilos!

Gianluca: That's it, when she finally lost weight, I remember her telling me: "Now I've dealt with this problem, but I see there are many other things I have to deal with"...

Gianluca (addressing Luisa): As if you had been caught out, is that right?

(Luisa nods.)

Emilio: I think that maybe she thought that this was her only problem, and saw it as her goal in life. Once I get over this, she said to herself, I won't have any more problems, but when she lost weight she realized that there might be bigger problems. So she said to herself: "it is better to go back to being fat, so my goal will be to lose weight and I won't have to think about other things!"

This brief excerpt allows us to observe first of all that in a group of peers, who are all aware of her issues — though everyone has a very different role: brother, friend, boyfriend — it is possible to speak frankly, simply and rapidly about such fundamental themes as the identity of an adolescent, adoption, obesity, the themes that are very present in Luisa's life, which can each be used as a joker behind which she can hide and avoid growing up, thus shirking the responsibilities that come with normality. You can be cheerful when you are fat, but you can also be happy when you are slim, if you can leave behind the "weights" that belong to others. All of this is the message and the positive reinforcement that the peer group offers Luisa, who will surely treasure this.

Practice illustration: Twelve friends... can be enough!

The case of Claudia and Roberto, two adolescent siblings who grew up with parents who emotionally abused them, was very different, and the participation of their friends in a session was strongly liberating.

The wife has requested couple therapy because of the husband's sexual impotence. He is dragged to the session with the same attitude used when going to court: she is very dissatisfied and attacks him verbally, without any respect. The wife's description of the sexual dysfunctions is very explicit and vulgar, and the husband appears to be totally "impotent" and powerless in the face of her insults. Moreover, the lady is quite unattractive and decidedly obese.

It seems quite difficult to begin couple therapy under these premises, but what seems more appalling is that the adolescent children have always been involved in the couple's dynamics, including their sexual problems. The mother constantly complains to them about the husband's sexual problems, while he elicits their pity with his passivity and total submission to the wife. There are no generational boundaries and the children are tossed around, without any respect or care for their feelings.

We propose a therapeutic approach whose primary goal is "taking the children out of the parent's bedroom," which, luckily, everyone accepts. It is quite a concrete and meticulous plan, based upon the essential principle that children should be kept out of couple issues for the entire day, to create a protective wall between generations. What happens during the week is regularly monitored in following sessions, and we later reach the decision that sessions should be held alternatively with the parents and with the children subsystem.

The agreement to keep the children away from their parents' bedroom actually frees the children from an extremely embarrassing and shameful situation, and allows the parents, for the first time, to do something productive for their children's wellbeing, and this is a huge step in itself. Once the dysfunctional triangulation in which the adolescents are caught is weakened, their direct collaboration during the sessions without parents becomes fundamental in rebuilding a strong generational understanding. At this point we suggest that we might invite their friends to a session, and the two siblings accept enthusiastically.

At the following session they bring twelve friends, as if to demonstrate that their friendship network is very solid; in fact, we realize how important it is for Claudia and Roberto to have a peer group to hold onto outside the family home. During this encounter we talk about many things: school, music, travels, and other things typically adolescent subjects, joking and laughing, as if the vital energy of adolescence had finally entered that room, where a lot of vulgarity and immaturity had been before. The adolescents then continue their meeting in a pizza restaurant.

Practice illustration: Giovanni and his dog

When there are pets in a home, especially cats or dogs, they always carry a very important emotional value for family members and for children and adolescents in particular. These are often very profound "love stories," especially when they involve abandoned or neglected animals and their saviors.

Dogs and cats can represent an anchor for marginalized people, and can help when mourning the loss of loved ones, absorbing the affection and attentions we had for those who passed away. They can often have functions that are complementary or substitute human relations (Bruni, 2009). A dog, for instance, on the one hand can enrich the world of emotions, and on the other have vicarious functions. As in Giovanni's case: we spoke about him in the previous chapter. He is the boy who laid down various times on unused railway tracks, ready to be run over.

Giovanni is a fourteen-year-old boy, the only son of two doctors. He is very depressed and sends very obvious and alarming signals to try and get his parents' attention, an extremely hostile couple constantly at war. His situation is desperate, alleviated only by his dog Charlie, a magnificent German shepherd. This is why we ask Giovanni to bring his dog to a session, and he accepts willingly, smiling broadly for the first time.

The family comes from Sicily, and faces a long car journey to bring Charlie to Rome. The following excerpt describes the value of this dog in Giovanni's life.

Therapist (addressing Giovanni): If there had been another child instead of Charlie, a brother or a sister, what would have happened at home? Would you have liked it?

Giovanni: No.

Father (with detachment): Let's say that there was a difficult situation at the time: Maria worked, I was also busy, and we didn't have a lot of time to spend with the boy. In fact, Giovanni grew up with his grandmother. We would have had to give his grandmother another child to bring up *(Giovanni beckons the dog.)*, and we wouldn't have been able to deal with two anymore than we were able to deal with one. If both parents work, I think it's difficult to have more children. This was the objective situation!

Mother (annoyed): No, no, we talked about the possibility that I might become pregnant, and you told me unequivocally that in that case I had to have an abortion, you know this very well!

Therapist (he comes near the boy, crouches between him and the dog and begins to stroke Charlie; then he addresses Giovanni): Is it easier to be a child or to be a dog in this family?

Giovanni: A dog!

Father: Giovanni's lying, you know it isn't so!

Therapist: But in this family another child couldn't have been...

Giovanni: A loser like me!

Therapist: Well, maybe you could have shared your misfortune...

Father (still in an annoyed tone): Why don't you tell him about all your privileges at home? Everything you do? You always do what you want, you always want to be in charge!

Mother (addressing Giovanni and completely ignoring the husband): Do you mean that the misfortune is about being an only child?

Father (annoyed): No, is nobody listening to me? At home it's the same, I talk but nobody listens!

Therapist (addressing the parents): I'd like you to remain silent for three minutes and to open your ears.

Therapist (addressing the boy): I asked mom and dad to remain silent for a few minutes, so they can listen to you, and maybe listen also to Charlie who, as you can see, always wants to be petted. What do you say? Will they be able to listen?

Giovanni (visibly moved): Who knows?

(The dog lies on the floor, at the foot of his owner.)

(After a few, sad moments...)

Therapist: So, what do you think? What if there was another child?

Giovanni (with tears in his eyes): I think he would have been very unlucky...

Therapist: Why, have you been very unlucky?

Giovanni: Very.

Therapist: You look so sad right now. Who do you think understood that you are sad?

Giovanni: Who understood? Charlie!

(When the dog hears his name he lies still on the floor, but looks up at Giovanni.)

Therapist (stroking the dog's head): Charlie understood, maybe because you feel a bit like Charlie?

Giovanni: Not completely like Charlie... at least I had the love of my mother for a while, before they started fighting.

Therapist: Do you think you still have it?

Giovanni: I think so.

Therapist: And dad's?

Giovanni: No!

Therapist: How do you think Charlie feels?

Giovanni: Alone.

Therapist: Alone? All alone like a dog?

Giovanni: Yes.

Therapist: And how do you imagine this loneliness, how do you think a dog feels when he's alone?

Giovanni: Unhappy!

This session would not have been the same without Charlie. The fact that the dog was present allowed us to highlight the boy's loneliness and sadness, representing it vividly, in the hope that these parents would be able to see what they could not hear. In fact, Giovanni seems to be more of a burden than a joy for this couple, who actually seem to function better as professionals than as parents, and are too busy competing to have time to collaborate. Giovanni is for them a son they have to deal with, an obligation that needs to be passed on to someone else, while for his dog he is his guiding star, the owner he loves, and who always needs to be looked after. These two relationships are at polar opposites.

The boy's non-verbal behavior during the session, the cuddles with his dog, the sadness he projects on the *imaginary brother* (Andolfi, Haber, 1994) are factors that contribute to the creation of a particular context where even the parents are able — perhaps for the first time — to feel their child's pain; a child who lives his adolescence by himself, locked up in his room, and who is luckily taken care of by a loyal dog. If even a dog can feel this boy's sadness, what will it take to make his parents aware of it, too?

NETWORK INTERVENTIONS

The concept of network refers to all those systems, whether primary or secondary in the life of each individual, which can act as resources to support therapeutic interventions.

Network therapy was developed during the Seventies by Ross Speck and Catherine Attneave (1975). It is a model of clinical intervention that characterizes itself as *expanded family therapy* (involving friends, relatives, neighbors, and so on) which activates the therapeutic forces found in the social fabric of those who are affected by psychiatric pathologies. The two authors further identified networks of networks they called "tribes," which can offer people a chain of relationships, and giving a sense of identity and belonging to a wider social context.

Thirty to forty years ago, the social level was the framework through which we observed the normal or pathological development of the family. It was not even possible to describe a family without highlighting the fundamental elements that showed the qualities and problems of its members' social relationships.

Community was the resource to be activated when a family was in difficulty because of marital problems or the individual psychological dysfunction of a family member. Home visits were a frequent and effective procedure in the vast majority of Institutional Health Services, especially so during crises. A similar social value was given to Team meetings, where different professionals caring for the patient, whether an individual, a couple or a family, all sat around the same table.

The first historical international conferences organized by Andolfi and the Institute of Family Therapy took place in Rome in 1975 and later, in Florence, in 1978. The title of these conferences was *Family Therapy within the Community*, to emphasize the community as the privileged place where therapists could observe and help families with problems.

We should now ask ourselves what has become of the social framework in therapy. On the one hand, there is a return to individual interventions, in line with today's increase in individualism: think about the number of publications on individual systemic-relational therapies or about the "postmodern" idea that even individual interventions are forms of family therapy. On the other hand, increased social exclusion, the social disintegration of Western-Country families and the increasing migration phenomena, with a huge presence of different cultures in these countries, should make us return to network interventions, the path of which was traced by family therapists during the Seventies. Suffice it to mention the extraordinary experiences of Ross Speck (Speck,

Attneave, 1975), Salvador Minuchin (Minuchin, Montalvo, Guerney, Rosman, Schumer, 1967), Albert Scheflen (1973), Dick Auerswald (1968, 1972), and Israel Zwerling (Andolfi, Zwerling, 1980), among others.

In March 2005, Andolfi wrote an article for a special edition of the Italian journal *Terapia Familiare*, entitled "Il ritorno al sociale; un utopia o una necessità per i terapeuti familiari?"

Among many thoughts concerning this question, he wrote: "Sometimes I ask myself where creativity has gone, the vitality of a movement that for so many years had looked for resources within the families in difficulty who came looking for help and within the world of their social relationships. I feel the same about case discussions by an open and passionate multidisciplinary team, in contrast with today's new and detached system paradigms, often built *on* patients instead of *with* their active contribution."

Following this line of thought, focused on a "return to the social," a year later the Accademia di Psicoterapia della Famiglia organized an international conference on *Working with Marginalized Families and Communities*, in the city of Oaxaca, in southern Mexico. The goal of this conference was to embrace the significant experiences of many professionals who work at grass-root level in the most different and remote places on the planet. The emotional context created there was touching: listening to experiences of work in environments that were violent, poor, and marginalized, such as Colombia, Mexico, Brazil, Egypt, or Palestine, just to mention a few. What was even more striking was the creativity and ideas of those who presented and represented — through footage and photo-montages of excellent quality — social and family contexts which were at once deprived and full of undreamed-of resources. In short, the framework consisted of community therapy and psychosocial interventions, where everyone dealt with the problems that arose. Barreto and his group of Fortaleza (Barreto, 2008) demonstrated network interventions reminiscent of the pioneering work of Ross Speck, where everyone dances, eats and talks together, feeling the strength that comes from solidarity on a concrete level and the reality of basic social needs. Each day of work was concluded by the Symphonic Orchestra of Medellín, made up of adolescents, 33 of whom participated in the conference, rescued from the streets and given the opportunity of becoming concert performers of the highest level. This is a psychosocial program which follows the motto: "A child who learns how to play a musical instrument will never carry a gun." This is how we move from armed gang to musical band!

We direct the interested reader to *The Oaxaca Book* (Andolfi, Calderón, 2008) for further information.

In fact, network interventions are still very useful today during situations of crisis, of personal, family or environmental danger and during emergencies, as they provide a strong response to a serious problem by using the greatest number of resources available. This work focuses on the value of primary networks, made up of the relationships a person builds during his life, not only with his family, but also with neighbors, friends, and work colleagues.

HOME VISIT

If we assume that we get to know families better within their own natural environment than in our offices, we can better understand how useful home visits are.

It is no accident that, during the Seventies and Eighties, when understanding the social and environmental components of specific individual symptoms or relational conflicts became particularly important, *home visits* became quite a common procedure in our Psychiatric Institutions, and provided an extraordinary contribution to the treatment of patients and families. Nathan Ackerman was the first who spoke about home visits, and experimented with them in the postwar period. At the Child Guidance Clinic, in the heart of a South-Philadelphia ghetto, Salvador Minuchin and Braulio Montalvo held supervision sessions in the supermarket and met families in the most run-down neighborhoods of the city. In New York, there were multidisciplinary teams who regularly had meetings with families in their own homes.

During those years, home visits were also common in Italy. This still happens today, but only sporadically, and in particularly enlightened centers. The reasons given for this are very diverse: traffic jams, lack of time, or heavy case loads. Even though these are valid reasons, we believe that the whole intervention philosophy has changed: it has become increasingly technical, mediated by drugs and by impersonal and bureaucratic procedures. The patient, alone or accompanied by someone, needs to come to our offices — the public ones bleaker, the private ones more comfortable — but they are all based upon the same principle: we, the professionals, will not give up our institutional certainties, because they, the patients, are the ones asking for help, and therefore have to adapt to our culture and our rules, as also happens with immigrants.

With the notable increase in biological therapies and individual interventions, home visits have become less and less frequent. Yet, if we resumed these experiences, we would be able to change many of our prejudices and develop a closer contact with our patients, reducing the gap between those who treat and those who are treated.

Many psychotherapists have told us that home visits carry the risk of "making us lose therapeutic power," as if being invited by patients to have a coffee or a bite together could represent a real threat to our expertise. They often ignore the fact that sharing something with them on their level is what makes our interventions truly therapeutic.

Experience and expertise cannot be lost while eating a plate of pasta with the family we usually see in our offices. Of course, if our humanity is constantly monitored by our role and therapeutic interventions, the situation could become uncomfortable and distressing!

However, if it is true that stories heal — as we have often asserted in this book — there is no better place than the homes where our patients live and which speak of their connections, to help us understand those stories and to enrich them with new elements.

Exploring family homes — the parents' and children's bedrooms, the kitchen, the living room, the bathrooms — provides us with much more information on the quality of family relationships and their problems than we can gather in our professional offices. In many cases, we would be able to understand, in a short time, the nature of many relational distortions.

Practice illustration: I know that you know that I know!

On the subject of very dysfunctional family dynamics, we remember a very significant home visit, carried out by Andolfi and a colleague of his, a psychiatrist, thirty years ago in a town two hours from Rome. They would never have understood as well the family's complicity and anorexic dynamic, had they not gone to visit their home.

The girl is not at home, and the visitors are met by the two elderly parents who are finally free to show them what happens in their home. They are taken to the kitchen first, which the daughter occupies all day long. The parents are not allowed to go there, while the daughter cooks fresh food several times a day, and later vomits it in the adjoining bathroom. The father is a farmer, and goes to market three times a day to buy food for his daughter. When he attends therapy in Rome he brings along an enormous quantity of receipts and grocery list. He has kept them all, as if to prove how much he loves his daughter and how desperate he feels.

The visitors leave the kitchen and are lead to the parents' bedroom, where an even greater surprise awaits them. Surreptitiously—as though the daughter might catch them at any moment—the parents show them what they keep under the bed: a small pantry of canned food, which they secretly eat in their room when they are hungry.

What is even more appalling is what they are shown next: it is a game of mirrors which allows them to spy on their daughter and allows her to spy on them. The girl keeps the kitchen door ajar, because she knows that her parents watch her through the mirror of the slightly open wardrobe door, so they can check on their daughter's eating rituals without being seen.

NEW YORK CRISIS INTERVENTION TEAM

Andolfi still recalls the experience he had in New York during the Seventies, when he was a member of the Crisis Intervention Team, a multidisciplinary team that twice a week would leave the south Bronx Mental Health Center to visit the homes of the families who had requested help for a family member's acute crisis. It could be a young adult having a psychotic episode, an adolescent behaving violently at home, a woman abused by her husband, and so on. They were always emergencies.

In theory, home visits during a threatening or violent episode might seem useless or, at the very least, very dangerous. But if we are willing to overcome fear and prejudice, we can discover differing human realities and unexpected resources: wherever there is violence, desperation is waiting in the adjoining room, and in the next room we may find unexpected hope. So, perhaps, we need to walk through the entire house instead of standing on the doorstep!

Practice illustration: The knife under the pillow

We mention as an example the story of an Italo-American family that had moved to New York many decades earlier. Someone called the Mental Health Service to say that the twenty-two-year-old son had threatened his mother with a kitchen knife. Apparently the boy kept this knife in his bedroom, under his pillow, as a weapon ready for use at all times.

The crisis intervention team is made up of three people: Andolfi, a social worker, and a professional nurse. The mother is visibly shocked, and welcomes them into the living room. She says that her son has locked himself in his bedroom. They ask her to call him so they can talk to him. John comes out: he is tall and well built, and does not seem hostile or to mind their presence.

The visitors introduce themselves and Andolfi tells him that he is an Italian professional temporarily living in the United States. Then he speaks a few words of Italian to the boy who doesn't speak the language well, but understands it. This verbal exchange is a good way of *joining*. Obviously, those who work with immigrants already know that going back to the past and to the migration journey is always an incredible resource, even more so when the one asking the questions comes from their motherland. They go back to their migration history, how they left the grandparents' town near Pisa during the Forties and migrated to New York. The most recent history is the hardest: the parents separated with much violence when John, an only child, was fourteen.

It was, in fact, the mother who thought it would be best for the son, and for the sake of an appearance of family unity, that the house should be divided into two parts: mother and son live on the ground floor, while the ex-husband lives upstairs with his new girlfriend, whom the mother calls "*the bitch.*" It is important to explain that these two levels are connected by an indoor wooden staircase clearly visible from the ground floor: the boundaries between the two homes are only virtual. The father is rarely at home, as he leaves early in the morning and comes back late at night. John has practically no contact with him, and detests him anyway, because he chose the bitch over his mother.

Mother and child live together as a couple, and there is no doubt that the boy, in adolescence, has started to show signs of aggression towards her. He went from being her bodyguard to detesting her for having brought him up in such a chaotic way.

John works as a caretaker in an apartment block, and there he is appreciated for his good conduct: his violence is therefore selective, and primarily directed towards his mother. Even though the issues are quite difficult and confronting, the meeting lasts over an hour: it seems that a safe context has made it easier for mother and son to address these themes without animosity. It seems the boy feels relieved of a burden, as if telling the story of the family, while painful, had a beneficial effect.

During the meeting, Andolfi asks the boy to get the knife, as he wishes to see it. It is like coming in contact with the object representing the relational violence of this family. John hands him a bread knife with a serrated blade. Andolfi takes it, looks at it, puts it on the coffee table and then starts connecting facts, emotions, and resentments in the family by means of the knife. He tries to redefine the threats that John makes towards his mother when he waves the knife in front of her: this gesture shows the impotence of the boy, who expresses through his anger the inconceivable violence which he has been fed all these years and which has, for so long, been present in the house, where a wooden staircase connects two parts of a family at war.

At the end of the encounter, the mother seems very relieved and offers everyone a coffee. With her son, she shows the visitors the family photos hanging on the living room walls. Lastly, Andolfi arranges a session for mother and child at the Mental Health Center, after the boy reassures him that the knife will go back to the kitchen, ready to slice bread.

Practice illustration: Go to Eritrea!

When working with immigrant families it is even more important to understand the problem and observe its familial and social contexts. There are an increasing number of foreign communities in Italy, and they seem to gather in neighborhoods and areas strongly characterized by the presence of their compatriots.

There was an interesting outcome following a home visit made after the Mental Health Department's team of a town in Tuscany requested a consultation from Andolfi after they experienced serious difficulty in treating Samba, a young Eritrean man, who had recently attempted suicide.

The family is made up of an Eritrean mother with three adolescent children from a marriage to an Italian man, who abandoned his family several years earlier to live with his children's babysitter in the north of Italy. From then on, the mother did everything possible to raise the children by herself and provide for their well-being, working all day as a cleaning woman.

Since childhood, Samba, the young man in question, took on the role of deputy father in the family, taking care of his younger sisters. But, as often happens with "parentified" children, Samba, when facing the typical identity crisis of adolescence, went from being the family's main emotional support to embodying its most serious problem through unexpected and serious suicide attempts.

Samba and his family are being treated at the Mental Health Department: a psychiatrist is in charge of his drug treatment, a psychologist does psychotherapy with Samba, and another does family sessions. The institution is heavily invested in this family, nevertheless the treating team says that the results are very unsatisfactory, also because of the family's insufficient cooperation.

The consultation is focused mainly on the team of professionals who are initially somewhat confused by the consultant's suggestion that they "go to Eritrea," a metaphor for the family's home. In fact, insisting that the team should "go to Eritrea" to understand the problem and resources of Samba and his family triggered the therapists' curiosity, and curiosity is an effective antidote to prejudice. In fact, their first reply was: "We don't believe they will accept us in their home and in their neighborhood!" Nonetheless, they were surprised to see the family's reaction to their proposal of a home visit, and felt welcomed by them. The mother had told many of her Eritrean friends that as many as three doctors would come to visit her, and would participate in the Sunday ritual of roasting the coffee, which is a very common practice within the Eritrean community.

What was even more interesting was the subsequent team meeting: the three therapists enthusiastically showed the slides of their visit with the family, singing the praises of Eritrean coffee, as though the doors to a completely unknown world had been opened to them.

At this point therapy could take a different path, because both therapists and the family were able to meet and face their challenges with increased trust. They entered a new territory, which we describe as a *third planet*, where skills are shared and there is no longer a separation between those who treat and are knowledgeable, and those who suffer and, therefore, do not know what to do (Andolfi, 2003).

Practice illustration: When a home visit can heal family grief

This family requested therapeutic support because they had been devastated by the sudden loss of a nineteen-year-old son, who was killed violently and accidentally by a mentally unbalanced person while volunteering in a war-torn country.

For months, the two caring parents and younger sister came to sessions with a deep sense of loss and desperation. Life didn't matter anymore, The mother, a primary school teacher, was unable to work for a while and the father was very concerned about her health. The family home was a recurrent theme during the session: the son's bedroom had been kept as he had left it before his departure, nothing had been touched since that tragic moment, and the father had hidden the key to the room in an attempt to protect his wife from further emotional distress.

Several months of therapy were needed to take a first step in this family's process of mourning: the mother, who actually knew where the key was (mothers always know everything!), steps into the room, which had been kept as a shrine and, crying, she touches the objects, the pillow, and her son's clothes. Entering the son's room was the beginning of a change in the family's emotional system and, by sharing their pain, the three were able to gain the strength to slowly return to normal living. When the two therapists (a male and a female professional) felt they had been fully accepted and trusted, they proposed a special home visit and the family readily agreed with a great sense of unity.

The home visit was an emotionally moving ritual for both family members and therapists: it began at the cemetery at the son's grave and continued later in the family home where the visit to the son's room took place and ended convivially in the living room.

The visit to the cemetery, to the son's room, and the shared lunch were all intimate and irreplaceable moments. Tears and emotions bonded and gave strength to the family and to the therapists, too. Their encounter was authentic and everybody was able to get in touch with the real essence of their common humanity, which is the core of any healing process.

**Practice illustration: An extraordinary session: twenty-three guests...
before Bianca's funeral**

The case of Bianca[6] is a prime example of the need to quickly widen the resources. She came to Andolfi for therapy several years ago in a very advanced state of anorexia: she is bony and haggard, and weighs only thirty kilos; she is 1.73 meters tall (ca. 66 lbs. and 5'8").

The parents are both successful professionals, desperate and powerless in the face of her tenacious refusal to any kind of help. She only agrees to go to therapy with her family. Besides her parents, the younger sister also takes part in therapy. The atmosphere of the sessions is characterized by a sense of hopeless inevitability. Paradoxically, the liveliest person during the session is Bianca herself, who answers the therapist's questions about the family environment when she was a child in a very animated way. She states that there has always been an air of

---

6   The description of this case was taken from the book *Le perdite e risorse della famiglia* (Andolfi, D'Elia, 2007), and later reviewed and improved.

sadness in the family, and that she never saw her mother smile, because she was always going from the sickbed of one relative to the other, both on her own and her husband's side. The latter, in the meantime, was much loved by the women of the house, but always away because of his job, and was detached from his daughter's problems.

The mother states that Bianca's condition had worsened between the first and second session: the girl had asked her to go to her room every night to check whether she was still breathing or not.

Given the dramatic objectivity of the situation and the family's eloquent images of a fine fading line between life and death, the therapist suggests that they should hold an extraordinary session, to which Bianca can invite relatives, friends and colleagues of the parents, everyone she thinks really cares about her and her family and would be present at her funeral, which is now a distinct possibility. Andolfi concludes his unusual request with these words: "Maybe, with their help, we can avoid the funeral!"

This suggestion comes from the realization that there is an announcement of suicide, and that the family seems to be totally powerless and understandably desperate, while Bianca raises the stakes. It also comes from the firm belief that when the nuclear family is in a serious impasse, we need to look for resources in the extended family and friendship systems.

A few days later, much to the therapist's surprise, Bianca's mother calls to tell him that there will be twenty-three people at the extraordinary session. This is the number of persons invited by Bianca.

During his clinical work, Andolfi had met large families several times, but he had never received twenty-three people at the same time. We should mention that the fact that Bianca was able to activate so many people is already a sign of hope and great solidarity.

The encounter is a kind of living representation of the family genogram. Bianca introduces all her guests to the therapist: she has chosen them personally, and only invited the people that she feels are closest to her, and most sincere. She has gathered grandparents, parents, uncles and aunts, cousins, friends and acquaintances, and they all become actors in a ritual of union, whose purpose is to give back life to a girl who seems determined to not want it. The atmosphere is almost festive, as though they are all there to celebrate something, maybe the collective desire to contribute to the rebirth of Bianca and her parents.

As often happens in situations of impending danger, they all offer concrete solutions, make suggestions or give advice on the value of life to Bianca, or the anguished mother, or the absent father, or to the therapist himself. And we believe that the strength of this extraordinary encounter came precisely from the presence of all these people, rather than from the verbal content exchanged during the session. Their presence today, to help Bianca, is a sign of their real interest in the girl and her parents, and represents an incredible therapeutic resource.

The first important outcome of this encounter is that, in the subsequent session, Bianca states that she wants to be hospitalized. Thus begins a long and complex family therapy that will last two years; Bianca and her parents will often say that they met these relatives, or that couple of friends, or those cousins, pointing out to the therapist where they were seated during the joint session. The twenty-three characters of this extraordinary session seem to be "engraved" in the therapist's office and continue to bear witness to the progress made by the girl and her family.

The girl uses the following words to describe the importance of authentic relationships in regaining a positive vision of life:

I try to be like Pollyanna, I look for the beauty in things. There has been a natural selection of persons that has done me nothing but good, as it is better to lose certain people than to find them. I also did the right thing in coming to therapy, as I got to know dad and salvaged my relationship with my sister.

THE SOCIAL CONSTRUCT OF DEVIANT BEHAVIOR AMONG ADOLESCENTS: THE EXPERIENCE OF SOUTH BRONX

South Bronx has been for Andolfi a school of life and a fundamental lesson for understanding the personality development of many adolescents who grow up in neighborhoods broken apart from a familial and social point of view. Through first-hand experience, during the seventies, of over two years spent in a junior high school situated in one the worst areas of the South Bronx (New York, USA)—he has been able to attest that the transgressive and deviant behavior of adolescents becomes an almost inevitable "criminal career" when the basic requirements to build a positive identity are missing. At the same time, he managed to observe the developmental plasticity of a group of adolescents—already heavily stigmatized and marginalized in previous years—and their incredible capacity for personal and social rehabilitation, once there had been the opportunity to create a space for personal growth for everyone at a scholastic and family level.

The project for this research was born from one of his previous experiences in the juvenile prison of Casal del Marmo in Rome, where he operated as a specialist advisor to the judge, supplying psychological and psychosocial profiles of the youngsters in preventive detention. Even back then, Andolfi observed the same elements that he would later find magnified in the South Bronx. The first and most tragic observation was that these kids, once they started breaking the law, transitioned from being people to simply becoming cases. From then on the procedures were strongly bureaucratized and the focus was on the criminal acts rather than on the personality or the potential resources of the adolescent at risk. The general attitude of the Juvenile Justice system was heavily paternalistic (incarceration in the South Bronx was a lot harsher and lacking real structures for rehabilitation) and what was missing wasn't so much the presence of motivated and competent professionals within the preventive detention system, but rather what came after: the need for real social rehabilitation of the adolescent once he returned to his natural environment. Thus the inside and outside of the prison structure became a *continuum* and the teenager progressively lost self-esteem and faith in others, and had no choice but to build himself a negative identity which became the only way he could face the adversities of life.

We now return to the Bronx, to a public school attended mainly by Afro-American and Puerto Rican teenagers, where even the walls exuded racial violence and the police, massively present near the school building, was an integral part of the scholastic system, always ready intervene whenever the school authority requested it or, in case of physical aggression, whenever teachers did. It was a school where boys and girls needed to get entry passes from their teachers to go to the bathroom, which was locked, and were supervised by a "warden." So an inevitable physiological need became confused with or expected to be possible criminal behavior, such as the use of, or dealing in, drugs.

In such a climate, it was difficult to distinguish the aggressor from the victim, since such a vicious cycle of violence made it difficult to understand when to intervene. However, there is no doubt that for students aged between twelve and fifteen the school had lost any educational value and became a school of life where kids learned to build, day by day, criminal careers, transitioning from being neglected and defenseless children to "tough guys of the neighborhood." The literacy and numeracy levels in these environments scored 70-80% below the national average, depriving these teenagers of a dignified working future. Their only other possibility was that of being exploited in occasional hard labor, so that they found it easier and more profitable to join a criminal gang.

The absence of a father figure at home (deviant careers begin in previous generations) and of a social consensus in the neighborhood were substituted by a repressive law, well represented by the police located within the school, that supported teachers who were at a loss and incapable of teaching, so that the idea that coming to school was like going to a house of correction took shape.

The local Mental Health Center, who knew what was happening inside these schools and was associated to the Albert Einstein College of Medicine of New York, accepted Andolfi's proposal (at that time, a Fellow in Social Community Psychiatry), whose aim was to do a systemic field study. They decided to engage the class for two hours per week, together with teachers and neighborhood families (or parts of families). The program also suggested that Andolfi should be integrated into the school council, the decision-making board—mainly concerned with punishments, such as suspension and sending kids to other schools—lead by the Principal, the guidance counselor (a social worker connecting the school to the family), and the teacher's representatives. His presence in this decision-making board also had the unexpected effect, over two years, of decreasing disciplinary action against the students, who knew there was a positive presence within the school council.

The meetings with the group of students, which had been difficult to organize at first, in the course of time became very profitable, as these young people had never felt listened to and taken into consideration by an adult. Andolfi was helped a great deal by Joy, an Afro-American therapist, born and raised in South Bronx—a precious collaboration we would today define as cultural mediation—and maybe because of his broken English and because he was a white foreigner who did not belong to the dominant American culture, never became an object of racist comments in spite of being the only white person there.

It was difficult to find an answer to the questions adolescents commonly asked concerning their identity: "Who am I?" or "Why am I bad?" But it was worth trying to go back to the origins of their "badness" and maybe rediscover a point where to change direction and start looking for values and positive feelings.

The numerous encounters done at school where the participants were, apart from Andolfi and Joy, a single boy or girl and a family member—the vast majority of whom were mothers or grandmothers—were aimed to research the positive. They asked the family members, in a warm and comforting tone, "Mom, can you tell me something positive about John or Michelle?" And often a long silence followed, or perhaps a disconsolate gesture as if to affirm that the son or the daughter was only bad. The question was asked a second and a third time, after which the mother would answer, under her breath, that John was good in playing basketball, or that Michelle could cook well. This was when the boy or the girl lightened up, as they had been able to see a glimpse of hope in their life. It was impressive to observe how a simple positive connotation could impact deeply these teenagers, who had grown up being deprived of everything!

The work with teachers was doubtlessly harder and more difficult, as they were scarcely motivated to find positive aspects in their students, that they addressed with heavy epithets and thought that had lost any chance in social rehabilitation. If anything, the main goal of school lessons was the physical survival of students, as there often was the chance of a negative cycle between teachers and students: the first threatened to suspend them and call the police, while the kids enacted violence. It must also be pointed out that teachers were often confined to South Bronx, so they often were the worst elements in the district. In any case, through support and attention to their complaints, they were able to recover some sort of appreciation of the positive changes in the behavior of students in the classroom.

The same procedure of looking for positive aspects in the single adolescent was extended to families and the neighborhood system in fortnightly encounters that took place in the neighborhood or in the courtyards of their homes, which were often organized by mothers, who had started to see changes in their children.

After two years of daily work in the school, Andolfi and Joy were able to see with their own eyes that the adolescents' personality structures and relational modalities radically transformed whenever these students were given space to find a meaning and a sense in existence, and families and social entities were included as well. This has also been described in a previous publication (Andolfi, 1979). The biggest problem was, and still is, turning researches such as the one described into stable systemic intervention in the school. Such a goal requires inevitably ideas, dedication, economical resources and collaboration between various systems: School, Family, and Justice System. When this motivation is absent within grown-ups those who pay are always the youngest ones: this is why we can state that deviant and criminal behavior are actually the result of a social construct.

Bibliography

ACKERMAN, N.W. (1958). *The Psychodynamics of Family Life: Diagnosis and Treatment of Family Relationships*. Basic Books, New York.

ADDAZI, A., MARINI, R., RAGO, N., editors. (2009). *Metodo e risultati di una comunità per tossicodipendenti. L'esperienza di Città della Pieve*. Franco Angeli, Milan.

ALONSO-FERNANDEZ, F. (1999). *Le altre droghe*. Edizioni Universitarie Romane, Rome.

ANDERSEN, T. (1991). *The Reflecting Team*. W.W. Norton, New York.

ANDOLFI, M. (1979). *Family Therapy: An Interactional Approach*. Plenum Press, New York.

ANDOLFI, M. (2000a). "Tre generazioni in terapia: un modello evolutivo di terapia familiare," *Gruppi*, vol. 2.

ANDOLFI, M. (2000b). "Terapia con l'individuo e terapia con la famiglia," *Rivista di Psicoterapia Relazionale speciale: Terapia sistemica con la famiglia e l'individuo*, vol. 11.

ANDOLFI, M. (2002). "Panta rei: la filosofia del divenire di Carl Whitaker," *Terapia familiare*, vol. 68, pp. 68-69.

ANDOLFI, M. (2003). *Manuale di psicologia relazionale. La dimensione familiare*. A.P.F., Rome.

ANDOLFI, M. (2005). "Il ritorno al sociale; un utopia o una necessità per i terapeuti familiari?," *Terapia Familiare*, vol. 77, pp. 79-92.

ANDOLFI, M., ANGELO, C. (1981). "The therapist as director of the family drama," *The Journal of Marital and Family Therapy*, vol. 7, no. 3, pp. 255-264.

ANDOLFI, M., ANGELO, C. (1985). "Famiglia ed individuo in una prospettiva trigenerazionale," *Terapia Familiare*, vol. 19, pp. 17-24.

ANDOLFI, M., ANGELO, C., D'ATENA, P. (2001). *La terapia narrata dalle
famiglie*. Raffaello Cortina, Milan.

ANDOLFI, M., ANGELO C., DE NICHILO, M. (1987). *The Myth of Atlas:
Families and the Therapeutic Story*. Brunner/Mazel, New York.

ANDOLFI, M., ANGELO, C., MENGHI, P., NICOLÓ-CORIGLIANO, A.
(1983). *Behind the Family Mask: Therapeutic Change in Rigid Family
Systems*. Brunner/Mazel, New York.

ANDOLFI, M., CALDERÓN, L. (2008). *The Oaxaca Book: Working with
Marginalized Families and Communities in the Trenches*. A.P.F., Rome.

ANDOLFI, M., D'ELIA, A., editors. (2007). *Le perdite e le risorse della
famiglia*. Raffaello Cortina, Milan.

ANDOLFI, M., FALCUCCI, M., MASCELLANI, A., SANTONA, A.,
SCIAMPLICOTTI, F., editors. (2007). *Il bambino come risorsa nella
terapia familiare. I seminari di Maurizio Andolfi*. A.P.F., Rome.

ANDOLFI, M., HABER, R., editors. (1994). *Please Help Me with This
Family: Using Consultants as Resources in Family Therapy*. Brunner/
Mazel, New York.

ANDOLFI, M., STEIN, D., SKINNER, J. (1977). "A system approach to
the child, school, family and community in a urban area," *The American Journal of Community Psychology*, vol. 5, no. 1, pp. 33-43.

ANDOLFI, M., ZWERLING, I., (1980). *Dimensions of family therapy*.
Guilford Press, New York.

ANDREOLI, V. (2006). "La violenza della metamorfosi," *Terapia Familiare*, vol. 81, pp. 5-15.

ARDOVINI, C., LIBERTI, S., RAMACCIOTTI, A., CAPUTO, G. (1998).
"Indicazioni alla psicoterapia." In BOSELLO, O., editor. *Obesità: un
trattamento multidimensionale*. Kurtis, Milan.

AUERSWALD, D. (1968). "Interdisciplinary versus ecological approach,"
Family Process, vol. 7, pp. 202-215.

AUERSWALD, D. (1972) "Families, change, and the ecological
perspective," *Family Process*, vol. 10, pp. 263-280.

AVENI, F., CAPUTO, G., CUZZOLARO, M. (1998). "La dimensione psi-
chica del soggetto obeso." In BOSELLO O., editor. *Obesità: un trattamento multidimensionale*. Kurtis, Milan.

BALDASCINI, L. (1993). *Vita da adolescenti*. Franco Angeli, Milan.

BANK, S., KAHN, M.D. (1982). *The Sibling Bond.* Basic Books, New York.

BARRETO, A. (2008). "Community Therapy: building webs of solidarity" (Abstract). In ANDOLFI, M., CALDERÓN, L. *The Oaxaca book. Working with marginalized families and communities in the trenches,* A.P.F., Rome.

BAUMAN, Z. (2000). *Liquid Modernity.* Polity Press, Cambridge, UK; Blackwell, Malden, MA.

BECKER, S., CURRY, J.F. (2008). "Outpatients interventions for adolescent substance misuse: a quality of evidence review," *Journal of Consulting and Clinical Psychology,* vol. 76, no. 4, pp. 531-543.

BELL, R.M. (1980). *Holy Anorexia.* University of Chicago Press, Chicago.

BLAZER, D.G. (2005). *The Age of Melancholy: "Major Depression" and its Social Origins.* Routledge, New York.

BOSZORMENYI-NAGY, I., SPARK, G. (1973). *Invisible Loyalties: Reciprocity in Inter-generational Family Therapy.* Harper & Row, Hagerstown.

BOWEN, M. (1978). *Family Therapy in the Clinical Practice.* Jason Aronson, New York.

BOWLBY J. (1980). *Loss: Sadness and Depression.* Basic Books, New York.

BOWLBY, J. (1984). "Violence in the family as a disorder of the attachment and caregiving systems," *American Journal of Psychoanalysis,* vol. 44, no. 1, pp. 9-27.

BRAET, C. (1999). "Treatment of obese children: a new rationale," *Clinical Child Psychology and Psychiatry,* vol. 4, no. 4, pp. 579-591.

BRUCH, H. (1973). *Eating Disorders: Obesity, Anorexia Nervosa, and the Person Within.* Basic Books, New York.

CARETTI, V., LA BARBERA, D. (2001). *Psicopatologia delle realtà virtuali.* Masson, Milan.

CIGOLI, V., GIULIANI, C. (1997). "La possibile trasformazione," *Famiglia Oggi,* vol. 10.

CLARK, D.M., & FAIRBURN, C.G. (1997). *Science and Practice of Cognitive Behaviour Therapy.* Oxford University Press, Oxford.

CRISP, A.H., JOUGHIN, N., HALEK, C., BOYWER, C. (1996). *Anorexia Nervosa: The Wish to Change.* Psychology Press/Taylor & Francis Group, Hove, UK.

CUZZOLARO, M. (2002). "Disordini alimentari in adolescenza." In AMMANITI M., editor. *Manuale di psicopatologia dell'adolescenza.* Raffaello Cortina, Milan.

DAMASIO, A. (1999). *The Feeling of What Happens: Body and Emotion in the Making of Consciousness*. Heinemann, London.

DEAS, D., THOMAS, S. E. (2001). "An overview of controlled studies for adolescent substance misuse treatment," *American Journal of Addictions*, vol. 10, no. 2, pp. 178-189.

DEVEREUX, G. (1980). *Basic Problems of Ethnopsychiatry*. University of Chicago Press, Chicago.

DE LEO, G. (1989). "Per un'analisi sistemica dell'azione violenta," *Terapia familiare*, vol. 30, pp. 21-35.

DE SHAZER, S. (1985). *Keys to Solution in Brief Therapy*. W.W. Norton, New York.

DIETZ, W.H., ROBINSON, T.N. (2005). "Clinical practice: Overweight children and adolescents," *The New England Journal of Medicine*, vol. 352, no. 20 (May 19), pp. 2100-2109.

DI NICOLA, F. (1990). "Tipologia familiare ed epistemologia sistemica: i due punti di vista che si fronteggiano a Milano," *Terapia familiare*, vol. 32, pp. 61-71.

DUNN, J., PLOMIN, R. (1990). *Separate Lives: Why Siblings are So Different*. Basic Books, New York.

EDWARDS, M., RUGGERI, G.C., WEIQUI, Y. (2004). *Measures of Obesity for Canada and New Brunswick*. Working paper. University of New Brunswick, NJ.

EHRENBERG, A. (2000). *La fatigue d'être soi: Dépression et société*. Odile Jacob, Paris.

EHRENBERG, A. (2010). *The Weariness of the Self: Diagnosing the History of Depression in the Contemporary Age*. [English translation of preceding.] McGill University Press, Montreal.

ELKAIM, M. (1990). *If You Love Me, Don't Love Me: Constructions of Reality and Change in Family Therapy*. Basic Books, New York.

EPSTEIN, L.H., VALOSKI, A., WING, R.R., MCCURLEY, J. (1994). "Ten-year outcomes of behavioral family-based treatment for childhood obesity," *Health Psychology*, vol. 13, no. 5, pp. 373-83.

FALCUCCI, M., MASCELLANI, A., SANTONA, A, SCIAMPLICOTTI, F., editors. (2006). *La terapia di coppia in una prospettiva trigenerazionale*. A.P.F., Rome.

FIVAZ-DEPEURSIGNE, E., CORBOZ-WARNERY, J. (1999). *The Primary Triangle: A Developmental Systems View of Mothers, Fathers, and Infants.* Basic Books, New York.

FRAMO, J.L. (1992). *Family of Origin: An Inter-generational Approach.* Routledge, New York.

GORDON, R.A. (1990). *Anorexia and Bulimia: Anatomy of a Social Epidemic.* Blackwell, Cambridge, MA.

GRIFFITHS, M.D., HUNT, N. (1995). "Computer game playing in adolescence: prevalence and demographic indicators," *Journal of Community Applied Social Psychology,* vol. 5, no. 3, pp. 189-193.

HAINER, V., TOPLAK, H., MITRAKON, A. (2008). "Treatment modalities of obesity: who fits whom?," *Diabetes Care,* vol. 31, no. 2, pp. 269-277.

HALEY J. (1973). *Uncommon Therapy: Psychiatric Techniques of Milton Erickson, M.D.* W.W. Norton, New York.

HALEY, J. (1980). *Leaving Home: The Therapy of Disturbed Young People.* McGraw-Hill, New York.

HALEY, J., HOFFMAN, L. (1967). *Techniques of Family Therapy.* Basic Books, New York.

HARRISON, T.R., FAUCI, A. (1998). *Harrison's Principles of Internal Medicine.* Manual, 16th edition. McGraw Hill, New York.

HAWKINS, A.J., CHRISTIANSEN, S.L., SARGENT, W.P. and HILL, E.J. (1995). "Rethinking fathers involvement in child care: a developmental perspective." In MARSIGLIO, W. *Fatherhood: Contemporary Theory, Research, and Social Policy. Research on Men and Masculinities Series,* 7, Sage Publications, Thousand Oaks, CA.

HOFFMAN, L. (1981). *Foundations of Family Therapy: a Conceptual Framework for System Change.* Basic Books, New York.

HORWITZ, A., WAKEFIELD, J. (2007). *The Loss of Sadness: How Psychiatry Transformed Normal Sorrow into Depressive Disorder.* Oxford University Press, New York.

KLEIN, M. (1959). *La psychanalise des enfants.* P.U.F., Paris.

LA PERRIERE, K. (1999). "Terapie con coppie in una società disgregante." In *La crisi della coppia.* Raffaello Cortina, Milan.

LAMB, M.E. (1981). *The Role of the Father in Child Development.* Wiley, New York.

LAMB, M. E., PLECK, J.H., CHARNOV, E.L., & LEVINE, J.A. (1987). "A biosocial perspective on paternal behavior and involvement." In LANCASTER, J.B., ALTMANN, J., ROSSI, A., SHERROD, L.R., editors. *Parenting Across the Lifespan: Biosocial Dimensions.* Transaction Publishers, New York, pp. 11-42.

LIDDLE, H.A. (2004). "Family based therapies for adolescent alcohol and drug use: research contributions and future research needs," *Addictions*, vol. 99, pp. 76-92.

MAGGIOLINI, A., PIETROPOLLI CHARMET, G. (1994). *Manuale di psicologia dell'adolescenza: compiti e conflitti.* Franco Angeli, Milan.

MARSIGLIO, W. (1995). *Fatherhood: Contemporary Theory, Research, and Social Policy.* Thousand Oaks, Sage Publications.

MINUCHIN, S. (1974). *Families and Family Therapy.* Harvard University Press, Cambridge, MA.

MINUCHIN, S. (1999). "Where is the family in the narrative therapy?," *Journal of Marital and Family Therapy*, vol. 24, no. 4, pp. 397-403.

MINUCHIN, S., MONTALVO, B., SCHUMER, F., ROSMAN, B.L., GUERNEY, B.G. (1967). *Families and the Slums: An Exploration of their Structure and Treatment.* Basic Books, New York.

MINUCHIN, S., ROSMAN, B.L., BAKER, L. (1978). *Psychosomatic Families.* Harvard University Press, Cambridge, MA.

NOWICKA, P., FLODMARK, C.E. (2011). "Family therapy as a model for treating childhood obesity: useful tools for clinicians," *Clinical Child Psychology & Psychiatry*, vol. 16, no. 1, pp. 129-145.

OSTUZZI, R., LUXARDI, G.L. (2007). *Un boccone dopo l'altro.* Baldini Castoldi Dalai, Milan.

PARKE, R.D. (2002). "Fathers and families." In BOORSTEIN, M.H. (editor). *Handbook of Parenting: Being and Becoming Parents*, vol. 3. Lawrence Eribaum Associates, Mahwah, NJ.

PIETROPOLLI CHARMET, G. (2000). *I nuovi adolescenti.* Raffaello Cortina, Milan.

ROUSTANG, F. (2004). "Che fare delle proprie sofferenze?," *Terapia Familiare*, vol. 76, pp. 5-18.

SANTONA, A., ZAVATTINI, G.C. (2007). *La relazione di coppia.* Borla, Rome.

SATIR, V. (1964). *Conjoint Family Therapy: A Guide to Theory and Technique.* Science and Behavior Books, Palo Alto.

SCABINI, E. (1985). *L'organizzazione della famiglia tra crisi e sviluppo.* Franco Angeli, Milan.

SCABINI, E. (1997). *Giovani in famiglia fra autonomia e nuove dipendenze.* Vita e Pensiero, Milan.

SCHEFLEN, A. (1973). *How Behavior Means.* Gordon & Breach, New York.

SELVINI PALAZZOLI, M. (1977). *Self-starvation: From Individual to Family Therapy in the Treatment of Anorexia Nervosa.* Jason Aronson, New York.

SELVINI PALAZZOLI, M., BOSCOLO, L., CECCHIN, G., PRATA, G. (1975). *Paradox and Counterparadox: A New Model in the Therapy of the Family in Schizophrenic Transaction.* Jason Aronson, New York.

SELVINI PALAZZOLI, M., CIRILLO, S., SELVINI, M., SORRENTINO, A.M. (1989). *Family Games: General Models of Psychotic Processes in the Family.* W.W. Norton, New York.

SELVINI PALAZZOLI, M., CIRILLO, S., SELVINI, M., SORRENTINO, A.M. (1998). *Ragazze anoressiche e bulimiche.* Raffaello Cortina, Milan.

SLUZKI C.E., RANSOM D.C. (1974). *Double Bind: The Foundation of the Communicational Approach to the Family.* Grune and Stratton, New York.

SPECK R.V., ATTNEAVE C. L. (1975). *Family Networks.* Pantheon Books, New York.

STERN, D. (2004). *The Present Moment in Psychotherapy and Everyday Life.* W.W. Norton, New York.

STIERLIN, H. (1981). *Separating Parents and Adolescents: Individuation in the Family.* Jason Aronson, New York.

SULLIVAN, R. (2000). "Fathering and Children: The Contemporary Context." Paper presented at the *Focus on Fathering Symposium* at 7th AIFS Conference, Sydney, July 24-26.

UGAZIO, V., DIXON, R. (2013). *Semantic Polarities and Psychopathologies in the Family: Permitted and Forbidden Stories.* Routledge, New York.

VARELA, F., THOMPSON, E., ROSCH, E. (1991). *The Embodied Mind: Cognitive Science and Human Experience.* MIT Press, Cambridge, MA.

VEGETTI FINZI, S. (2008). *Nuovi nonni per nuovi nipoti: la gioia di un incontro.* Mondadori, Milan.

WALSH, F., editor. (1982). *Normal Family Processes.* Guilford Press, New York.

WATZLAWICK, P., BEAVIN BAVELA, S.J., JACKSON, D.D. (1967). *Pragmatics of Human Communication: A Study of Interactional Patterns, Pathologies, and Paradoxes.* W.W. Norton, New York.

WHITAKER, C. (1958). "Psychotherapy with couples," *American Journal of Psychotherapy*, vol. 12, pp. 18-23.

WHITAKER, C. (1989). *Midnight Musings of a Family Therapist.* W.W. Norton, New York.

WHITAKER, C., KEITH, D. (1981). "Symbolic Experiential Family Therapy." In GURMAN, A.S., KNISKERN, D.P. (1981). *Handbook of Family Therapy.* Routledge, London, pp. 187-225.

WHITAKER, C., SIMONS, J. (1994). "The inner life of the consultant." In ANDOLFI, M., HABER, R., editors. *Please Help Me with This Family.* Routledge, New York, pp. 66-70.

WILLIAMSON, D.S. (1981). "Personal Authority via Termination of the Inter-generational Hierarchical Boundary: A 'New' Stage in the Family Life Cycle," *Journal of Marital and Family Therapy*, vol. 7, no. 4, pp. 441-452.

WOODSIDE, D.B., SHEKTER-WOLFSON, L. (1991). *Family Approaches in Treatment of Eating Disorders.* American Psychiatric Press, Washington, DC.

YOUNG, K.S., ROGERS, R.C. (1998). "The relationship between depression and internet addiction," *Cyberpsychology and Behavior*, vol. 1, no. 1, pp. 25-28.

ZATTONI, M. (2009). "Accettiamo la tristezza dei figli," *Famiglia Oggi*, vol. 1, pp. 36-42.

The Authors

Maurizio Andolfi.
Child Psychiatrist, Full Professor in the Department of
Psychology at Sapienza University of Rome, Director of
the Accademia di Psicoterapia della Famiglia of Rome.
Editor-in-chief of the journal Terapia Familiare
(Rome, Italy).

Anna Mascellani.
Family Therapist, Teacher, Supervisor, and Deputy
Director of the Accademia di Psicoterapia della
Famiglia, in charge of the Clinical Services of the
Accademia della Famiglia Onlus, and a team member of
its Couples Therapy Unit.